THE
SOVEREIGN
COLONY

THE SOVEREIGN COLONY

Olympic Sport,
National Identity,
and International Politics
in Puerto Rico

ANTONIO SOTOMAYOR

University of Nebraska Press
Lincoln and London

An earlier version of chapter 5 was previously published as
"The Cold War Games of a Colonial Latin American Nation:
San Juan, Puerto Rico, 1966," in *Diplomatic Games: Sport,
Statecraft, and International Relations since 1945*, ed. Heather
L. Dichter and Andrew Johns (Lexington: University Press of
Kentucky, 2014), 217–49.

Library of Congress Cataloging-in-Publication Data
Names: Sotomayor, Antonio, author.
Title: The sovereign colony: Olympic sport, national identity,
and international politics in Puerto Rico / Antonio Sotomayor.
Description: Lincoln: University of Nebraska Press, 2016. |
Includes bibliographical references and index.
Identifiers: LCCN 2015021065
ISBN 9780803278813 (hardback: alk. paper)
ISBN 9780803285385 (epub)
ISBN 9780803285392 (mobi)
ISBN 9780803285408 (pdf)
Subjects: LCSH: Olympics—Participation, Puerto Rican. |
Olympics—Political aspects—Puerto Rico. | Nationalism
and sports—Puerto Rico. | BISAC: HISTORY / Latin Amer-
ica / General. | POLITICAL SCIENCE / Political Ideologies /
Nationalism. | SPORTS & RECREATION / Olympics.
Classification: LCC GV721.4.P9 S68 2016 | DDC 796.48—dc23
LC record available at http://lccn.loc.gov/2015021065

Set in Minion Pro by M. Scheer.

Para mi padre, Antonio Sotomayor Mora, y madre, Sandra Carlo Santana.

To Nicole, who proves that dreams can come true.

Para Paio y Amalia, son la luz en mi vida.

Contents

Illustrations

Acknowledgments

This book is the result of a dream, a dream that often looked as elusive as the mere writing of these few words of acknowledgment. This dream was never clear and set, but went through different versions as I traveled the winding roads of scholarly training. Most important, it was a dream fostered and nurtured by the support I have received directly or indirectly from family, friends, and colleagues throughout the years. A few sincere words of appreciation are in order for so many people, most of whom, for lack of space, will have to stay in a collective heartfelt *¡gracias!* From my cherished and never forgotten twelve years of schooling at Colegio Espíritu Santo in Hato Rey, Puerto Rico, to my life-changing and character-building years at Universidad de Puerto Rico–Recinto de Mayagüez (¡Colegio!), this book owes a little bit to all of you. Contrary to the stereotype for a Latin American, I play basketball, not soccer, and not baseball (although I did play little league baseball). Hence my early passion for sports derives from this sport and the friends I played with back in the Joyuda beachfront Liga de Punta Arenas in Cabo Rojo and during four years of high school varsity and street games. I was never any good, but I did love the game. I still remember watching, celebrating, and mourning the 1990 World Championship of Basketball, where the Puerto Rican team, after beating the great and eventual champion Yugoslavian team, finished in fourth place after losing the bronze medal game in overtime by two points against the United States. Although Puerto Rico had beaten the United States earlier in the tournament, it was Puerto Rico's highest finish in FIBA's championship. I believe this 1990 team, which included Federico "Fico"

López, Georgie Torres, Mario "Quijote" Morales, José "Piculín" Ortiz, Ramón Rivas, and Jerome Mincy, among others, was Puerto Rico's best national squad. Thank you, guys, for so many thrills!

There is a select group of people, in Puerto Rico and the States, who throughout the first few years of graduate school were a central source of support; they know who they are, and to them I give my deep gratitude. I found much inspiration, encouragement, and support from faculty and friends during my graduate work at Indiana University–Bloomington and at the University of Illinois at Urbana-Champaign. My introduction into the scholarly study of history was with Arlene Díaz. During my stay at IU she published her book on the history of Venezuelan law and women (coincidentally also with University of Nebraska Press) and gave me a dedicated copy, which motivated me throughout graduate school. As promised, and eleven years later, here's my book! As a master's student at Illinois, I was equally lucky in having a great history mentor and friend, Nils Jacobsen. My initial sustained training as a historian occurred under his guidance, and for that I remain eternally thankful. Also at Illinois I found much encouragement and advice from Arlene Torres, a great scholar of Puerto Rico and mentor to many. Thank you. Other scholars and friends were influential in my initial training at Illinois, for which I am equally grateful; they include Maria Todorova, Carol Symes, Alejandro Lugo, Ellen Moodie, Dara Goldman, and my CLACS cohort, Amy Firestone, Courtney Fuoss, and Cuauhtemoc Mexica.

The details of this project began to take clear shape during my PhD work at the University of Chicago. There I found many supportive colleagues that made my stay an enriching experience, both academically and personally. For this I thank José Ángel Hernández, Pablo Ben, Patrick Iber, Jaime Pensado, Nicole Mottier, Sarah Osten, Heather Allen, Mikael Wolfe, Sara Hirschhorn, Darryl Heller, George Ironstrack, Samuel Lebovic, Toussaint Losier, Alejandro Maya, Theodore Francis II, Richard del Rio, Johnhenry "Hank" Gonzalez, Emily

Remus, Zachary Chase, Jeevan Devassy, María Balandrán-Castillo, Jackie Summer, Casey Lurtz, Diana Schwartz, Janette Gayle, Tessa Murphy, and Laurencio Sanguino. Particular thanks to my cohort in Latin American and Caribbean history; without them the program would have been a very lonely road: Sabine Cadeau, Matthew Barton, Stuart Easterling, Amanda Hartzmark, Ananya Chakravarti, and Romina Robles Ruvalcaba.

Concrete ideas for this book began to take shape at Chicago with the encouragement, guidance, and supervision of a great team of scholars and mentors, including Dain Borges, Emilio Kourí, and Agnes Lugo-Ortiz. I am deeply grateful for their excellent advising, critical evaluation, and thoughtful suggestions. I also benefited from the mentoring and supervision of different scholars at Chicago, including Julie Saville, Stephan Palmié, Mauricio Tenorio, and John MacAloon. Early versions of this book received great feedback and suggestions by colleagues at the Latin American History Workshop and the Caribbean Studies Workshop, both at the University of Chicago, and at the Conference on Latin American History, the International Congress of the Latin American Studies Association, and the Puerto Rican Studies Association Conference.

Throughout the long process of thinking, writing, and presenting different parts of this book I have received valuable feedback, motivation, and support of colleagues who deserve my sincere appreciation and respect: Francisco Scarano, William Beezley, Lillian Guerra, Margaret Power, Brenda Elsey, Joel Horowitz, and María Alejandra Pérez. Special words of gratitude to the late Joseph Arbena, a pioneer of Latin American sports history and a source of encouragement and good humor. He'll be missed. April Yoder read and provided poignant and motivating feedback to a longer version of this project, for which I am profoundly grateful. I also received much appreciated words of encouragement and feedback from colleagues at Historicizing the Pan-American Games: An International Colloquium at the University of Toronto–Scarborough, including the organizers

Bruce Kidd and César Torres, and Thomas Carter, David Sheinin, Russell Field, Sarah Teetzel, Francesco Ragno, Mariadele di Blasio, Mark Dyerson, John MacAloon, and many more from the engaging audience.

I want to thank the head of my department, Steve W. Witt, for giving me the space and time to finish this book. To the rest of the faculty, staff, and graduate student colleagues at the International and Area Studies Library and the University Library at the University of Illinois at Urbana-Champaign, thank you for your support. I would like to thank especially my library colleagues Paula T. Kaufman, past dean of libraries, and John Wilkin, current dean, for their support and needed words of encouragement; University Archivist William Maher and his staff for helping me navigate the Avery Brundage collection; Sarah L. Shreeves, who introduced me to the complex world of copyrights; Daniel G. Tracy, whose support of all of us researchers at the library is invigorating; Jenny Marie Johnson and James V. Whitacre for their masterful and visionary work with maps; and Paula M. Carns for patiently helping me transition into my position. I would also like to thank other librarians and historians, Luis A. González from Indiana University–Bloomington and José O. Díaz from Ohio State University, whose support and mentorship on navigating two distinct yet complementary fields have been crucial in my growth as a scholar and librarian. Equal thanks go to other fantastic scholar librarians at the Seminar on the Acquisition of Latin American Library Materials (SALALM).

I thank my colleagues in the Department of History—Augusto F. Espíritu, Nils Jacobsen, Jerry Dávila, Marc Adam Hertzman, Joseph L. Love, Matthew Sakiestewa Gilbert, Vicente Miguel Diaz, Ikuko Asaka, Craig M. Koslofsky, and others—for their collegiate encouragement on the book and overall research. Other scholars of Latin America and the Caribbean on campus, particularly in the Department of Spanish and Portuguese, including Silvina Montrul, Mariselle Meléndez, Anna María Escobar, Dara Goldman, and Glen Goodman, have given me a warm welcome to campus and much motivation. The University of Illinois is truly a special place for Latin American and Caribbean studies, and I am thrilled to be part of it. Special thanks go to the members of the First Book Writing Group of the Office of the Vice Chancellor for Research in the Humanities and Social Sciences, excellently led by Nancy A. Abelmann, Craig M. Koslofsky, and Maria Gillombardo. Their feedback and suggestions were instrumental in the later stages of this book. Many thanks to Angelina Cotler and the Center for Latin American and Caribbean Studies at Illinois for the opportunity to present my work at their Lecture Series, and to Carla Santos for giving me a space on her graduate seminar in the Department of Recreation, Sport, and Tourism to present part of this research. Thanks to Seth Meisel for inviting me to present and share this research at a workshop on Latin American sports sponsored by the Center for Latin American and Caribbean Studies at the University of Wisconsin–Milwaukee.

I would like to acknowledge the staff at the Regenstein Library at the University of Chicago for early research into this topic. A part of this book was discussed during my Colonial Puerto Rico under the U.S. Empire course at the University of Chicago. Thanks to the students for a great class and engaging discussion. Very special thanks to the faculty and staff at the Seymour Library in Knox College for giving me access to their resources and for the overall support in my research. A part of this book was discussed in my National Identity in the Caribbean course in the History Department at Knox College, and I thank those students for their thoughtful comments and rewarding discussion. The students at both Chicago and Knox prove that learning is a two-way street. I am glad to have had the opportunity to share my thoughts on this topic with them and learn from their insights.

Significant appreciation goes to Bridget Barry, history editor for the University of Nebraska Press, who invited me to send a book proposal and supported my work throughout the publishing process. Thanks to the anonymous peer reviewers and their generally positive reviews, words of encouragement, and very thoughtful and pertinent critiques. Very special thanks to Wendy Kapp and Judith Hoover for their excellent and much needed copyediting work. Sincere thanks to William Beezley and Francisco Scarano for agreeing to read and comment on this book; I am humbled by your support. Additional thanks to the University Press of Kentucky for allowing me to reproduce chapter 5, which was previously published in one of their anthologies. Obviously any faults, omissions, and shortcomings in this book are not due to any of them or anyone else mentioned so far, but solely my responsibility.

I owe much gratitude to the financial support of the Mellon Foundation, as well as Freehling and Kunstadter research grants, all at the University of Chicago, for initial work on this project. At the University of Illinois I wish to thank the Office of the Vice Chancellor for Research for granting me travel awards to present parts of this research at scholarly conferences, and especially the Research and Publication Committee of the University of Illinois at Urbana-Champaign Library, which provided much needed support for the completion of this book. Special thanks to the great interlibrary loans team at the University of Illinois Library in Urbana, for they work magic in finding the rarest of materials across oceans.

I would like to thank the staff at the Archivo General de Puerto Rico, the Fundación Luis Muñoz Marín, the Archivo Central and the Archive of the Board of Trustees of the Universidad de Puerto Rico, the Library of the Legislature of Puerto Rico, the Ateneo Puertorriqueño, and the Comité Olímpico de Puerto Rico. Particular thanks to Jaime Partsch McMillan from the Colección Jesús T. Piñero of the Universidad del Este and Félix Ortiz of the Museo Olímpico de Puerto Rico. I thank Benjamín Lúgaro Torres for opening the doors to his home and personal archive.

Special thanks as well to the diligent and friendly staff at the Colección Puertorriqueña of the Universidad de Puerto Rico at Río Piedras, including María Ordóñez Mercado and Miguel A. Vega Rivera, and the student workers who willingly and assiduously provided me with hundreds of newspaper microfilms: José Manuel Dávila Marichal, Yahira Aguilar, Giselle Cordero Arroyo, Juan Dávila Reyes, Christian Rivera, Joshua Escalera, Reinaldo Ruiz, William Ortiz, Viviana Betancourt, and the rest. I am grateful for the collaboration and generosity of Carlos Uriarte González for permission to use some of his collection of sports images. I am grateful to the staff at the National Archives and National Records in Washington DC and their permission to use confidential material.

I have been privileged to have had conversations with the following leaders of Puerto Rican sports, who have found part of their lives and points of view in the pages of this book or were an early source of inspiration: Joaquín Martínez-Rousset, José "Fufi" Santori Coll, Vidal E. "Anicetito" González, Vicente "Tito" Nieves Mora, the late Eddie Ríos Mellado, and the late Ricardo Alegría (not a leader of sports but certainly a source of inspiration).

Finally, and certainly not least important, I thank my family. Although I left "mi viejo San Juan" many years ago, I never felt that their presence, tenderness, and support were left behind. For all of this I am most thankful. To my sisters, Rebeca and Mónica—who year after year asked, "When will you finish studying?!"—thank you for your support and understanding that in my line of work I don't stop studying. To my niece, Patricia, and my nephew, Sebastián, sports fans, thank you for keeping it down to earth. To my dear Ream family from Ohio and beyond, but especially to Brian, Becky, and Elyse, I could not ask for a better and more loving (and a bit crazy) acquired family. Love you guys! To my father, Tony "Gallego," who taught me, among many other things, the value of perseverance, without which this book (and my professional career) would not have been completed, gracias. My success rests on your unwavering shoulders. To my loving mother, Sandra (my Lady Laura), who taught me to be a fan of the Puerto Rican national team, yet most importantly the value of appreciating life, gracias (ciertamente "lo importante es que emociones viví"). To my wife, best friend, academic partner, soul mate, and love of my life, Nicole, thanks for being there for me during the ups and downs of academe and throughout this journey of life. I am truly fortunate to have you by my side. Go Browns! To my children, Paio and Amalia, thank you for your laughter, smiles, and never-ending pursuit of play. In the innocence of your being I find the best antidote for the stress of life. The world is yours; go and get it!

Abbreviations

AGPR:	Archivo General de Puerto Rico
AOA:	American Olympic Association
BLPRTBF:	Biblioteca Legislativa de Puerto Rico Tomás Bonilla Feliciano
CACG:	Central American and Caribbean Games
CACSO:	Central American and Caribbean Sport Organization
COC:	Cuban Olympic Committee
COPR:	Comité Olímpico de Puerto Rico (Puerto Rican Olympic Committee)
FC:	Fútbol Club
FDPR:	Federación Deportiva de Puerto Rico
IAAF:	International Association of Athletics Federations
IOC:	International Olympic Committee
MPI:	Movimiento Pro Independencia
NBA:	National Basketball Association
NOC:	National Olympic Committee
NP:	Nationalist Party
OAPR:	Olympic Association of Puerto Rico
PAPC:	Public Amusement and Parks Commission
PASC:	Public Amusements and Sports Commission
PASO:	Pan-American Sports Organization
PE:	physical education
PIP:	Partido Independentista Puertorriqueño
PN:	Partido Nacionalista
PNP:	Partido Nuevo Progresista
PPD:	Partido Popular Democrático
PRPA:	Public Recreation and Parks Administration
PRRA:	Puerto Rican Reconstruction Administration
UHS:	University High School
UPR:	University of Puerto Rico
USLTA:	U.S. Lawn Tennis Association
USOA:	U.S. Olympic Association

THE
SOVEREIGN
COLONY

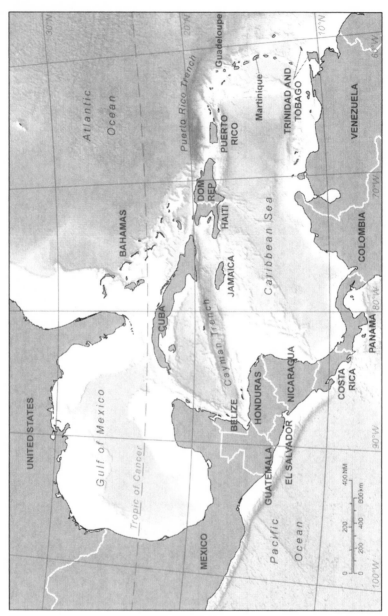

Map 1. Central America and the Caribbean. Map by James V. Whitacre.

/ Introduction

On August 15, 2004, Puerto Rico faced the United States during the
first day of basketball competition in Athens at the twenty-eighth
Summer Olympic Games. Since their debut in 1960, this was the ninth
Olympic Games appearance for the Puerto Rican basketball team.
There was much anticipation; they faced the dreaded U.S. "Dream
Team," composed of the National Basketball Association (NBA) stars
after the International Olympic Committee (IOC) allowed profes-
sional players to participate in the 1992 Olympic Games in Barcelona.
The so-called Dream Team had not only been undefeated since 1992;
they had crushed their opposition, winning the gold medal in 1992
by a margin of 44 points per game. I watched the game that day in
the media room of my apartment complex with a group of friends
(Mexicans and other Puerto Ricans) while a graduate student at the
University of Illinois at Urbana-Champaign. I, a faithful fan of the
Puerto Rican national team, endearingly called "Los 12 Magníficos,"
followed the game closely.

The game started when Carlos Arroyo, Puerto Rico's point guard,
led the charge along with Puerto Rican legend José "Piculín" Ortiz,
Larry Ayuso, Rolando Hourruitinier, Eddie Casiano, and Daniel Santiago, among others. The U.S. Dream Team included the usual NBA
stars and some future Hall of Famers, including Allen Iverson, Tim
Duncan, Lamar Odom, Dwayne Wade, LeBron James, and Amare
Stoudemire. The game began at 8:00 p.m. Athens time, in front of
11,560 people. The first quarter was close, as each team made baskets
and the defense cleared the boards. The quarter ended with Puerto
Rico leading 21–20; I had no idea my heart could beat so fast. After

Fig. 1. Carlos Arroyo, point guard for the Puerto Rican national basketball team, during the U.S.–Puerto Rico game in 2004 in Athens. AP Photo/Michael Conroy.

the second quarter began, something utterly unrealistic and highly improbable happened: the Puerto Ricans took over the game and closed the second quarter on a 28–7 run, stunning the crowd and, indeed, the entire sports world. Meanwhile the Dream Team had fallen into a deep hole. The rest of the match resembled the first quarter. The U.S. "Nightmare Team," as they were later called, tried unsuccessfully to make a comeback. Puerto Rico won the game. Carlos Arroyo made a name for himself, becoming a Puerto Rican hero, finishing with 24 points, 7 assists, and 4 steals as he proudly displayed the corners of his jersey showing the name "Puerto Rico." The image was captured in an iconic photograph that traveled across the world (see fig. 1).

More significant, the game ended with the Puerto Ricans defeating the United States by an embarrassing 19-point margin, 92–73. This margin of defeat stands as the largest for any U.S. basketball team in Olympic history.[1] It was only the third loss in U.S. basketball Olympic history: twice to the Soviet Union, first in a controversial gold medal game in 1972 at the height of the cold war and then in the 1988 semifinals in Seoul.[2] At the end of the game the U.S. Olympic record was 109-3, although they lost two more times at Athens, to Lithuania in the preliminary round and to Argentina in the semifinals, winning a bronze. That moment in Urbana felt like the greatest achievement in Puerto Rican basketball, greater even than winning a gold medal.

On campus the next morning, colleagues, professors, staff, and other friends commented on the Puerto Rican victory over the Americans. They congratulated me as if I had been playing on the team. I could sense that some of them had been talking among themselves about the game, discussing the great victory for Puerto Rico, debating whether the U.S. team was still the Dream Team, and speculating about the up-and-coming talent of "international" basketball. Newspapers, sports networks, and newscasts commented on the lopsided defeat of the Americans to the Puerto Ricans and what this defeat meant to U.S. basketball.[3] Many questioned basketball's status as an "American" sport.[4]

Many sports commentators debated the tactical reasons for the loss, whether the U.S. team just had a bad game or the Puerto Rican team had a good game in terms of shooting, playing defense, or coaching.[5] Admittedly I too questioned the potential of Puerto Rican basketball. After training as a scholar of Latin America and the Caribbean, I began to question the deeper meanings of this performance. I came to realize that what is most significant about this Puerto Rican victory against the United States, yet seldom acknowledged by the media, public, or scholarly community, is that it came at the hands of a small unincorporated island territory of the United States. That is, the U.S. team was defeated by other U.S. citizens. While analysts commented on the strength of international basketball, they did not observe that this Puerto Rican team was not technically international.[6] Rather than evaluating how the Puerto Ricans managed to beat the indestructible Dream Team, it is more pertinent to ask why this nonindependent island territory has a sovereign international athletic presence in the first place.

For Puerto Ricans who have been living under colonialism for more than five hundred years under two different empires, Olympic participation became a way to demonstrate that they are in fact a nation, a process that can be labeled colonial Olympism. This book relates the story of how Puerto Ricans, despite their colonial relation with the United States, were able to participate at regional and world Olympic events, and in doing so foster a strong sense of national identity and engage in international politics. Pierre de Coubertin, founder of the modern Olympics, anchored his neo-Olympism beliefs in classical Hellenic ideals of democracy and the human body in order to sponsor modern practices of physical education and foster international goodwill among the nations of the world.[7] Keeping this in mind, colonial Olympism is in effect the process by which a colonial territory or postcolonial nation becomes fully immersed not only in Olympic competition but also in the struggle over cultural survival and political agency. In this regard colonial Olympism puts in a subaltern light two interlaced processes of modern Olympics: nationalism and international diplomacy. This story is not simply a negotiation over the terms of Olympic inclusion but also a negotiation over a hegemonic relation and colonial authority that tests the limits of sports and political autonomy and ultimately the meaning of the nation. Involved in these negotiations were Puerto Rican state and sport leaders, chief among them Julio Enrique Monagas (the father of Puerto Rican Olympism), different U.S. administrations, Latin American sport leaders, and the IOC.

Colonial Olympism encompasses more than world Olympic Games. It analyzes the roots, ideology, and meanings of the Olympic movement as it relates to small peripheral nations and the larger international repercussions. While many Olympic studies center on the inter- and multidisciplinary analysis of world Olympic Games, I view Olympism in a more comprehensive and inclusive light, paying particular attention to regional games patronized by the IOC, including the Central American and Caribbean Games and the Pan-American Games. This is particularly relevant to peripheral small nations who send delegations to world Olympic Games but who may not stand a chance to win and excel. Regional games constitute a perfect platform on which to perform and showcase the nation competing on a more or less equal playing field. Still, for peripheral countries, being able to participate at world Olympic Games is the ultimate show of national pride. Attendance in the opening parade proves that the nation belongs and has a right to play, perhaps even a chance win, among the nations of the world. Yet for many other smaller countries, regional games are as relevant as the Olympics. This is even more pressing when these neighboring countries, whether politically friendly or antagonistic, compete and engage in athletic diplomacy. Hence it is imperative to consider regional international meets and the political context in which they occur, as they often have larger diplomatic implications.

Several questions were the impetus for this book: How does an Olympic nation exist if it is not an independent nation-state? What is the relationship between Olympic sovereignty and colonialism? How did Olympic participation help to foster a colonial national identity? What were the roles played by key individuals in Puerto Rico, the United States, Latin America, and the IOC in the negotiation between Olympic participation, colonialism, and diplomacy? What does the Puerto Rican Olympic story tell us about twentieth-century colonialism and postcolonialism, nationalism, Latin American sport and political cultures, and the Olympic movement? In answering these questions, this book contributes to four broad and interrelated areas. First, it contributes to Puerto Rican, Caribbean, and Latin American political histories of sport; a study of sport at this length and conceptual depth has never been undertaken in Puerto Rican historiography. While there have been various studies on Puerto Rican national identity, colonialism, and popular culture, this is the first attempt at capturing the significance of Olympic sports for Puerto Rican culture and politics, contributing as well to a broader understanding of the Olympic movement in the Caribbean and Latin America. Second, this book seeks to broaden our understanding of Olympism and Olympic sports in general. Histories of the Olympics, nationalism, and diplomacy often center on the Summer Olympics and on more influential countries of the North Atlantic. In this book the focus is equally on regional and world Olympic Games, as they have been central in the formation of national identity and the engagement of international athletic diplomacy. Focus is also placed on a small peripheral nation in order to demonstrate that size is not always a sign of relevance. Third, this book seeks to contribute to our understanding of colonialism. Puerto Rico, being the oldest colony in the world, challenges notions of Latin American decolonization, adding an important case for twenty-first-century colonial and postcolonial studies. The reasons why this island and its people have endured 507 years of colonial rule, and why the past 117 have been under the United States—former colonies themselves and now the world leader in freedom and democracy—should be comprehended in all of their complexity and should be included in discussions of Latin American coloniality.[8] Fourth, this book contributes to the literature on nationalism and national identity, especially as it relates to Caribbean and Latin American nationalisms. Colonialism for Puerto Ricans has not meant a full rejection of nationalism as a source of collective identity. Although many Puerto Ricans first and foremost identify as U.S. citizen residents of Puerto Rico (as they legally are), many others identify first and foremost as Puerto Rican nationals who have U.S. citizenship. The seemingly contradictory nature of these two concepts attests to the need to differentiate between political nationalism and cultural nationalism. Puerto Rico's nationalism, for the most part, is cultural but also resides and thrives within the constraints of colonialism, owing much to the power and popularity of Olympic sports.

When I refer to the Puerto Rican nation I do so under Benedict Anderson's framework of imagined communities.[9] Nations are a social, political, economic, and cultural construction of human action, both elite and popular, and not a natural expression of distinct peoples.[10] That is, nations are created by human action; they do not evolve naturally from "time immemorial." Nonetheless, while nations are artificial, in the sense of being artifacts of "recent" historical production, they are real for many, and many have given their lives or killed for them. In terms of sport and the nation, Latin American soccer, for example, has been vital in the construction of national identities.[11] This is especially true with the advancement of mass media.[12]

Olympic delegations are great vehicles to explain nationalism because they represent the nation internationally in competitive events. In his classic book *Nations and Nationalism*, Eric Hobsbawm eloquently writes, "The imagined community of millions seems more real as a team of eleven named people."[13] Referencing Uruguay's world soccer success in the 1920s, the Uruguayan writer Eduardo Galeano says, "The sky-blue shirt was proof of the existence of the nation: Uruguay was not a mistake. Soccer pulled this tiny country out of the shadows of universal anonymity."[14] Therefore this study will enrich our understanding of the Olympic movement because it sheds light on the political process of culture making and the cultural process of nationalism to which the Olympic movement is intrinsically tied. Olympism has been a medium par excellence for cultural nationalism, in addition to international sport politics.

I particularly place my argument in line with the nationalism scholar Partha Chatterjee and the argument that nationalism and national identity are present in the colonial world, and not solely an experience of Western nation-states.[15] To be sure, Puerto Rican nationalism was not necessarily the "anticolonial nationalism" that Chatterjee describes, since some Puerto Ricans consented to colonialism under the commonwealth, but the "spiritual" and "cultural" aspects of identity in the colonial world are surely applicable. In this regard I also locate my theoretical framework on nationalism next to John Hutchinson's argument that cultural nationalism can be a separate experience from political nationalism.[16] Nationalism in Puerto Rico was constructed, performed, and celebrated within the parameters of colonial politics that gave preference to cultural expression rather than a political struggle for independence,[17] constituting a unique case in Latin American history. As the historian Luis López argues, the Partido Popular Democrático (PPD), under the leadership of Luis Muñoz Marín, redefined the meanings of Puerto Rican nationalism from a political quest for freedom to a quest for socioeconomic reforms in association with the United States. For the autonomist wing of the PPD, liberty meant escaping the strictures of a backward agricultural economy and entering a progressive industrial age. Independence became an obsolete concept, and association and alliance, especially in the postwar world, became the centerpiece of political action.[18]

Puerto Rican cultural nationalism fits the parameters of the political autonomist tradition. The goal of Puerto Rican nationalism is to portray a sense of uniqueness that reflects centuries of Caribbean history and traditions yet does not aim for full independence. Instead Puerto Rican identity celebrates politically "safe" figures such as the peasant *jíbaro*. Studied by scholars such as Francisco Scarano, Lillian Guerra, and Arlene Torres, since the late eighteenth century the *jíbaro* has become a figure with multiple meanings.[19] From being the symbol of backwardness and a figure of scorn to being celebrated as the soul of the traditional Puerto Rican, the *jíbaro* represents the complexities of Puerto Rican identity. When celebrated, the *jíbaro* symbolizes the white male farmer who lives and works in the rural highlands, who silences not only women but also the pervasive presence of African culture, the result of hundreds of years of the Caribbean slave plantation system.[20] The *jíbaro* has been the PPD's official symbol since 1938.

Despite Puerto Rican colonialism, participating at regional and world Olympic Games has been the most preeminent, if not the ideal, way to mingle with the international community as a sovereign nation.[21] Granted, Olympic sport is not the only venue available for Puerto Ricans to perform the nation. Music, the fine arts, culinary traditions, literature, and beauty pageants are all powerful expressions of national identity and have played key parts in creating a Puerto Rican imagined community. Yet sports actually represent and are directly sponsored by the Puerto Rican state, especially Puerto Rico's Olympic Committee. The Miss Universe Puerto Rico pageant is perhaps the other important cultural event to showcase the Puerto Rican nation, and future research should focus on it. However, given the competitive nature of sports, with clear winners and losers, the Olympic delegation conveys a sense of community and nation different from a single individual.

While reading this book, remember that modern Olympism, as conceived by Coubertin and upheld by the IOC, sought to sponsor and nurture patriarchal values.[22] Although the role of women in Puerto Rican Olympism is significant, they were relegated to a secondary level in the creation and justification of Puerto Rico's Olympic Committee. Women, notably the 1938 Central American and Caribbean Games gold medalist Rebekah Colberg, have featured prominently in the construction of the Puerto Rican Olympic nation. The same can be said of black and mulatto Puerto Ricans. As a movement based in aristocratic circles and in Western racialized societies, Olympism favored and actually intended to support white racial superiority.[23] (It should be noted that two of the most important men in Puerto Rican sports were Julio Enrique Monagas, a mulatto, and Eugenio Guerra, a black Puerto Rican.) While gender and race dynamics were and are relevant within the Olympic movement, a full analysis is beyond the scope of this book. Future research should unravel this complex and essential problem in Puerto Rico's Olympic movement.

In the absence of other formal venues, Puerto Rico's Olympic Committee provides a good vehicle to represent the Puerto Rican state through athletic diplomacy. Puerto Rico is not a member of the United Nations, the Organization of American States, or the Community of Latin American and Caribbean States. However, despite their absence at the UN, Puerto Ricans have the support of many UN members. At the June 2013 UN meeting, many Latin American states expressed their support for Puerto Rican self-determination and affirmed Puerto Rico's Latin American identity. Additionally the Special Committee on Decolonization drafted yet another resolution calling on the United States to accelerate a process that would allow Puerto Ricans to implement their inalienable right to self-determination and independence.[24] The International Olympic Committee has more members than the UN. Given that the Olympic Games attract more attention, sporting and political, than meetings of the UN, being a member of the IOC and participating at the Olympic Games are the best ways for both independent and non-independent nation-states to engage in diplomatic agency. As a Latin American and Caribbean Olympic nation, Puerto Rico has absolute legitimacy to join its regional neighbors in the celebration of international goodwill, but most important in showcasing the national self.

At the heart of the problem in Puerto Rican Olympic history is the process by which an Olympic "sovereign" delegation can provide a sense of autonomy, or even decolonization, while still being bound to its colonial strictures. While Puerto Rico is considered a Latin American country and nation, it is the only one in the region owned by the United States. For Puerto Ricans, having a National Olympic Committee while still holding and benefiting from U.S. citizenship (unrestricted travel to and from the United States, employment opportunities in the United States, welfare benefits), actually prolongs the colonial relation. With a stable sense of Puerto Rican nationhood, having an Olympic representation fulfills the need to see the nation performed. At the same time, with growing economic dependency on the United States, increased federal welfare assistance, and trans-national migrations, territorial status becomes for many a despised necessity. In light of this political and cultural paradox, Puerto Rican Olympism has actually helped consolidate a colonial relation by allowing Puerto Ricans to have the best of both worlds: a sovereign Olympic nation and a close association with the United States.

While Puerto Rican Olympism has accommodated the contin-uation of colonial relations, it should not be taken as the desired outcome of Puerto Rican national identity or among the political leadership. To the contrary, since the late nineteenth century Puerto Rican political culture and tradition have centered on a desire for cul-tural and political autonomy in association with either Spain or the United States or as a fully annexed state of the United States rather than independence.[25] In the dawning decades of the nineteenth cen-tury, Puerto Rican liberals struggling against Spanish colonialism sought a diplomatic arrangement for provincial autonomy rather than embarking on an outright independence insurrection. Despite an influential conservative sector loyal to Spain, Puerto Ricans saw themselves as both Spaniards and Puerto Ricans and in 1897 obtained the long coveted Autonomic Charter from Spain that granted full local autonomy and more representation at the Spanish Cortes. When the United States invaded during the Spanish-American War of 1898, Puerto Rican politics switched gears, seeking autonomy within a very different imperial system. Different political factions welcomed the new regime, with its promise of democracy, liberalism, and progress. Major political parties were divided along lines of full annexation as a state of the Union or independence. Yet the wide gap between the promise and the practice of democracy led to active criticism and negotiation over the terms of colonialism.[26]

Much of the story in this book revolves around the autonomists, not because the other movements (independence and U.S. statehood) were irrelevant to Olympic sports but because Puerto Rico's incursion into the Olympic cycle mainly occurred within the autonomist movement. Although there are many followers of U.S. statehood (called *estadistas*) who enjoy Puerto Rico's success in Olympic meets, most of them would accept eliminating Olympic representation as the price of U.S. statehood. Due to the nationalistic overtones of the Olympics, it is understandable why *estadistas* might frown upon it, given that as a U.S. state Puerto Rico would not be able to have its own Olympic team.[27] However, one might think that pro-independence followers (called *independentistas*) would cherish, support, and nurture national Olympic representation. While this is true today, it was not always the case. Of the thousands of documents and newspaper articles in libraries and archives in Puerto Rico and the United States, only a handful indicated or suggested an *independentista* perspective on Puerto Rico's Olympic movement during the 1930s, 1940s, and early 1950s. The majority of those involved in Puerto Rico's Olympic movement, the autonomists, worked within and for a stronger relationship with the United States, openly using Olympic delegations as a diplomatic envoy to foster the U.S. Good Neighbor policy in Latin America in the 1930s, to showcase a decolonized commonwealth in the 1950s and 1960s, and for tourism and economic benefits. While performing the nation was certainly in the minds of some Olympic athletes, leaders, and followers during these decades, for those in the administration it was more a matter of U.S. diplomacy, economic interests, and local hegemony.

The 1930s was a decade of significant nationalist activism and the rise of Puerto Rico's Partido Nacionalista, led by Pedro Albizu Campos. However, the PN did not have an official position on Puerto Rico's Olympic representation. Albizu Campos's major speeches during the 1930s, including ones given after Puerto Rico's participation at the Central American and Caribbean Games in 1935 (where the flag bearer was a nationalist student), did not mention Puerto Rico's Olympic delegation.[28] Scholars so far have not studied this side of Albizu Campos's ideology.[29] In trying to understand the PN's silence on Puerto Rico's early Olympic strides, two points must be acknowledged. First, some prominent PN leaders, including Albizu Campos, were not athletes themselves and did not see the importance of sports or Olympic participation in the struggle for Puerto Rican independence during the 1930s and 1940s.[30] Second, the PN did not recognize U.S. authority in the island. Calling for abstention in the 1936 general election, Albizu Campos's PN affirmed, "Yankee rule in Puerto Rico is null and the Yankee Empire does not have the right to convene the Puerto Rican nation for elections under its flag."[31] Given this posture, one explanation of the PN's silence on Puerto Rican Olympism might be that they did not recognize a Puerto Rican delegation that officially represented the United States and carried the U.S. flag. In other words, the nationalists were not going to endorse or celebrate an Olympic delegation convened and organized by the colonial state in compliance with and representing the United States. It was only after the recognition of the increasing popularity in Olympic sports, the creation of the commonwealth, the official use of the Puerto Rican flag in international competition, and a new generation within the movement in the 1960s that the nationalists, now organized under the Movimiento Pro Independencia, recognized the importance of Olympic sports for the nation and would defend it at all costs.

However, the nationalists did have representation and a voice at regional and Olympic Games. Some athletes, including Juan Juarbe Juarbe and Manuel Luciano, made sure to showcase their nationalist or anti-imperialist sentiments at the Games. Their acts were well received by some throughout the region and were scorned by other Puerto Ricans and by U.S. officials. Margaret Power's insights into the transnational Latin American solidarity networks nurtured by the PN and Albizu Campos since the 1920s can help explain these incidents as examples of Latin American solidarity with Puerto Rican nationalists.[32]

A key idea behind the paradox of Puerto Rican colonial Olympism is that U.S. citizenship, granted in 1917, and Puerto Rican national identity were not mutually exclusive. By participating under the name Puerto Rico, showcasing their nationhood, and doing this as U.S. citizens, Puerto Rican Olympic athletes defined the terms of their colonial existence. Nothing in the terms of the Jones Act of 1917, which granted U.S. citizenship, included a ban on a Puerto Rican Olympic delegation. The 1952 Constitution, which did not alter the U.S. citizenship statue of 1917, also did not mention the Olympic delegation. Puerto Rico's Olympic participation as U.S. citizens was negotiated on the spot—between different agencies and individuals in the United States, Puerto Rico, and the IOC—at every meet they were invited to or participated in.

Puerto Rico's Olympic story is as much a story of cultural survival as it is a story of politics and international diplomacy. Puerto Ricans used, and still use, the limits of their colonial structures to claim national existence and continue an autonomist political tradition. They used a central feature of twentieth-century U.S. colonialism and Olympism, mainly the championing of democracy, to participate in Olympic sports, and by doing so showcasing the national self. They took advantage of Coubertin's Hellenic inspiration and desire for national inclusiveness, whether sovereign or not, in his revival of the Olympic Games.[33] In this regard, Coubertin was convinced of the necessity to spread Olympism to all corners of the world. Similarly Puerto Ricans understood the U.S. interests in the region and embraced their role as the Latin Caribbean representative for the U.S. Good Neighbor policy at the Central American and Caribbean Games. These Games were the perfect place to practice political diplomacy by showing they were as Puerto Rican as they were U.S. citizens.

Diplomatically Puerto Ricans were a part in the U.S. imperial sphere of sports as a means to spread U.S. political influences abroad, as Robert Elias shows in the case of baseball.[34] More generally Gerald Gems demonstrates how the United States used sports in spreading cultural imperialism through an "athletic crusade." The U.S. expansionist zeal in the phrase *manifest destiny* would shape imperial ambitions.[35] Once the United States had firm roots in the island, the Puerto Rican Olympic delegation of the 1930s, in their capacity as U.S. citizens, became diplomatic athletes to bridge Anglo and Latin American political and cultural differences. This role was actually welcomed by Puerto Ricans who had decided early in the occupation, and as part of an Americanization project, to accept the progressive and modernizing influence of the United States. When the United States took over the island in 1898, it sought to convert locals to fit the cultural values and politico-economic interests of its growing empire. As such it carried out an Americanization project that included, among other things, an overhaul of the education system in place under Spanish rule. Similar Americanization projects had been implemented in the continental United States for Native Americans, African Americans, and Irish immigrants. The goal of Americanization was to make English the lingua franca in Puerto Rico and to replace Spanish with American traditions and values, among them sport and physical education.

If sport was a source of diplomacy and Americanization, this occurred as part of a negotiation process between U.S. political interests and Puerto Rican struggles for national progress. As the historian Solsiree del Moral skillfully argues in *Negotiating Empire*, Puerto Ricans negotiated the elements of this Americanization project, rejecting the ones they perceived as threatening identity and pride but accepting the ones they believed helped them to progress. While adhering to their Spanish Caribbean traditions and cultures spanning four hundred years, Puerto Ricans welcomed in their visions of nation U.S. ideals of progress, including the promise of democracy, civil equality, popular and progressive mass education, and more and better sports and physical education. Besides Americanizing in their adoption of sports, Puerto Ricans also immersed themselves in U.S. capitalist and consumerist culture, rock music, and Protestantism. However, they managed to keep those elements at the core of what made them a unique Latin and Caribbean people. In this regard they are similar to other Latin American countries where baseball, rock music, and Protestantism have thrived.

Puerto Ricans did not integrate into U.S. Olympic structures and rejected a proposal in 1948 to merge with the U.S. Olympic Committee, as Hawaii and Alaska had done prior to their incorporation as states of the Union. Moreover Puerto Ricans overcame colonial Olympic suppression and claimed a legitimate place among Olympic nations, aided by external factors such as other Central American countries, the International Olympic Committee, and Avery Brundage, president of the U.S. Olympic Committee (1928–53) and International Olympic Committee (1952–72). These external factors go beyond the national boundaries that aid in the creation of national identity and add another layer to the complex and multifactorial process of nationalism and national identity.

This book departs from older histories of colonialism that focused on clearly drawn lines between oppressor and oppressed. Instead the story of Puerto Rican Olympic sports confirms that some Puerto Ricans were as responsible for their colonial strictures as some Americans were champions of the Puerto Rican Olympic nation. For example, sport leaders such as Justo Rivera Cabrera and even Julio Enrique Monagas in the 1930s and 1940s upheld the primacy of Puerto Rico's association to U.S. sports and citizenship rather than willfully advancing international athletic participation. On the other hand, Blanton Winship, a U.S.-appointed governor known for his repressive administration during the 1930s, was an open supporter of Puerto Rico's athletic participation abroad, and Brundage supported Puerto Rico's continuing participation in Olympic international competition.

While many Puerto Ricans viewed sports and Olympism as a source of national identity, others viewed sports as beneficial to physical health, tourism, and goodwill; some even viewed sports as a political contribution to athletic diplomacy. The popularity of sport and Olympic competition moved many to follow the Puerto Rican delegation as it competed abroad. For others, sport was a way to represent U.S. democracy and progress internationally as U.S. citizens. Some athletes were proud of being Puerto Rican; others just aspired to compete and prove themselves against other elite athletes, often other college students.

The construction of a Puerto Rican national identity through sport was intertwined with international politics. The Good Neighbor policy, World War II, the decolonization movements, and the cold war all had profound roles in Puerto Rican Olympic participation. Puerto Rico was not the only Latin American country involved in this process. In his study of President Juan Domingo Peron's use of sports in Argentina, Cesar Torres concludes, "The Peronist state comprehended the powerful symbolism and high visibility of international sport, especially in light of its competitive character, and invested profusely in it. In doing so, it fully included sponsoring, bidding, participating, and hosting large international sporting events to the repertoire of available diplomatic instruments. Thus the athletes of the New Argentina were conceived as effective ambassadors, capable of multiplying, or even surpassing, the efforts of traditional diplomacy."[36] For Puerto Rico, the Olympic delegation became not only proof that the nation existed but also an athletic diplomatic envoy to demonstrate U.S. goodwill and to help support the International Olympic Committee's own existence.

International politics and Olympic Games are good platforms on which to test national and sport strength. In the case of Puerto Rico, these developed within the limits of empire and the construction of an autonomist political culture. Having experienced the lack of development of mass sports and physical education under Spain,

Puerto Ricans welcomed a new system. The YMCA entered Puerto Rico in 1899 as part of the U.S. Army and Navy to provide religious, moral, and recreational support to the soldiers and civil society. The "Army and Navy YMCA" set an example of the importance of sports and recreation for physical and spiritual well-being. U.S. federal and local colonial authorities also sponsored athletics and physical education through the overhaul of the public education system and the establishment of the University of Puerto Rico in 1903. By hosting the Tenth Central American and Caribbean Games in San Juan in 1966, Puerto Ricans consolidated their sport culture and its relation to international politics with the development of a national identity.

The focus of this story is the twentieth century, roughly from 1898 to 1966, although some events in 1980 and 2010 are discussed in the last chapter. I have chosen to end the story in 1966 because this year marks the climax of Puerto Rico's Olympic trajectory. The problems of being recognized as a legitimate Olympic nation had been, for the most part, clarified by this time. By hosting the Central American and Caribbean Games of 1966, their first ever mega-sporting international event, Puerto Ricans tested their infrastructural and programmatic Olympic capabilities. The problems faced at the 1966 Games, mainly dependence on the United States to set foreign political policy in relation to communist Cuba, continued in the decades that followed until the present. The negotiations and dilemmas of Olympic politics as seen in the 1980 Olympic Boycott (although here the Puerto Rican Olympic Committee did go against the boycott and participated in the Games) and in the 1993 and 2010 Central American and Caribbean Games are reminiscent of the experiences of 1966. After 1966 Puerto Rican Olympism shows the continuation of political negotiations and clashes between the pro-statehood and pro-commonwealth groups and the small but vocal pro-independence groups.

Although I am aware of the problems of periodization in history, I trace the development of sport across five loosely conceptualized political periods: (1) the late nineteenth century and the end of Spanish colonialism; (2) the early negotiations over U.S. colonialism and its Americanization policies from 1898 through the 1920s; (3) the instability of the 1930s and the definition of national identity; (4) the PPD's populism of the 1940s; and (5) the evaluation of autonomy and the commonwealth after 1952. This division of Puerto Rican history also correlates to international political events: the first period corresponds to the emergence of the United States as an imperial power that covers the Spanish American War of 1898, the Good Neighbor policy of the post-Depression 1930s, World War II and the near postwar years, the waves of decolonization of the late 1940s, 1950s, and 1960s, and the cold war.[37]

At the center of this book is a wide range of interrelated governmental and private agencies that together contributed to the framework of Puerto Rican colonialism and national identity. These institutions, created under the banner of progress and modernization, actually served the dual purpose of identity formation and colonial consent. These included the YMCA, the public education system, the University of Puerto Rico, the Puerto Rican Legislature, the governor of Puerto Rico, the sport and recreation government agencies, and the Puerto Rican Olympic Committee. In the search for Puerto Rican political and cultural autonomy, these institutions morphed, grew, and sometimes disappeared only to surface again, eventually consolidating to create a healthy, educated, and progressive citizenry.

While studying institutions is elemental in dissecting the development of sport and Olympism in Puerto Rico, they are ultimately meaningless if we do not analyze the individuals commanding them. Leading these government agencies were central figures in politics, education, and sports, both elite and nonelite, who together gave meaning to Puerto Rico's colonial Olympism. Central among them was Julio Enrique Monagas, a figure perplexingly nonexistent in Puerto Rican historiography. Monagas played a crucial role in the development of local sport in Puerto Rico through his sports and recreation agencies and as head of the Comité Olímpico de Puerto

Rico (COPR) and an ally of the populist hegemonic project of the PPD. Monagas's role in the politics of sport and nation building in Puerto Rico actually transcended insular politics. His international credence and presidency over the Central American and Caribbean Sport Organization (CACSO) was a significant accomplishment.

Indeed Monagas was one of the PPD's key contributors to Puerto Rico's dramatic modernization, which became an example to the developing world.[38] My analysis of Monagas contributes to the idea that for all the charisma, dynamism, and strong leadership of Luis Muñoz Marín (Puerto Rico's twentieth-century political *caudillo*), there were key figures whose loyalty, intelligence, cleverness, and drive were indispensable to the success of the PPD's reforms.[39] These include Teodoro Moscoso and Operation Bootstrap, Jaime Benítez and the Universidad de Puerto Rico, Ricardo Alegría and the Institute of Puerto Rican Culture, Rafael Picó as chairman of the Puerto Rico Planning Board and president of the Government Development Bank, Secretary of State Roberto Sánchez Vilella, and Antonio Fernós Isern and his ideological basis to establish the commonwealth.[40] Monagas deserves a place in this team of political, economic, and cultural leaders who, working within the parameters of U.S. imperialism, created a pro-American populist colonial state.[41]

Most of these men coincided almost exactly in their tenure as head of their respective institutions during the heyday of PPD hegemony. Monagas served as commissioner and administrator of sports and recreation from 1942 to 1966, and Jaime Benítez served as chancellor of the UPR from 1942 to 1966. Rafael Picó served as chairman of Puerto Rico Planning from 1942 to 1955, as treasurer of Puerto Rico from 1955 to 1958, and as president of the Government Development Bank from 1958 to 1964. Teodoro Moscoso served as president of the Puerto Rican Industrial Development Company from 1942 to 1950, as administrator of the Economic Development Administration from 1950 to 1961, as U.S. ambassador to Venezuela in 1961–62, and as coordinator for the Alliance for Progress from 1962 to 1964.

Puerto Rican modernization aimed at fulfilling the needs of a colonial nation. Modernization comprised a project of political dignity and economic industrialization that lifted Puerto Ricans from centuries of colonial exploitation, without necessarily abandoning a special relationship with the metropole. In this regard, despite the creation in 1952 of a seemingly autonomous status (commonwealth, or Estado Libre Asociado de Puerto Rico) and the establishment of an economic industrialization program (Operation Bootstrap) that lifted Puerto Ricans from poverty, Puerto Rican modernization actually consolidated colonialism and increased economic dependence within the U.S. economic system.[42]

Although modernization is usually discussed in terms of economic, social, and political policies of industrialization, institutionalization, urbanization, and political consolidation, the development of Puerto Rico's Olympic movement occurred as part of these politico-economic and infrastructural changes in relation to cultural activities. Cultural studies examines the traditions, practices, and beliefs of a group or community that provides entertainment and leisure but also shows its uniqueness and cultivates a sense of identity.[43] In this regard, I am distancing myself from the highly criticized modernization theory with a one-style development model for the "Third World" in order to "catch up" with the world's industrial centers. I am also distancing myself from the often inconclusive and elusive concept of modernity.[44] Instead I use modernization not as a global model of development but as a series of fundamental reforms by and for a particular society that sought to increase standards of living. For Puerto Ricans, modernization, or progress, entailed the creation of an industrial society following a populist and social justice program, with a degree of autonomy.

Monagas was not alone in the task of sport development and leadership. Other major players were no less influential; they include Zerah Collins, William Coxhead, George Keelan, Cosme Beitía, Justo Rivera Cabrera, Eugenio Guerra, Teófilo Maldonado, Luis Guillermety, Emilio Huyke, and Germán Rieckehoff Sampayo. Not all of these individuals agreed on the purpose, shape, or goals of Puerto Rican sports and Olympism, but each of them left an enduring mark on Puerto Rican colonial Olympism. Sport policies did not occur in a leadership vacuum or separate from the political, economic, or social issues. These policies were designed, enacted, and enforced by different individuals representing different ideologies and interests that ranged from full Americanization to Olympic and political sovereignty. Athletes and the masses also had varying reasons to partake in and follow Olympic activities. Some athletes believed they were representing a nascent Puerto Rican nation; some just wanted to compete against other good athletes and were clearly detached from political ideologies. Developing Olympism in Puerto Rico was a process characterized by multiple meanings, not always dictated from the top of the colonial venture but defined by multiple actors from different segments of society.

While the present story focuses on Puerto Rico, parallel developments are cited. As a Latin American nation, Puerto Rico shares with its neighboring Latin American countries a history of Iberian colonization, encounters of diverse ethnicities, similar cultural and political traditions and socioeconomic concerns, and U.S. interventions.[45] As eloquently put by Antonio Benítez-Rojo in *The Repeating Island*, as a Caribbean nation Puerto Rico also has a history multicultural Atlantic cultural chaos and polyrhythms characteristic of the Plantation society.[46] Yet as Franklin Knight explains, the island's history also shows the particular local processes of nation within larger Caribbean national identities.[47] We must understand as well identities in both a geopolitical and a "geohistorical" sense.[48] That is to say, European colonization patterns and imperial wars in the Caribbean, including that of the United States, have shaped the construction of national identities in the region. Varying degrees of forced African immigration, European immigration, a sugar plantation economy, and militarized societies have caused the Caribbean islands to have similar national characteristics. Nonetheless I agree with Stephan Palmié and Francisco Scarano, who state that the history of the Caribbean ought not to be understood as a byproduct of empires and migrant civilizations that fought for and lived in the region, but as its own area full of similarities and differences, all centered on the societies that inhabit it.[49] To understand Puerto Rico is also to understand Latin America and especially the Caribbean. Even though the particular contexts of these societies may be very different, the political, social, and cultural processes, including sport and Olympism, are fairly similar.[50] Examination of the institutions and people that regulated, supervised, controlled, scrutinized, and reacted to sport in Puerto Rico will shed light on other places.

Sport and History

Amy Bass, writing for an American academic audience, has cleverly framed the suitability of sport as a window to understand history:

> The possibilities are vast, and much is demanded of the sports historian. Sport is a commercial industry that deals with concepts of labor and capitalism, often within the landscape of urban studies; a cultural realm that takes in the politics of media and spectacle, constructing and contesting identities such as gender, race, and sexuality, class, religion, ethnicity, and nationality (and their multiple combinations); a scientific domain with focal points on the psyche of both athlete and spectator, as well as the physical achievements of humans on any given playing field; and an arena for foreign policy and cultural diplomacy.[51]

The historical study of sport does not view sport as representative of society but as forming an integral part of it. Sport in modern societies has become an inescapable variable in the study of the human experience in all its complexities. Leaving it aside as a mundane activity of entertainment means leaving our comprehension of our past and present incomplete.

Andrew Johns states that sports as politics "can be a peaceful tool of goodwill or used as leverage to coerce behavior. It can exacerbate existing nationalistic tensions or be used to promote developments and strengthen alliances. It can have a significant economic impact on a country or region, and it can be used as an effective weapon of propaganda. In short, sport is at once parochial and universal, unifying and dividing, and has the potential to fundamentally affect relations between individuals and nations."[52] On the cultural side, sport is an activity that resembles a theater where heroes, villains, myths, and legends are formed.[53] The story of Puerto Rican Olympic sport points to a historical process of sport as both politics and culture.[54] The power of sport in political affairs results partly from the ways in which human emotions drive and react so powerfully to these performances.[55] Accordingly this story is framed with reflections on sport and its role in modern society offered by scholars such as Allen Guttman, John Hargreaves, John MacAloon, and James Mangan.[56]

Different factors account for the rise and consolidation of sports as an integral and unavoidable feature of modern societies. Although some scholars argue that sports have been practiced since antiquity, other scholars point to the rise of industrialization in the North Atlantic, mainly in England, France, and the United States.[57] Industrial societies became more technological and technical, which led to the formalization of games, including written rules, record keeping, and recurring schedules. This was achieved due to an emphasis on rationalization, standardization, secularization, specialization, and quantification. At the same time, physical education became more important in an already developing emphasis on scientific education. Physical education was considered an essential part of the formation of modern and rational individuals. Indeed Coubertin was first and foremost an educator and an advocate of physical education.[58]

As a feature of modern society, sports are essential in their relation to politics and social coercion. Although sports involve a large degree of play, they also need rules and a degree of social control and formalization, which turns into relations of power. Scholars have traced the formalization of sport to nineteenth-century England, where the rising political and economic supremacy of the bourgeoisie used sport to gain dominion over the popular classes.[59] Elite white men with leisure time controlled the regulations of different sports; they dictated who could play what, where, when, and how, while also codifying social hierarchies. Take, for example, the establishment of private elite clubs to play golf or tennis, while another set of rules and public spaces were for the popular masses to play sports or attend soccer games. Blue-collar factory workers (teammates) working together under a supervisor (coach) offered a perfect analogy to team sport. As sports became popular among the working classes, competing within and between factories, they became an integral part of society. In the United States, especially after the Civil War, sports became a leading form of modern, capitalist, and Protestant identity.[60] For instance, Donald Mrozek shows that U.S. sports, such as baseball, with its emphasis on regulation, precision, and social order, became the emblem of citizenship, patriotism, and the "American" way of life.[61]

Clearly, then, sport is a cultural phenomenon of national identity. As Andrew Blake asserts, "Patriotism and nationalism . . . are available more powerfully and effectively through aspects of sports—its performance and technology, language and representation—than through any other set of human activities and beliefs." By producing great victories, heroes, and villains, sports enter into the realm of myth making and in turn feed an integral part of national myths essential to the formation of a national past. Indeed the role of sports can be seen in the idea of progress in the nineteenth century.[62] Western civilization's progress can be measured in part by the development in sports of formal rules and organized tournaments and the revival of the Olympic Games in 1896. Transportation made attending games easier, mass media communication brought games into one's household, and electricity made night games possible. Sport became a unifying factor in nation building.

There is no doubt that sport at the international level, such as the Olympic Games and the Soccer World Cup, has been a leading forum to not only display and compare levels of development but also to actively engage in political contests and negotiations and create national consciousness.[63] International sporting events played an integral part in the dramatic political and cultural scene after 1945, as recently evidenced in the essays gathered by Heather Dichter and Andrew Johns.[64] Stephen Wagg and David Andrews effectively show how "international sporting competition provided a hitherto unprecedented—and, arguably, cathartic—vehicle for the expression of the new order of nation-based antagonisms within the post-war world."[65] That is, the culture of sport became the stage on which to display and peacefully play out the ideological, civil, and moral differences between capitalism and communism. When these tensions met at the Olympic Games, competition provided a way to contend for the supremacy of new world orders yet also became a space where these orders proved their willingness to relate in diplomatic capacities. Needless to say, in the context of cold war Olympics, there was an inherent competition to prove which side was more developed.

Puerto Rico is an excellent place to study this idea of how sports, culture, and politics are intrinsically tied together. Puerto Rico's status as a U.S. territory challenges our notions of sovereignty and nation. Yet this paradox is not unique to Puerto Rico. The IOC has recognized nonindependent nations such as Palestine, Chinese Taipei (Taiwan), Bermuda, Aruba, and Hong Kong, while also recognizing Jamaica and the Philippines before independence. Coubertin himself believed in letting all nations participate at the Olympic Games, regardless of their political situation.[66] Laurent Dubois's *Soccer Empire* shows how soccer in the Caribbean became a source of national identity not only for the French overseas departments of Guadeloupe and

Martinique, but for the French national sphere overall.[67] In World Cup soccer Guadeloupeans and Martiniqueans are as much nationals of their islands as they are French nationals. Sports historian John Hargreaves argues that one of the IOC's reasons for denying Catalonia recognition and Olympic representation was that a separate Catalonia National Olympic Committee would present a challenge to the cohesiveness of the Spanish nation.[68] Coubertin used his own judgment to determine which nations would be recognized as Olympic nations. During the 1916 Intermediate Olympic Games in Athens, he declined national Olympic status to Catalonia and the Basque Country, while allowing separate Olympic delegations from Bohemia when it was part of the Austro-Hungarian Empire and Finland when it was a grand duchy within the Russian Empire. Thus, regardless of Coubertin's "all games—all nations" belief, the IOC does engage in discriminatory guidelines and sets international hierarchical lines within its governance, especially in the decolonized world.[69] This book contributes to the historiography of Olympic politics by presenting how Puerto Rico's Olympic trajectory has contributed to prolonging the life of Latin America's last colony.

In Latin America the study of sport has shown promising advances since C. L. R. James's classic *Beyond a Boundary* from 1963.[70] Like James, Joseph Arbena and Allen Guttmann can be considered pioneers in the field of sports history in Latin America and beyond.[71] Guttmann's emphasis on sports' secularism, equality, bureaucratization, specialization, rationalization, quantification, and records defines the modern qualities of sport.[72] Eduardo Galeano's beautifully written *Soccer in Sun and Shadow* portrays in simple yet enduring narrated images the political, national, personal, social, and economic complexities of soccer in Latin America. Sport historian J. A. Mangan captured the importance of sport in Latin America when he said that sport can produce "an ecstasy as potent as any religion, an escapism as real as any cinema, [and] an enjoyment as intense as any carnival."[73] Sports are the driving force in Latin America's modern political dynamics.

Joseph Arbena stands as the pioneer historian of sport in Latin America. He has traced the three paths of Latin American sport nationalism: (1) "the establishment of domestic physical education programs, sport competitions, and the permanent institutions necessary to oversee athletic programs"; (2) "the preparation of individuals and teams capable of competing successfully on the international level"; and (3) "the hosting of international sporting events."[74] This book confirms Arbena's model by detailing how this three-step process occurred in Puerto Rico. For example, the first condition was achieved under the establishment of the public school system and the University of Puerto Rico in 1903 with the development of their athletic and physical education programs. The second stage was fulfilled through the creation in 1927 and then development of the government's sport and recreation agency, and the third became a reality when Puerto Rico hosted the Tenth Central American and Caribbean Games in San Juan in 1966.

Other scholars have followed a similar model in the study of sport. For example, the recent work of Brenda Elsey, *Citizens and Sportsmen*, skillfully analyzes the role of soccer in Chile and the ways the organization, institutionalization, and performance of soccer clubs aided in the "democratization of the public sphere" and the bridging of formal and informal politics. Joshua Nadel's *Fútbol! Why Soccer Matters in Latin America* demonstrates the multifaceted impact that soccer has had in different Latin American countries. The historian Louis Pérez Jr. has studied sport in its intersections with politics, nationalism, and revolution in Cuba.[75] Sport in Cuba has been a marker not only of identity but also of modernization and even Americanization. In *On Becoming Cuban*, Pérez describes how Cubans welcomed and adopted sports as a symbol of the levels of modernization their country was achieving after the U.S. intervention in 1898.[76] That this modernization was a result of specific U.S. national games and recreation entailed acceptance of American values. Modernization for Cubans meant baseball, and baseball meant Cubanness. Hence the line between Americanization, modernization, and Cubanness was blurred in the creation of Cuban national identity.

While the few works of Puerto Rican Olympism have addressed the ways national identity has been forged through sports, few have taken a profound look at the institutional scaffolding of such dynamics. Without a close scrutiny of the creation, motives, actions, and complex web of politics of such Olympic and sports institutions, our understanding of the process is incomplete and misleading. The history of sports on the island has usually been documentary or celebratory, without paying much attention to political complexities within the nation.[77] Writers assume that there is indeed a Puerto Rican nation that can be seen through the Olympic athlete rather than examining how that idea of a nation may have been constructed and made up through sport. Emilio Huyke's classic *Los deportes en Puerto Rico* (1968) is a good example of the documentation of the variety of games and sports. Other equally valuable documentary contributions to the history of sport in Puerto Rico have been made by the works of Carlos Uriarte González, which contain rich statistical and anecdotal accounts of Puerto Rican participation at Central American and Caribbean Games, Pan-American Games, and Olympic Games. Joaquín Martínez-Rousset uses an array of primary documentation in *50 años de Olimpismo* to narrate the political and colonial stages of Puerto Rican Olympism. The value of this work is that it does not present an uncritical view of Puerto Rico's road to Olympism, but unabashedly presents it in its full drama as a colonial project of nation building. The present book is an attempt to continue, elaborate, and deepen Martínez-Rousset's work.

Baseball has been the best studied of all sports practiced in Puerto Rico. However, most of this literature falls within the descriptive or celebratory approach.[78] Félix Huertas González stands out as one recent scholar who conceptualized sport and identity in colonial politics and constructions of nationalism. In his book *Deporte e identidad: Puerto Rico y su presencia deportiva internacional (1930–1950)* of

2006, Huertas González shows how the introduction of Puerto Rico into international competition marked the strength of Puerto Rican identity. This work is a good introduction to the long and complex history of the institutions and individuals that aided in the development of a sport culture, paying particular attention to Olympic and local politics. Huertas González bases his theoretical framework on the work of scholars of nationalism such as Benedict Anderson, Ernest Gellner, and Eric Hobsbawm. Yet he does not make it clear whether sport is the reflection of a national identity or the process of constructing a national identity.

Many of today's Puerto Rican Olympic enthusiasts still exemplify the nationalistic essentialist approach toward sports that Antonio Pedreira took in the 1930s. Antonio Pedreira's classic work, *Insularismo* (1934), is representative of a generation of scholars in the 1930s who sought to assert a Puerto Rican Hispanic nationality, a part of the larger and similar Hispanismo movement in Spanish America.[79] While his work has been criticized for being pessimistic, paternalist, and racist, Pedreira did include sports as a strong marker of *puertorriqueñidad* and of a sense of individual and collective will. He stated that sport "lay a note of joviality in our somber night, developing a hygienic, happy, and battling youth." Yet for Pedreira, Puerto Rican sporting spirit, exemplified in horse racing, was inherited from the aristocratic Spanish culture, which "manages to truly discover an enlightened manifestation of the national soul."[80]

This book moves beyond the celebratory, documentary, descriptive, and tactical approaches to sport and assumes a more critical study of sport politics, following an analytical approach to Puerto Rican sports similar to that of other scholars. Roberta Park has recently undertaken the academic study of sport in Puerto Rico; in "'Forget about That Pile of Papers': Second World War Sport, Recreation and the Military on the Island of Puerto Rico," she studies the intersections of sport and recreation with U.S. imperial and militaristic interests in Puerto Rico in the building of hegemony in the island. Her most recent essay, "From *la bomba* to *béisbol*: Sport and the Americanisation of Puerto Rico, 1898–1950," looks at the role that sport played in the U.S. interest in fully turning Puerto Rican culture into American values. Frances Negrón-Muntaner has critically studied professional boxing as it relates to complexities of contemporary Puerto Rican national identity and colonialism.[81]

As Kevin Witherspoon asserts for Mexico's Olympic movement, this book is as much about Olympism and institution building as it is about the politics of sports and the sport of politics.[82] John MacAloon gave an excellent start to the academic study of Puerto Rican sport when he said that Puerto Rico's Olympic Committee in the 1970s was the axis around which much of politics and culture revolve. His essay "La Pitada Olímpica" (1984) analyzed how Puerto Rican international sport representation was the source of political and cultural identities; in addition to Martínez-Rousset, it informs my basic ground for analysis. MacAloon sees sports in Puerto Rico and elsewhere not as a curiosity of culture and political relations but as culture and politics in and of themselves.[83] In other words, sport is politics and sport is culture.

MacAloon argues that the status of Puerto Rico as a nation is politically ambiguous, but in international sporting events it is not. Regardless of previous setbacks and defeats, every new Olympic cycle brings hope of victory and redemption. However, regardless of the result, Puerto Ricans look forward to being present and participating in every new cycle. This is one of the few times that the Puerto Rican flag is hoisted and carried alone in an official public event, the other one being the Miss Universe pageant. However, MacAloon's study, while a good start, only scratches the surface of the story of the creation and development of sport institutions and their leaders. I take MacAloon's basic analytical parameters and present a comprehensive view of the story behind sport development in its political and nationalistic complexities.

The chapters' decade-by-decade story line should not be taken as a strict periodization. The process of creating and maintaining a sport and recreational culture is not that neat. But in order to show the progression of events in a more visible way, I have opted to break the story into decades. The events discussed in each chapter do not cover all regional games and all Olympic Games, as this is not a sport chronicle. Instead I focus on certain events that for different reasons highlight how Olympic sports, national identity, colonialism, and international politics interact.

In chapter 1, I develop the details of why sport became the perfect tool to show the differences between an obsolete and backward Spanish regime and a progressive U.S. regime, which helped in the exchange of empires in 1898. After a brief outline of the use and purposes of sport and games in Spanish Puerto Rico, I show how sport was used by the United States to Americanize and firmly establish hegemonic control. The YMCA and the newly created education system were the key institutions for spreading athletic culture. U.S. sports in Puerto Rico were welcomed and quickly gained popularity, as they represented the dawn of a new progressive, democratic, and physically fit society.

In chapter 2, I describe how Puerto Ricans began to organize their Olympic institutions despite growing discontent with the colonial regime and much social, economic, and political distress in the 1930s. With increasing local sporting leadership, Puerto Rican incursion into international competition became an advertisement for tourism, a performance of identity, a showcase of progress, and a tool for diplomacy. The Good Neighbor policy and regional diplomacy were the backdrop to international play that ultimately made many Puerto Ricans question both U.S. imperialism and Puerto Rican progress and identity.

Sport became integral in solidifying Puerto Rico's relationship to the United States in the 1940s, as illustrated in chapter 3. As sport became more centralized and autonomous, the goal of the United States and local governments was to consolidate a political relationship in order to aid Puerto Rican pro-American populism and socio-economic development. The international concerns over imperialism and colonialism that accompanied World War II, coupled with the International Olympic Committee's need for Olympic nations to recover from the war, allowed Puerto Ricans to showcase their Olympic nationhood. In 1948 Puerto Ricans participated for the first time in the Summer Olympic Games, demonstrating the performance of the nation on the global stage as well as the unyielding persistence of colonialism. Revealing interviews with some Puerto Rican athletes who were there provide a personal view of the politics of the London Games.

Chapter 4 demonstrates the intricate ways in which the commonwealth and Olympic sport interacted in the 1950s as a colonial territory became a sovereign sporting nation. This occurred within internal sport-political power struggles that spurred debates over patronage, centralization, and communism that split Puerto Rican Olympism. In turn, Puerto Rican internal problems placed the International Olympic Committee in a philosophical conundrum over the role of the state in Olympism, which became known as "the Puerto Rican Case." Regardless of this, the commonwealth, now in a growing movement of decolonization, continued to participate in the Olympic Games. However, parallel to a perception of autonomy, Olympic participation legitimized and cemented U.S. colonialism due to the still colonial political basis of Puerto Rico's new status.

During the 1960s and as a result of the Cuban Revolution, Olympism in Central America and the Caribbean became more deeply involved in volatile cold war politics. Chapter 5 sets the context for the 1966 Central American and Caribbean Games in San Juan and explains how regional Olympic tournaments embodied cold war hostilities. The 1966 Games represented the perfect scenario, indeed the pinnacle for the commonwealth and many Puerto Ricans to display their Latin American and Caribbean nationhood. These Games confirm that while the government kept developing sport infrastructure, the commonwealth became dangerously entangled by cold war tensions when the Cuban delegation was prohibited from entering San Juan. Sport and politics clashed once again, ultimately evidencing a colonial relationship, revealing Puerto Rico's leading (yet still invisible) role in Central American and Caribbean cold war affairs. Indeed these Games, although today remembered as a governmental and Olympic diplomatic success, actually came close to unleashing a major international conflict.

Chapter 6 provides an overview of the career of Puerto Rico's sport czar, Julio Enrique Monagas, in light of his accomplishments and shortcomings during his tenure developing Olympic sport in Puerto Rico. By 1966 he had renounced his leadership positions in the institutions of sport locally and the Central American and Caribbean Sport Organization, yet his legacy had just begun. He managed to consolidate a sport culture locally and internationally, and future issues of sport revolved around the base he had laid in his twenty-four years of service, from 1942 to 1966. Serving as a conclusion to the book, this chapter highlights the most important topics in Puerto Rican Olympic participation, intertwining them in a brief recollection of major Olympic incidents since 1966. The intersections among sport, politics, and national identity continued from 1967 until the present, yet were highlighted in 1980, 1993, and 2010. Together they exhibited the strength and endurance of sport institutions, the power of colonial Olympism, the consolidation of national identity, and the persistence of an autonomous political culture despite challenges from other political forces.

1/ Sport in Imperial Exchanges

"I speak more truth than God." These were the words that captain general and governor Juan de Velasco (1660–70) used in the midst of a challenge during a game of *pelota* in colonial Spanish Puerto Rico.[1] The expression appalled the bishop of San Juan, who, under the rules of seventh-century Catholicism, could have censured him as a heretical blasphemer.[2] But for Velasco, winning that point was so important that he challenged the meaning and applicability of heresy and, in turn, established himself as the absolute authority, even higher than the island's bishop. Velasco was not deposed from his position, and the heretic comment did not take away his legitimacy as supreme commander. To the contrary, the game was another venue to showcase Velasco's power and authority. More than a curiosity of colonial history, this event portrays several aspects of games and sports in Spanish Puerto Rico.

The process of establishing a culture of sport in Puerto Rico is extensive and goes back centuries. This culture of sport was affected by colonialism, which in turn affected and shaped sociopolitical dynamics. Colonialism, periphery, isolation, geopolitics, and centralization all play important roles in how Puerto Ricans view themselves and how sports developed in this small Caribbean island. For nearly four hundred years under Spanish rule (1508–1898), games in Puerto Rico were similar to those in other parts of colonial Spanish America. Sport was another stage for colonial authority and hierarchy to be displayed and defined. Once the United States entered the scene, formally in 1898, Puerto Rican sports entered a more institutionalized and democratic stage.

As mentioned in the introduction, sport has been defined generally by Allen Guttmann in *From Ritual to Record* as an activity of play that includes an emphasis on secularism, equality, bureaucratization, specialization, rationalization, quantification, and an obsession with records.[3] While this definition is accepted in modern sports—and is inherently tied to my analysis—it runs the risk of privileging the North Atlantic's athletic culture because it was developed under the historical perspectives of Europe and the United States. However, when we look closely to how sports were practiced in other places of the Western world, such as the Iberian Peninsula, we see that people played games that resemble modern sport long before the nineteenth century.

Just as the political leaders in Puerto Rico transferred their loyalty and their claims for autonomy from Spain to the United States, so did the political uses of athletics for authority and empire building. Sports and games did not suddenly appear in 1898 with the U.S. Army and Navy troops. They were present in the island well before then and played a particular role in Spanish Puerto Rican colonial life. Games and sports were used for recreation but also to define lines of authority, by different groups to challenge such authority, and by liberals to modernize society. The lack of a popular mass modern sport and recreation system in Spanish Puerto Rico is also relevant: it became another reason to welcome and incorporate U.S. modern sports in the ideals of the Puerto Rican nation.

In this chapter I discuss the games and sports present well before the entry of North Atlantic sport into Puerto Rico to demonstrate how these games were utilized to define lines of colonial authority. By observing the role of sport in Spanish Puerto Rico, readers will have a better understanding of the nuances in Puerto Rico's acceptance or rejection of U.S. and North Atlantic sport. When the United States invaded the island in 1898, its claims of political and sporting democracy were positively received by different groups. The institutions responsible for the early introduction of organized sport were the YMCA and the new education system. These institutions served to unabashedly Americanize Puerto Ricans and mold them into desirable colonial subjects. Because baseball was one of the first and most popular of the U.S. sports introduced to the island, much has been written about it, and it would be redundant to repeat its long history here.[4] The story of sports in Puerto Rico is more than the story of one sport. While there are definite points of comparison and contention between baseball and the development of physical education and Olympism, these are part of a bigger picture, a bigger historical process.

Spanish Sport and Games

The games that the Spanish brought to the island (and to other parts of the New World) after 1508 were ones that were practiced in the Iberian Peninsula. These games held the same value for the Spanish as those that drove their religiously charged militaristic expansion against Moorish kingdoms: a culture of Reconquista.[5] One of the instruments of war in Medieval Spain was the horse. When not at war, the horse served as a work tool but also as recreation. Horse races were organized in and near the urban area and with a set finish line. Bernal Díaz del Castillo records that as part of peace celebrations between Emperor Charles V of Spain and Francis I of France in colonial Mexico, horses raced from the plaza at Tlatelolco to the *plaza mayor*. The winner of the race received yards of velvet and satin for the horse.[6] While this activity might resemble an apolitical entertainment, it served another purpose: by determining the parameters of the race and limiting its participation to the upper classes, the colonial state proclaimed itself the source of authority. These races were not frivolous events; they were reserved for special occasions, as a celebration of elite power, while the common people were limited to observing them at play.

The same can be said of the game of *cañas*, or jousting. As in medieval tournaments, two riders held a lance in one hand and a shield in the other. Separated by a barrier, the two riders charged at each other in an attempt to knock the other from his horse. The game was usually played in the main plaza between the town's church and the city hall. The *cabildo* (city mayor) and other dignitaries observed from specially crafted benches around the plaza. The last mention of such activity in Puerto Rico occurred in San Germán in 1711.[7] Again only the upper classes were actively involved in this event, as they were the ones who could afford the horse, the lances, shields, attire, and privilege to perform in front of the city's dignitaries. Games like these were always confined within the limits of colonial power such as the main plaza and its surrounding streets, always close to the buildings that represented the top colonial hierarchy, the church and city hall.

Other recreational practices in Spanish Puerto Rico, also reserved for the elites, were known as lounge or skill games and included cards, billiards, fencing, and bowling, among others. Billiards had been practiced in Spain since the seventeenth century and became popular in Spanish America in the early nineteenth century. Benjamín Lúgaro Torres found that by 1852 there was a casino for these types of lounge games in the town of Ponce.[8] And there is evidence that fencing and duels were present during much of the Spanish colonial period; José Celso Barbosa and Manuel F. Rossy, two autonomists under Spain who became annexationists under the United States, were known for their ability with the sword.[9]

Despite this athletic activity, sports and recreation were not officially institutionalized or widely practiced in Spanish Puerto Rico, as they would later be under the United States. There was no system in Spanish Puerto Rico to provide the lower classes with recreational activities; they only could watch these games from the outside, constantly reminded of the colonial lines of hierarchy. This does not mean that the popular classes did not play. People were allowed to gather during the patron saint festivities to play popular games, such as *sartén*, *pescaito*, climbing greasy poles (*palo ence-*

bao), and others.[10] These games involved very little equipment and organization. Others, such as cockfighting, appeared to breach class and racial lines as both the upper and lower classes took part in the events. However, the interaction between these men (women were not allowed to participate) still upheld traditional patriarchal and hierarchical power relations.

As the nineteenth century entered the industrial age, games received new attention in Europe and the United States. Innovation, science, democracy, and education paved the way to new conceptualizations of recreation and physical fitness. Skilled labor was increasingly in demand, which produced a demand for educated workers. The continuing rise in democratic ideals opened opportunities for more people, though still only men, to acquire an education. Changing attitudes on education and modernity in England suggested that only a healthy body would allow for a healthy mind, a healthy individual, and a better citizen. English public schools were the main force behind the development of a widespread sport culture that included track and field and soccer.[11]

Physical education in Spain, and consequently Spanish Puerto Rico, was almost nonexistent. If anything characterizes the Spanish education in colonial Puerto Rico it is the absence of systematic instruction. Indeed education during Spanish colonialism, and for that matter education in nineteenth-century Spain, ran significantly behind the standards in Europe and the United States.[12] Schools were scarce and ill equipped, and teachers lacked proper training. If physical education was underdeveloped in Spain, in Puerto Rico the situation was worse.

Along with the absence of physical education in the Spanish education system since 1883, overall physical education in late nineteenth-century Spain was primarily ineffective and militarily oriented.[13] Thus physical education was not promoted with any sort of consistency or curriculum value in Puerto Rico. At the time of the U.S. arrival, the Puerto Rican education system had gone through numerous reforms and revisions and could not achieve any stability or consistency in order to flourish and reach its full potential. This might have been true for the Spanish experience as well. The Spanish education system in its entirety in the nineteenth century was as fragile as the Spanish Empire. Consequently education in Puerto Rico had a low priority, even lower than in Cuba.

As previously stated, when the United States invaded in 1898 and established a colonial education system, which included athletics, it did not enter into a vacuum. Games in Spanish Puerto Rico had a particular role in shaping the state's spectacle of authority and hierarchy.[14] Although ideas of physical education as part of the education system were not present until the 1890s in the normal schools,[15] new forms of sport as practiced in the United States and Europe certainly arrived before 1898. For example, baseball (outlawed by the Spanish for being American and threatening colonial order) was introduced from Cuba in the 1890s.[16] Gymnastics was introduced with the German immigration of the nineteenth century.[17] Nonetheless, Spain's failure to establish a free and popular practice of sports and a working education system with a strong physical education component made Puerto Ricans welcome the educational reforms and sponsorship of sport brought by the United States. Those reforms included a wide range of sports and a school curriculum with a strong physical education component.

Soccer, the YMCA, and Americanization

In 1897 Puerto Rico under the leadership of Luis Muñoz Rivera obtained the long awaited Autonomous Charter from the liberal Spanish government and full representation in the Spanish Cortes. The Charter gave Puerto Rico rights over its internal affairs with an elected legislature, freedom of international trade, and the authority to establish tariffs. However, on July 25, 1898, eight days after the new legislature held its first assembly, the U.S. Army invaded. Bombarding a peaceful San Juan and entering through the bay of Guánica, U.S. generals, including Nelson A. Miles, claimed they had come in order to liberate Puerto Ricans from the yoke of Spanish colonialism and repression. The Autonomous Charter was abolished and a military government installed amid some local, yet short-lived, instability.[18]

Between 1898 and 1900 the U.S. government instituted a military government even though there was no war for independence in Puerto Rico, as there had been in Cuba.[19] In 1900 the U.S. Congress passed the Foraker Act, establishing a Puerto Rican civil government. The U.S. president appointed a governor and an Executive Council of eleven members while thirty-five members of the House of Delegates and a resident commissioner were elected by qualified voters.[20] Yet, unlike Hawaiians, who were granted U.S. citizenship in 1900, the Foraker Act did not grant U.S. citizenship to Puerto Ricans.[21] As a result of several court cases, today known as the Insular Cases, the Supreme Court of the United States approved the colonial relation of several U.S. possessions by upholding the theory that Congress had plenary powers over them, without having to extend the full benefits of the U.S. Constitution and without the promise of eventual admission as a state of the Union.[22] In 1917 the U.S. Congress enacted the Jones Act, granting U.S. citizenship to Puerto Ricans, despite opposition by local leadership.[23] This citizenship did not carry the full benefits of other U.S. citizens residing in the mainland (such as voting for the U.S. president and full representation in Congress), which some suggest proves the hegemonic intent of Congress rather than recognition of legal equality.[24]

Puerto Ricans welcomed the new U.S. regime that hailed democracy and freedom, yet quickly realized it as a colonial project of the United States. As early as 1899 the local political leadership, including Eugenio María de Hostos, protested against the new regime. Luis Muñoz Rivera stated, "The North American Government found in Puerto Rico a degree of autonomy larger than that of Canada. It should have respected and enlarged it, but only wanted to and did destroy it [autonomy]."[25] Soon after, local politics reorganized into three general viewpoints on the status question: those who wanted full independence from the United States, those who wanted full annexation as a state of the Union, and those who aspired to some sort of autonomous relation with the United States.[26] These three main ideological groups mirrored the previous ones under Spanish colonialism. The pro-independence liberal factions continued their fight, while the autonomists who had managed to obtain the Autonomous Charter formed the Partido Federal Americano and, after a very brief consideration of U.S. statehood, formally sought a degree of sovereignty under the name Partido Unión de Puerto Rico. Another branch of the autonomists under Spain, which included José Celso Barbosa, morphed into the Partido Republicano Puertorriqeuño, which sought political equality and full annexation by the United States. Although there was some disappointment with U.S. policies right after the occupation, the fact is that most Puerto Ricans benefited from the U.S. presence, including large landowners who gained access to U.S. markets.[27] Most important, the intellectual elite viewed the United States as the exemplar of democracy and progress and believed in the promise of political modernity.[28]

Socially Puerto Rico benefited in its early relationship with the United States from much needed improvements in health care, communications, roads, the civil service, and education. For example, for four hundred years of Spanish rule, only 1,660 miles of roads had been constructed. After the U.S. occupation, 5,730 miles were constructed between 1898 and 1918.[29] With the majority of the population living in previously inaccessible rural highlands, isolation began to diminish and communication eased. These improvements did not cover the majority of the population, however, and were instituted in order to benefit U.S. interests, be it economic or geopolitical. Most important, the new education system replaced the inefficient Spanish system and had the cultural-political goal of Americanization.[30] The number of rural schools increased from 313 in 1899 to

2,390 by 1914.[31] The new system also included a strong component of physical education and athletics;[32] new sports introduced by the United States included baseball, basketball, volleyball, and track and field. Unlike other Latin American countries that experienced the introduction of similar North Atlantic sport practices,[33] these sports entered Puerto Rico as a colonial territory.

The new colonial relation between Puerto Rico and the United States affected the way sport developed early on. If changes and improvements in roads, health care, and education were made to benefit U.S. interests, development of sport was also imbued with political interests. For example, soccer, organized and favored by local Spaniards and a select group of the white middle and upper-middle classes, was associated with Spanishness; under the new regime preference was given to U.S. sports,[34] which became another element in Americanization. Thus although soccer is the dominant sport throughout Latin America, in the areas where the United States had a strong presence and influence, such as in Puerto Rico and the greater Caribbean, soccer did not become the premier sport.[35] Instead U.S. sports followed U.S. imperial interests.[36]

Historians do not agree on exactly when soccer was first played in Puerto Rico.[37] The establishment in 1911 of the Comercio Sporting Club in San Juan may have been the first soccer club on the island. The club's membership included the owners and employees of San Juan's businesses. Puerto Rico's first Soccer Cup was held on April 23, 1911, on the grounds of the old Spanish fortress El Morro, and included the teams Minerva and Mercurio. Centro Español (Spanish Center) soccer club in San Juan organized soccer matches in 1913. The San Juan Fútbol Club and the Ponce Sporting Club were founded in 1913, with San Juan FC rapidly becoming one of the winningest teams of the time. Soccer kept developing with the establishment of the Liga Insular de Fútbol in 1915 with fierce competition between the San Juan FC, Ponce SC, Arecibo FC, España FC, and Celtics FC. More teams were established after 1916, including the Hércules FC, Borinquen FC, and Mayagüez FC. Games were originally played on the grounds of El Morro, but because they had to share the space with baseball—the game preferred by Americans—they had to move to the area of Puerta de Tierra in San Juan.

From the start soccer was associated with the old Spanish rule and, though some Americans played the sport (mainly the Irish Catholics),[38] many of them were not willing to support it. For many Puerto Ricans, the San Juan FC, Arecibo FC, and the Ponce Sporting Club offered a way to resist U.S. rule by playing a non-U.S. sport.[39] The España FC especially was seen as the embodiment of loyalty to Spain. To make matters worse for Americanization, in 1920 the San Juan FC became the Real (Royal) San Juan FC when King Alfonso XIII granted this honorific title, at the same time assuming the honorary presidency of the team.[40]

Although by the end of Spanish rule many Puerto Ricans, especially the lower classes, blacks, and the liberal white elite, despised Spanish exploitation and absolutism,[41] others maintained loyalty to Spain. More than a Hispanophile sentiment that threatened the Americanization project, soccer proved to have actual institutional ties to Spain, as seen in the Real San Juan FC. Puerto Rico and Cuba were the last possessions of Spain in the New World. However, unlike Cubans, Puerto Ricans were not in an open war for independence but had actually voted to keep relations with Spain under the Autonomous Charter of 1897. In fact all Puerto Ricans born on the island before December 10, 1898 (the date of the Treaty of Paris that signaled the official surrender of Spanish rule in Puerto Rico), were Spanish citizens by birth.[42] As such, many would have considered themselves both Spanish and Puerto Rican. Although there was a strong independence movement during the nineteenth century, the fact is that the majority of Puerto Ricans wanted to keep political ties with Spain and had developed a political culture based on autonomy rather than independence. The endorsement by King Alfonso

XIII of a Puerto Rican soccer team could have been seen as a direct institutional threat to Americanization and political hegemony. For this reason soccer players often had to compete for playing fields with U.S.-sponsored sports, which were brought to the island by two main institutions: the YMCA and the new education system.

The process of making U.S. sports easily accessible to children while creating obstacles for soccer had a profound impact upon the inability of soccer to cement itself as a popular sport on the island. As a result baseball, basketball, volleyball, athletics, and boxing would spearhead sporting culture. Yet while Puerto Ricans accepted U.S. sports as a form of progress, they used these same sports to develop their own national identity through Olympic representation.

Although created in England, the YMCA developed more profusely in the United States after its arrival there in 1851.[43] Beginning in 1858, the YMCA was present in U.S. colleges, upholding its evangelical mission against growing secularization in U.S. cities. Immersed in the muscular Christianity movement, the YMCA in the United States developed superior centers for physical activity such as the International Training School of the YMCA in Springfield, Massachusetts, founded in 1887 under the leadership of Robert J. Roberts, Luther Halsey Gulick, and James Naismith.[44] As an institution of Christian fellowship through sport and recreation for young white men, it also reproduced male gender norms, privileges, and access to civil society.

In the late nineteenth century the YMCA was already well established in Italy, France, Egypt, Syria, Japan, China, India, and Hawaii, and in Latin America the organization was in Argentina, Chile, and Brazil.[45] By the late 1890s the rising sentiment of Manifest Destiny, in addition to a missionary muscular Christianity, was firmly in the minds of YMCA leaders. Indeed the Spanish-American War could be viewed as the catalyst for the association's newest alliance with the U.S. military as the United States expanded its political sphere of influence.[46] Claiming "War is Hell," the YMCA sought to make living conditions in the battlefield and in military camps more "humane" and more Christian.[47] The YMCA was not the only religious missionary organization to enter Puerto Rico after 1898; dozens of the major Protestant denominations divided and secured different parts of the island to carry out their evangelization projects.[48]

Having obtained permission from the invading commanders, the YMCA officially established their army and navy offices in Cuba and the Philippines in 1898; contrary to historical accounts that assert the YMCA began operations in Puerto Rico in 1903,[49] the Army and Navy YMCA were there as early as 1899. Armed conflict continued in Cuba and the Philippines, yet in Puerto Rico the war lasted only a few months. However, the persistence of random popular violent unrest toward waning Spanish authority and incoming U.S. military occupation required the presence and activity of the U.S. armed forces for some time after the war.[50] Regardless of this, the Army and Navy YMCA were better established in Puerto Rico than in Cuba or the Philippines.

According to the 1899 Army and Navy YMCA report, the YMCA in Puerto Rico had managed to secure a building in the San Juan center, at 42 Calle Sol (fig. 2).[51] By 1899 the association had established a reading room (fig. 3), a café (fig. 4), and a recreation room, and by 1900 had a permanent library.[52] The YMCA had not only the intention but the financial and political means to civilize, evangelize, and make the soldiers physically fit. In doing so it influenced the institutionalization of recreation and sport.

Rev. Zerah Collins was in charge of the San Juan Army and Navy YMCA. Collins was a staunch believer in the missionary qualities of the YMCA, especially as they related to war efforts. Deeply patriotic, he was very enthusiastic to aid the troops and begin religious work in Puerto Rico. Among the different activities he led, he was most proud of establishing a Sunday school for local children near San Juan.[53] The central offices in New York only covered the salary of the YMCA secretary for Puerto Rico; the rest was covered by the

Fig. 2. U.S. Army and Navy YMCA, San Juan, Puerto Rico, 1899. Source: YMCA, *Yearbook of the Young Men's Christian Association* (1899).

locals. A report by Army and Navy Secretary W. B. Millar indicated that the work being done in Puerto Rico had been favorable, a view that he corroborated during a personal visit to the island in 1902.[54]

With the establishment of a civilian colonial government after 1900 and the withdrawal of fighting forces from Puerto Rico, the Army and Navy YMCA most probably closed between 1905 and 1909 or merged with the civilian YMCA. Organizing for a civilian YMCA had begun as early as 1909 and, after raising funds locally, was built in 1912. With five thousand guests in attendance, the new YMCA building was inaugurated on Sunday, June 1, 1913, complete with an indoor pool, a gymnasium, and a basketball court.[55] By 1914 the YMCA had 599 members and held competitions in or practiced the sports of basketball, volleyball,

Fig. 3. (*above*) U.S. Army and Navy YMCA Reading Room, San Juan, Puerto Rico, 1899. Source: YMCA, *Yearbook of the Young Men's Christian Association* (1899).

Fig. 4. (*below*) U.S. Army and Navy YMCA Café Room, San Juan, Puerto Rico, 1899. Source: YMCA, *Yearbook of the Young Men's Christian Association* (1899).

athletics, fencing, gymnastics, *frontón* (also called Jai-alai and Basque ball), swimming, and handball, among others. During the 1910s the YMCA's San Juan secretary, William Coxhead, wrote of the benefits of expanding into the education system to reach wider audiences.

The civilian YMCA set an example as an institution dedicated to sport and recreation. By introducing modern sports it aided in the colonial Americanization agenda of Puerto Ricans, in turn providing Puerto Ricans with a part of the liberal society under the United States that they had been hoping for. The YMCA's early incursion into the school system made it particularly popular for those interested in sports. However, its connections with missionary activities, though loosening up in the 1910s, did not go over well in a predominantly Catholic society. Although Puerto Rican Protestantism existed before 1898 and continued to grow afterward, Spaniards still living in Puerto Rico and conservative Catholic Puerto Ricans were distrustful of this Protestant institution.[56] An unofficial boycott of the YMCA that hindered connections to the wider public caused the YMCA to go through an unstable period that lasted through the 1930s. Still, it survived and by the 1950s and 1960s had expanded to the cities of Ponce and Mayagüez. Before the presence of the YMCA and throughout the early part of the twentieth century, the education system had accepted its role in the development of sports, which was what the people were interested in.

Physical Education and Sport: The Public School System, the UPR, and Athletics

As Joseph Arbena explains, the establishment of modern local education systems was paramount for the development of sport nationalism in Latin America.[57] Jorge Humberto Ruiz Patiño, in his study of Colombia, similarly demonstrates that the 1903 establishment of a liberal education system, with a focus on physical education, became the foundation of a larger bourgeois project for political control and the crafting of Colombian national identity.[58] In El Salvador, Chéster Urbina Gaitán writes, gymnastics entered the school system in the nineteenth century but became a part of the curriculum in 1907. In 1912 the future dictator Maximiliano Hernández Martínez published his book *Manual de Gimnasia* as a preamble to the important role his regime gave to physical education and international sports in the 1930s and 1940s.[59] In Puerto Rico physical education became an integral part of the new public education system in the early 1900s but acquired particular meaning after 1917, when Puerto Ricans were granted U.S. citizenship and the United States entered World War I.[60] For Puerto Ricans physical education was a way to prove their physical literacy as U.S. citizens going into war and was important for a future healthy, modern, and strong Puerto Rican nation.

Just as in other islands of the Caribbean,[61] the U.S. occupation in Puerto Rico established a comprehensive and free public education system. The establishment in 1903 of the University of Puerto Rico (UPR) culminated a centuries-long desire of local leaders and intellectuals to provide local higher education. The relation between education, sport, and liberal ideas was active at the turn of the twentieth century. Furthermore education was a top priority for the founder of the modern Olympic movement, Pierre de Coubertin.[62] Considered an educational reformer, Coubertin equated education with democracy, progress, and physical health for modern ways of living. As such he thought it ideal to revive an ancient Greek athletic festival in celebration of these values in international goodwill.[63] For Coubertin education was first and foremost in the development of Olympism.

The public education system instituted after the U.S. occupation was therefore a dream come true for many leaders and commoners. However, the system was implemented more as a political tool of incorporation through the imperial project of Americanization than as a benign democratic innovation to uplift and civilize.[64] The University of Puerto Rico, more than a center for higher education in the spirit of intellectual pursuit, was a center to train teachers of English to support the newly founded schools modeled after the ones in the United States.[65] As English became compulsory in all grades in a Spanish-speaking society, instruction in Spanish became a medium of cultural and political resistance, sparking one of the central points of conflict between Puerto Ricans and U.S. officials in the first half of the twentieth century.[66]

But the story of education and Americanization in Puerto Rico is not just the story of cultural imperialism and national resistance. As Solsiree del Moral argues in *Negotiating Empire*, Americanization in Puerto Rico actually became more of a negotiation over the terms of U.S. imperialism and of Puerto Rican notions of progress in the future *patria* (homeland). Puerto Ricans welcomed those Americanizing elements they thought would uplift their *patria* and help them create a better society. While rejecting discriminating language policies, they welcomed other parts of the project, such as physical education and sports. The autonomist political tradition won the battle over colonial educational politics, and Puerto Ricans developed a U.S. physical education program while nurturing growing ideas of Puerto Ricanness.[67]

Notions of physical education (PE) in Latin America also began to develop in the early twentieth century. Many of its proponents were greatly influenced by ideas of athletics and education as developed in Europe and the United States. As early as 1908 physical educators from Latin America met at the Pan-American Scientific Congress in Santiago, Chile, in order to "incorporate sports into plans to address cramped housing, epidemics, and other health hazards." As a result of this congress PE teachers in Chile, led by a Swedish doctor, Henrik Ling, founded the Chilean Physical Education League. This league traveled through Europe and used advances in PE in the United States to "bring the most modern techniques to Chilean education."[68] Hence Puerto Rico's PE influence under the United States should also be understood—with the significant caveat of colonialism—as part of a broader Latin American exposure to European and

U.S. advances in physical education. As we will see, Puerto Ricans also developed Swedish ideas of physical education.

Teachers working in the development of education played a big role not only in students' general education but also in their physical education. Soon after the invasion, Puerto Rican educators had the backing of the commissioner of education, which included developing initial infrastructure to practice gymnastics and athletics. Contrary to UPR's official history of athletics,[69] the normal school was allotted the necessary equipment for the practice of physical education as early as 1902. The school had "two small gymnasiums, one for boys and one for girls—equipped with showerbaths and lockers and all necessary appliances for physical training."[70] When the normal school became the normal college of the UPR in 1903, the board of trustees appointed the first instructor of athletics, Sgt. Maj. Rafael A. Segarra, for the year 1904–5 with the title "instructor of gymnastics" and a salary of $150.[71]

High-ranking education leaders in the early years of the occupation advertised progressive education and the benefits of sports. In 1902 some of these leaders, mainly from the United States, embarked on an education propaganda tour around the island with the purpose of "raising a healthy and active interest in normal education and in the public school."[72] Commissioner of Education Samuel McCune Lindsay invited two guests to travel the island and talk about the benefits of education. One was James Earl Russell, dean of the Teachers College of Columbia University, and the other C. Hanford Henderson, a preeminent figure in manual training and physical culture. Their public lectures were given to groups of students, teachers, and the general public at schools and public squares in San Juan, Río Piedras, Manatí, Arecibo, Camuy, Quebradillas, Aguadilla, Mayagüez, Cabo Rojo, Sábana Grande, San Germán, Yauco, Ponce, Cayey, and Coamo. Though the trip was intense (on one day they gave seven lectures), Russell and Henderson believed it was worthwhile because the reception was "enthusiastic."

These supervisors, teachers, and invited guests cooperated with soldiers and social leaders—who also attended the YMCA—to organize athletic meets. An Athletic Committee within the Puerto Rico Baseball Association was created to organize track and field meets in 1902. Track and field, often referred to as *atletismo* or athletics, became the premier international sport. It was the standard by which Olympic nations were measured, certainly at the Central American and Caribbean Games. Early in the occupation, track and field challenges became a way to distinguish between Americans and Puerto Ricans. Sportsmen in Ponce were particularly passionate about athletics. In 1904 an athlete by the name of Machín published a challenge in the newspaper *Boletín Mercantil* to any athlete, American or native, to race him. He bet $200 and exclaimed, "Á ver quien desbanca al gallo jíbaro" (Let's see who overthrows this Puerto Rican rooster).[73] Although we do not know if the race took place, Machín's athletic pride is obvious, as is the belief that there was a clear difference between Puerto Rican and American athletes.

With athletic fever increasing within the general public, politicians did not waste time promoting sports, whether as a form of Americanization or for the *patria*'s well-being. On November 21, 1902, the Executive Council assembled to organize an athletic club in the presence of forty U.S. leaders. The Athletic Club of San Juan was the result. The meeting of the mainly American Executive Council and the Puerto Rican House of Delegates, the two top political institutions, reveals the early collaboration between U.S. and Puerto Rican politicians in the sponsorship of athletic institutionalization. The hope behind these early phases of sport institutionalization was that Puerto Rico would receive official state recognition.

From 1905 on, a degree of athletic activity continued developing in the school system, which included the UPR, the Central High School in San Juan, and the other selective high schools in Ponce, Arecibo, and Mayagüez. Since mass athletic facilities had not been established during the first decade of the U.S. occupation, Puerto

Ricans waited until the 1940s for mass athletic modernization. Small steps were taken to provide a sample of athletic infrastructure. In January 1906 the board of trustees of the UPR agreed to provide $200 for "laying out and improving an athletic field to be located near the Normal School building." Later that same year, on October 1, and in response to a request from Puerto Rico's secretary of education Paul G. Miller, the trustees agreed to increase the funding for the athletic field to $500 over a period of two years.[74] There was no opposition to this improvement; on the contrary, it seems that the planning for the upgrading of athletic facilities was rather fast.

The impact of athletics needs to be contextualized in a broader local educational scope that included the university and the high schools. The UPR was not the sole entity responsible for the development of athletics, as it was a collaboration of different schools, secondary and college level, in recurrent meets. In addition to the UPR there were the high schools in Ponce, Mayagüez, Santurce, Guayama, and a few others. They did not serve the whole island, much less the majority of the children, who lived in the rural areas. Nevertheless they were the home institutions of future Puerto Rican Olympians. The first Track and Field Interscholastic Cup was held in 1906 at Ponce High School, under the legendary leadership of an American principal, Charles Terry. Under Terry, Ponce became the leader in sport infrastructure, to the point of securing funds to build the first state-of-the-art athletic field in 1909, a scaled-down replica of the field at the University of Pennsylvania.[75] This Ponce High School team was so successful that they won six of the ten athletic meets celebrated between 1906 and 1915.

The playgrounds built in the 1910s were mainly used to practice these sports and teams that were being formed in increasing numbers. In 1913 baseball had some forty-four teams, which had increased to seventy-three by 1915; in 1913 track and field had eighteen teams, which increased to thirty-nine by 1915. However, the most dramatic increase in team organization occurred in basketball. Even though basketball had only two organized school teams in 1913, by 1915 there were fifty-eight (see table 1). This increment in basketball popularity was the result of the work of the YMCA and of schoolteachers in local high schools who had learned from the same institution. Basketball was played as early as 1905 in Ponce High School in an all-female match between teachers and students. The students beat the teachers by 10 points, and a reporter described the match as being a "very pleasant and interesting spectacle."[76]

Table 1. Sport teams in public schools in Puerto Rico

SCHOOL YEAR	BASEBALL	TRACK AND FIELD	BASKETBALL	TOTAL
Prior to 1913	44	18	2	64
1913–14	55	28	27	110
1914–15	73	39	58	170

Source: Osuna, A History of Education in Puerto Rico, 240.

These numbers portray a positive picture of sports development and Americanization through sports. However, they do not reflect the reality of sporting facilities and Americanization. First, 170 teams of baseball, track and field, and basketball is a minute number if we compare the increase in teams with the increase in classrooms. In 1910 there were 522 classrooms; in 1920 there were 1,422.[77] In other words, in 1920 only 12 percent of classrooms had a sports team. For the mass of Puerto Rican children, athletic activity and physical education were not being developed on par with the facilities at the elite institutions in the city centers.

A bigger issue was at stake in the early development of sports and physical education in Puerto Rico. As del Moral argues, physical education after 1917 developed in response to the rejection of 75 percent of Puerto Rican volunteers to World War I due to illiteracy and physical deficiency.[78] For Puerto Ricans and their national project this rejection was an embarrassment, and an urgent call was made for written and physical literacy. At stake was the meaning of their recently granted U.S. citizenship, their visions of a healthy and progressive Puerto Rican *patria*, and the benefits of sports Americanization.

Del Moral analyzes the essay "Educación Física" by Pedro Gil, school principal and athletic director of Yauco High School, in which he argues that physical education in Puerto Rico needed separate attention from athletic teams, in addition to more emphasis on education. The emphasis should be on physical health for all, not on winning athletic meets with teams of elite athletes. Gil's proposal represented those teachers who saw education as a means to create a new citizenry, one that was more democratic and that encompassed a vision of progress for all Puerto Ricans in hopes of creating a better *raza* (race, citizenry, people, or nation).[79] While I agree with del Moral that Gil was exposing the autonomist tradition of negotiating the terms of Americanization, U.S. citizenship, and Puerto Rican education, there is more to this analysis that reveals another significant message by Gil and the educators he represented.

In a previous issue of the *Porto Rico School Review*, where Gil's essay appeared, is an essay on sports and education by Edwin Schoenrich, an American principal of Guayama High School, titled "An Interscholastic Basketball League for Porto Rico." Schoenrich was concerned about the awful state of athletics, the shortcomings of education, and Puerto Rico's overall well-being. What he inadvertently demonstrates, however, is the detached attitude of some of the American teachers in Puerto Rico, their imperial Americanization mission, their paternalistic view of Puerto Ricans, and the chauvinistic view of American competitive sports.

Schoenrich begins his article by stating, "Athletics—I mean real, intensified athletics—is the final stamp of Americanization upon the Puerto Rican high school. A school without athletics is a dead school." By athletics he means competitive sports. He argues that students need to develop "school spirit," and he cannot understand why local schools have not developed their athletic programs. According to him, money is not the reason for athletic underdevelopment, but proper allocation of funds. Basketball, he asserts, is the perfect sport to develop this school spirit; baseball fields are too far away and the game is boring and lacks physical contact. Football and tennis are too expensive; volleyball is really a playground game, and soccer is not American. What Puerto Ricans need is an inexpensive, aggressive, and accessible sport, such as basketball, in order to develop school spirit and escape "tropical stagnation."[80]

If we follow the argument of the negotiation over the terms of Americanization in Puerto Rico, Gil's essay is a direct response to Schoenrich's. Gil's article reflects the group of teachers who navigated the complex waters of Americanization, Puerto Rican self-respect, and nationhood. First, the six-page essay is written in Spanish. Second, contrary to the idea of school spirit as a result of a few elite team players, Gil argues for the development of "physical education" for all students. Third, he makes a plea for more physical education class time and teachers rather than simply more basketball teams. Fourth, he recommends teachers focus on gymnastics rather than basketball.

In addition to these pedagogical points, Gil clearly situates his broader vision of physical education in the Greek tradition of celebrating the body and the development of gymnastics. He elaborates on the glories of Greek thought and positions Puerto Ricans as their inheritors. This viewpoint is reflected in his many references to the concept of *nuestra raza*, "our race." Del Moral argues that Puerto Rican teachers used the idea of *raza* to differentiate themselves from Anglo-Americans and to protect Puerto Rican Hispanic traditions. However, the concept was used on a larger scale at this time and not only by Puerto Ricans. The pride of *raza* was part of a broader international Hispanismo movement led by intellectuals in Spain and other Spanish-speaking places.[81] For Spaniards, Hispanismo is a reaction to the "Disaster of '98," when Spain lost its remaining overseas colonies—Cuba, Puerto Rico, and the Philippines—to the United States. For Spanish Americans and Filipinos, it was also a reaction to U.S. imperial interests in their regions. Hispanismo claimed moral and spiritual superiority over what they considered a materialistic, Protestant, and power-driven United States. It was also the last claim to the glories of a lost Spanish Empire as heirs of Roman-Hellenism and Catholicism. For Gil the *raza*, "full of vices and weak," had come to admire athletes with such American names as "Jeffries or Johnson."[82] Instead Puerto Ricans, connected to the cultural public sphere of Hispanismo, should nurture the *raza*, making it strong and healthy again.

Also significant is Gil's appeal for gymnastics. More than an alternative to basketball, gymnastics had a particular ideological root. Claiming that Puerto Ricans should hear the echo of their Greek ancestors' love for athletics and physical education, Gil saw gymnastics as preventative health care rather than a cure for Puerto Rico's physical illiteracy. He believed the "art of gymnastics" should be considered a path to illness prevention but also a source of health, hygiene, and physical strength—"Mens sana in corpore sano." All of these factors were necessary if Puerto Ricans wanted to "raise a people [levantar un pueblo]" in order to mingle alongside the "concert of civilized nations."[83] While these ideas carry a neo-Lamarckian and eugenics value,[84] there is another ideological component that ties physical educators in Puerto Rico to Olympism.

First, not only was Gil reacting to Schoenrich's "American" model of athletics to modernize Puerto Ricans and raise their "school spirit," but he also aligned with a particular model of physical education: the Swedish system. The Swedish system of physical education was established by Per Henrick Ling, who saw physical training as a way to prepare strong war-able citizens and as a balance between mind and body.[85] It followed the laws of the natural sciences and merged the fields of biology, anatomy, kinesiology, and physiology. Ling founded the Chilean Physical Education League in Santiago in 1908, the start of his enduring influence in the region. The Swedish system, in addition to the German and the English, was another model of physical education that influenced U.S. educators during the nineteenth century. However, it was mainly the German and English systems that helped to create the American system, the New Physical Education System, based on interscholastic competition and the education of the body.[86] Aware of Ling's Swedish system, Gil negotiated Puerto Rico's need for holistic physical education without denying the importance of U.S. interscholastic competition.

The second point of significance for Gil's appeal for gymnastics is the Swedish role in the development of early Olympism. Coubertin's Olympic dream, while coming from the point of view of physical education and the celebration of Hellenistic culture, was actually more in line with the English tradition of competitive sports than with the holistic, mind-body, and physiology approach of the Swedish. As a matter of fact Coubertin created his own motto, "Mens fervida in corpore lacertoso" (an overflowing mind in a muscular body), to try to supplant the medical motto, "Mens sana in corpore sano" (a sound mind in a sound body). With some reluctance from Coubertin, the Swedish capital of Stockholm hosted the fifth Olympic Games in 1912. With Sweden winning the overall medal tally (sixty-five; the United States was second with sixty-two), their physical education system became a leader in modern physical pedagogy.[87] Gil, writing just eight years after the Stockholm Olympics, used what he thought were leading ideas in the field of physical education. Puerto Ricans may not have participated in any of the early Olympiads, but various physical education teachers were in accord with current international pedagogy. If Gil was aware of basic elements of the Swedish system, a system that proved successful at the Olympic Games, then his vision for a strong, physically literate citizenship was ready to mingle with the "concert of civilized nations." Puerto Rican culture would be negotiated between U.S. and Puerto Rican values and traditions and would incorporate broader notions of Hispanidad and physical education.

The new *raza* that many Puerto Rican educators envisioned was already being displayed athletically at limited venues. Some Puerto Rican students attended U.S. universities and participated in U.S. competitions. Some of these Puerto Ricans willingly represented the Puerto Rican "nation" at athletic meets. For example, in 1912 Nicasio Olmo represented Puerto Rico at the Bronx Marathon in New York. Olmo won the marathon, repeating his victory from 1911. What is out of the ordinary is that Olmo, from Arecibo, ran wearing a jersey with the image of the Puerto Rican flag. (During these years the Puerto Rican flag was not officially in use since the official flag was that of the United States.) According to a news report, the U.S. Athletic Union would not approve the use of the Puerto Rican flag and insisted he wear the emblem of the New York Athletic Club, which he belonged to; failure to do so would result in his expulsion from the club. Olmo refused, wore a jersey printed with the Puerto Rican flag, and quit his association with the NYAC.[88] After this incident he returned to Puerto Rico, where he organized the Porto Rican Athletic Club.

In the early years of U.S. colonization, Puerto Ricans experienced the full benefits of their association with the United States. The ill-equipped and badly executed Spanish education system was modernized by the U.S. education system. The differences in quality between the Spanish and U.S. systems were obvious, and many welcomed the new system. However, welcoming the system did not mean accepting it fully. Puerto Ricans negotiated the terms of Americanization, including the meaning and purpose of physical education and athletics. In the end Puerto Ricans incorporated international visions of physical education and sports, including some elements of Olympism.

Although Puerto Ricans did not participate in any Olympic events sponsored by the International Olympic Committee during the late nineteenth century and first two decades of the twentieth, they did begin to build the basis of Olympism. As the founder of modern Olympism, Coubertin believed that education was its basis. Physical education was an extension of the values of democracy and progress, as seen in the ancient and admired Greek societies. Taking this into account, Puerto Ricans were ready to develop their Olympic spirit and persona. It was in the 1930s that this Olympic persona was performed on the international scene, testing the limits of democracy and evidencing the existence of colonial Olympism.

2 / The Rise of a Colonial
Olympic Movement, 1930s

The 1930s are considered transcendental for Puerto Rican politics, culture, and economy. After three decades of U.S. presence, Puerto Rican politics and culture mainly revolved around a single crop economy—sugar—dominated by absentee owners from the United States. During the first two decades of U.S. occupation, the local economy did not experience the widespread progress that the military governors of 1898 had promised. With the effects of the Great Depression in the island, Puerto Ricans faced even more pronounced and dire conditions.[1] As a result, social and political instability swept the island, producing numerous strikes that brought clashes, often fatal, between the police and the Partido Nacionalista. In response autonomists and other liberals formed new alliances and new parties, including the Partido Popular Democrático in 1938, to tackle different ways of solving the country's crisis. Although the punitive Tydings Bill was introduced in the U.S. House of Representatives in 1936 and would have granted independence to Puerto Ricans, it failed. Puerto Ricans then sought ameliorative reforms to maintain an association with the United States. President Franklin Delano Roosevelt's administration (1933–45) instituted a comprehensive set of economic reforms and relief programs exemplified by the New Deal. In Puerto Rico these programs took the form of the Puerto Rico Reconstruction Administration and the Puerto Rican Emergency Relief Administration.

To some extent sport during the 1930s was a cultural and recreational way to mitigate the political and social instability of the decade. Like the country's economic and social conditions, sports and athletics developed to a limited extent until the 1940s and 1950s, when they flourished. The public education system, led by the U.S.-born University High School (UHS) principal George Keelan, continued organizing athletic meets and spreading athletic culture throughout the island. The UHS became the leader and model of a sound educational institution for the promotion and success of interscholastic sports. Athletics evolved despite setbacks and struggles for athletic equipment and facilities. The role of the education system in the development and modernization of sport in Puerto Rico was not unique within Latin America; there are many similarities, including the premier role of state agencies in the centralized regulation of sport and recreation in Latin America and elsewhere.[2]

The development of sport through the public school system was not limited to the high school level but continued at the University of Puerto Rico. Under the leadership of Cosme Beitía as director of athletics, a program in physical education was created in 1937, and the UPR became the producer of Puerto Rican national athletes and the leader of athletics in the island. Beitía obtained a master's degree in physical education at Columbia University and a law degree from UPR and became a lieutenant in the 65th Infantry of Puerto Rico of the U.S. Army. One of Puerto Rico's best athletes, he was considered, along with the brothers Ciqui and Fabito Faberllé, and Gacho Torres, one of Puerto Rico's "four horsemen of baseball." He was a devoted follower of Coubertin's Olympism and the value of sportsmanship.[3] With the growth of PE as a legitimate pedagogical subject, leaders in the education system saw it additionally as a practical way to improve social conditions. That is, the healthy human body was seen as the first and most important component of a modernized Puerto Rico. Beitía viewed sports and athletes as necessary to lift up the nation. Because of his passion for and leadership in sports he was made the official trainer of the Puerto Rican National delegation at the Central American and Caribbean Games of 1935 in El Salvador and 1938 in Panama.

The 1930s were also characterized by a growing concern over ideas of the nation. Defining the nation was a concern in the minds of many Puerto Rican intellectuals, most prominently Antonio S. Pedreira, but also for other Caribbean and Latin Americans, including Fernando Ortiz and Jorge Mañach in Cuba, José Vasconcelos in Mexico, and Gilberto Freyre in Brazil. Puerto Ricans were ready to partake in a broader current of identity that had been present in other parts of the continent.[4] In his analysis of sport in the Southern Cone, César Torres writes, "During the first thirty years of the twentieth century sport is transformed into a social practice in which national identities are constructed, disseminated, and affirmed."[5] Yet what is special about the construction of national identity through sport in Puerto Rico is that it was carried out in a colonial context. Other nations, such as Scotland and Catalonia, have gone through similar processes of sport and identity in a subjugated political relationship, and in his classic *Beyond a Boundary*, C. L. R. James analyzes the pervasive relation between cricket, colonialism, and identity in his home country of Trinidad, but also within the larger context of British imperialism.[6] Yet Puerto Rico presents a different case, one that is pertinent to the Spanish Caribbean in its relation to Latin America and the growing U.S. Empire. Puerto Rican incursion into the Olympic cycle in 1930 proved to be an ideal method to cultivate a sense of nationhood, which had been denied in the political realm.

This chapter shows that Puerto Rico's Olympic representation was in fact the embodiment of different political interests. That is, at stake in Olympic athletics was the very meaning of colonialism and imperialism, Olympic diplomacy, tourism, and insular authority. The political, economic, and social instability of the 1930s occurred alongside accomplishments in the sporting arena, producing along the way multiple cultural and political meanings. Primarily, different people utilized achievements in sports to claim the success of their own nationalistic, colonial, hegemonic, or economic agenda. Ultimately the negotiation over Puerto Rican Olympism in the 1930s helped to shape the ways the autonomist groups on the island envisioned the existence of the Puerto Rican nation while still holding, consenting to, and defending their U.S. citizenship. In this way the 1930s saw the beginning of the autonomist meanings of Puerto Rican national identity, colonial sovereignty, and colonial Olympism.

Organizing Insular Sports:
The Politics of Colonial Games

The regulation of sport and games has been used in contemporary societies, as in colonial Spanish Puerto Rico, to set the parameters of what is allowed and what is prohibited. In Puerto Rico such authority was exercised consistently in the twentieth century in a series of laws. Cockfighting and horse racing were the sports that received the most scrutiny and the most detailed and lengthy regulations. To discuss these two sports is beyond the scope of this book; suffice it to say that at stake was the regulation of large amounts of money involved in gambling and betting, in which the state participated. In terms of Olympism, many saw these games as traditional and backward Spanish sports, not part of the dream for an athletically modern and progressive Puerto Rican nation. My analysis focuses on the so-called modern sports of the Olympics and the source of Puerto Rican desires for a new *patria*.

One of the first laws in Puerto Rico to regulate sports was enacted in 1927, creating the Athletic Commission under the supervision of an athletic commissioner.[7] Horace Mann Towner became the first commissioner, and the commission was created specifically to regulate boxing and Greco-Roman wrestling. The commissioner was appointed for two years by the governor and approved by the senate. Among the duties of the commission was to issue licenses to sanctioned establishments, to schedule boxing and wrestling matches, and to establish a minimum participation age. It also set the sports tax rate, determined the necessary protective equipment, controlled the business of betting and ticket sales, and issued licenses to judges, physicians, and other personnel. While it is true that these measures were meant to uphold necessary safety standards for boxing, it is also true that the state needed to control every aspect of a violent sport that was already making huge profits. To a large degree the state was catching up with the requirements of professional sport and, at the same time, making its place in Puerto Rican sport official. Recognizing the public euphoria over sports, the legislature increased the number of members on the commission to five in 1928 and defined further details and duties of the regulating body.[8] In 1932 the legislature created the position of boxing commissioner, separating the sport into its own category.[9] The Athletic Commission supervised all other sports, also taking charge of the athletic field at the Parque Luis Muñoz Rivera, which had been managed by the Parks Commission since 1917.[10]

The Athletic Commission of 1932–33 reported to Governor James Beverley on a monthly basis during its fiscal year. In 1933 the members of the Commission were Eduardo González; William Guzmán; Teófilo Maldonado; Francisco Pons, commissioner of the interior; and Justo Rivera Cabrera, boxing commissioner. One of the two most important individuals in the organization and establishment of sports was Teófilo Maldonado, a leader in Puerto Rico's effort to regulate and supervise athletic competitions and to appeal for more athletic facilities. The Commission reported an increase in boxing matches from seven in 1932 to 124 in 1933, with gross receipts of $12,731.91. Despite the gains in boxing, the Athletic Commission was actually reporting net deficits in general operations of $1,323.38 and liabilities amounting to $1,672.88. Regardless of the Depression, they were still hopeful about the development of sports, saying, "It is expected that the general conditions of all sports in Puerto Rico will be greatly improved during the next fiscal year, and in consequence, our economic conditions will be better."[11]

Another group of sport enthusiasts were organizing athletics on their own terms. With Puerto Rico's participation at the second Central American and Caribbean Games (CACG), held in Cuba in 1930, a group of private citizens, with the help of the leading politicians, sought to create the Puerto Rican Olympic Committee (Comité Olímpico de Puerto Rico, COPR).[12] The COPR was actually born within the structure of the Federación Deportiva de Puerto Rico (FDPR) of 1933, a federation approved by the Constituent Assembly under the leadership of Maldonado on January 8, 1933, at the Ateneo Puertorriqueño. However, contrary to the Olympic spirit, Maldonado sought government support, which suggests his desire to supplant the Athletic Commission. As president of the newly created federation, he communicated on January 13 to Governor Beverley seeking his support to develop sports throughout the island. Beverley, who had served as attorney general, then as interim governor in 1929, and then as governor proper between 1932 and 1933, was a staunch supporter of sports, especially track and field and basketball. His response affirmed his interest: "I am convinced that this federation is destined to play an important part in the development of all sports in the Island. Both personally and officially I shall consider it a pleasure to cooperate in every way possible with your federation. The development of wholesome sports, especially among the younger generation is of great social importance in any country and I am glad to know that your federation is arousing general interest."[13]

Though the COPR of 1933 was a section of the FDPR, it was formally created by Law No. 8 on April 7, 1933. The resolution listed reasons for establishing the Committee:

The Puerto Rican youth has always demonstrated its love and interest to its physical development, participating in insular sport competitions and various times in international tournaments. . . .

In 1930, Puerto Rico participated in the Central American Olympics in the city of Havana, Capital of Cuba, finishing in fourth place with only four native athletes representing our island. . . .

A year later a native basketball selection visited the Republic of Venezuela, ending unbeaten in all games on this sport in said country. . . .

Puerto Rico presently lacks solvent associations that can carry costs of sending our best athletic delegations to the Antilles, Central American and international competitions. . . .

The cultural development of the Puerto Rican youth greatly depends on their physical development.[14]

The creation of this COPR was a direct result of Puerto Rico's participation at the Central American Games in Havana in 1930 and a later basketball tournament in Venezuela. But because neither the COPR nor the sport leadership of the time, could undertake the financial responsibility for such an enterprise they needed the support of a populist New Deal government.

The insular treasury would provide $5,000 to the Puerto Rican Olympic Fund, which would support the organization and defray the costs of the Olimpiadas Puertorriqueñas (Puerto Rican Olympics), "the preliminary selection tournaments and first step to send our best delegation to the next Central American Olympics."[15] The law was supposed to go into effect immediately after its approval on April 7, 1933.

The law that established the first COPR stipulated that the Committee would be composed of the governor, Commissioner of Education José Padín, President of the House of Representatives Miguel A. García Méndez, President of the Senate Rafael Martínez Nadal, Chancellor of the UPR Carlos E. Chardón, the city manager of San Juan, and the mayors of Ponce, Mayagüez, Arecibo, Aguadilla, Guayama, and Humacao. (All of these are large cities with good sports records.) Other members included the industrialists Pedro Juan Serrallés, Frederick Krug, and J. Adalberto Roig. The list of politicians on this original COPR points to the political nature of the institution, and the inclusion of powerful industrialists indicates the attempt to secure financial backing. In no way did this Olympic Committee follow the official IOC parameters of nongovernmental involvement. The governmental involvement in Puerto Rico's Olympic Committee would lead to an unprecedented conflict within the IOC in the 1950s and is the subject of a subsequent chapter. Ideologically the composition of this first COPR was diverse. Its members belonged to different political sectors, ranging from pro-statehood conservatives to pro-independence liberals.

The COPR's first meeting was held on May 13, 1933, at 4:00 p.m. in the Governor's Palace and was presided over by Governor Beverley himself. According to the minutes, Beverley stated that the COPR should be concerned most of all with the "practical and rapid benefits of sports for the country."[16] A reporter from *El Mundo* covering the meeting recorded the following statement: "Let us go determined to save amateurism and we will prevail. The spirit of sport arises in all of Puerto Rico and the athletic feeling of all our classes unite to form a formidable and vigorous bloc. We feel that a new era, a new epoch, is coming; like a clearer and diaphanous awakening for athletic sports in Puerto Rico and for the youth that until recently were orphans of unselfish mentors, organizers, and counselors."[17]

With Padín and Krug on the Puerto Rican Olympic Committee were Francisco Porrata Doria, an architect and leading engineer for the Puerto Rico Reconstruction Administration; Emilio Calderón Carrión, a poet and physician; and Blas C. Herrero, a politician with the Puerto Rican Republican Party. All echoed the support for sport, and specific plans for proceeding were examined. As commissioner of education, Padín recommended that all possible information regarding the next CACG, in 1934, be obtained so that enough funds could be collected to send a delegation. Following this recommendation, Calderón Carrión suggested eliminatory trials by district to select the delegation of athletes. The current selection system, whereby each town sent its representatives, was too complex and took too much time. According to Calderón Carrión, a district elimination system would be simpler and more disciplined. One of the successful motions approved in this first meeting was the creation of an executive subcommittee that would organize the first Insular Olympics; Beverley appointed Maldonado as its president. Also on this executive subcommittee were Frank Campos from the Department of Public Instruction, Eduardo R. González from the Athletic Commission, Juanito C. González from the Asociación de Cronistas de Puerto Rico (Puerto Rico Journalists Association), María Luisa Arcelay from Mayagüez, Oscar Loubriel from the Gran Asociación Deportiva de Puerto Rico (Grand Sports Association of Puerto Rico), and Tomás Cuerda from the Asociación Deportiva de Ponce (Ponce Sports Association).[18]

The next meeting of the COPR was scheduled for June 15, and Beverley's tenure ended soon thereafter. On July 1, 1933, Robert Hayes Gore was sworn in as the eleventh civilian governor of Puerto Rico. Soon after his arrival at Fortaleza, Rafael Santiago Sosa, secretary of the COPR, sent him a letter explaining the existence of the committee and listing its members. As any good politician would do, Gore offered his cooperation. However, the FDPR wanted to make sure that they were getting all the support possible from their new governor and drafted a memorandum for sport development on August 2, 1933. By this time Maldonado had ceased to be the president of the FDPR, replaced by Miguel Diez de Andino; Rafael Santiago Sosa was named secretary and Camilo Crossas the auditor-treasurer. In the memorandum to Governor Gore, the FDPR stated that they had the support of forty-five island-wide sporting associations in their attempt to manage and direct the development of physical culture for the betterment of the Puerto Rican youth.[19] This "manifesto" included six main points the FDPR thought necessary if Puerto Rican sports were to advance:

1. Protesting state centralization of sports, the FDPR argued that the state should stop enacting laws that lumped together amateur with professional sports such as horse racing, boxing, and cockfighting.
2. The FDPR was fully committed to insular amateur Olympism, and for that reason local organizations were holding eliminatory meets by districts to facilitate the selection of the Puerto Rican Olympic squad.
3. The FDPR reminded Governor Gore that the Beverley administration had approved the Puerto Rican Olympic Committee and informed him that plans to organize the Puerto Rican Olympiads were under way.
4. Referring to the Central American Games of 1935 in El Salvador, the FDPR suggested that the $5,000 approved by the legislature was not enough to defray the costs to the delegation. They hoped the governor would try to obtain free round-trip tickets on a ship to and from Panama.
5. On numerous trips around the island sponsoring sports programs the FDPR noted a dearth of physical education teachers. They reported parents' complaints and request that the legislature fund more positions for PE teachers for the "scientific" physical education of their children.
6. Acknowledging that the legislature approved funds for the building of a baseball field in El Escambrón, the FDPR requested that funding be allotted to establish similar playing fields in the principal cities of the island that serve as heads of their districts.

These six points reveal an apparent contradiction. On the one hand, the FDPR wanted to take sports from the government and give them to the citizens. Their Federation, which represented forty-five smaller local federations, achieved this purpose. Yet they requested monetary aid from the central government. This push-and-pull tendency between Puerto Rican amateur sports and the state was char-acteristic of the 1930s and 1940s and reached its conflictive climax in the 1950s. Such conflict was not exclusive to Puerto Ricans; sport supported by state funding is abundant in other places, especially when the state tries to prove its stature as a sports power.[20] In Puerto Rico the citizens who composed the FDPR reminded Governor Gore of the power of sports for a healthy society. They reminded him as well that in his first state address he had promised to support the development of sport for future generations and for the "happiness of our people."[21]

The FDPR sent a similar letter to the members of the legisla-ture on August 1, 1933. In this letter, Diez de Andino, a representa-tive of FDPR, urged the legislature not to mix professional sports such as boxing, horse racing, and cockfighting with amateur sports in the law creating a new Amusement Commission. Ignoring the Soviet Union and other communist countries, he argued that in no other country did the state centrally regulate all sports, except horse racing and boxing. Instead, he stated, the organization of sports needed to be left to the "natural free will of the individual Puerto Rican youth, demonstrated in his affection for the practice of sports as an efficient method of obtaining his best physical and cultural development."[22] Finally, he affirmed that in Puerto Rico no one was more knowledgeable about the "scientific" regulations needed to properly develop sports than the leaders of the FDPR.[23] As sports enthusiasts, they had the knowledge to enrich the coun-try's athletic culture. According to Diez de Andino, placing central-ized control over sports in three mediocre, government-appointed individuals—the governor, the president, and the secretary of the Athletic Commission—would mean a regression in Puerto Rican athletic progress. Despite the appeal, the legislature ignored the FDPR's recommendations, and in 1934 the Public Amusement and Sports Commission was created.

The creation of the first COPR in 1933 points to the serious desire to organize sports in accordance with Olympism and, in doing so, to modernize society. Nevertheless the fact that the committee was mainly composed of politicians demonstrates that the leadership of athletics and sports was still in the hands of the government.

Olympics are a political event by default simply because the athletes represent nation-states. Nation-states, whether independent or not, compete for bragging rights and medals, symbols of wealth and prestige. The fact that the founders of COPR included a U.S.-appointed colonial governor, many U.S. pro-statehood Republican leaders, and industrialists begs a question: Why was a Puerto Rican Olympic Committee created? Wouldn't having a COPR imply to other Olympic nation-states that Puerto Rico was an independent country? To answer this apparent contradiction, one must understand the political gains from supporting sports within the colonial context. It was not necessarily a patriotic project.

Due to the great following and popularity of sports, politicians could not afford to ignore or defeat anything related to its development. The Olympic movement was seen as a worldwide progressive and growing movement. The Games were designed to display advances in physical training, and Puerto Ricans too wanted to demonstrate their athletic progress. Also, sports enthusiasts might be voters and politically involved citizens, so supporting sports helps politicians gain popularity and possibly reelection. Controlling the institutions of sport became a great tool to define and dictate popular behavior. The reason a Puerto Rican Olympic Committee under a colonial relationship with the United States existed lies in the mentality of the colonizers (including locals in alliance with the imperial state) more than the colonized. As readers will learn, some U.S. and Puerto Rican officials thought Puerto Rico's participation in the Olympic movement was an excellent opportunity for Olympic diplomacy to show off the athletic prowess of a U.S. possession. However, the negotiation of this Olympic project was full of experimentation and, at points, confusion.

Before considering this topic, it is necessary to examine the fate of the initial COPR. In 1934 the COPR and the Athletic Commission were repealed under Law No. 11, which stated in Section 3 that "the office of Amusements and Sports Commissioner is hereby created and also a Public Amusement and Sports Commission to be composed by three persons to be appointed by the Governor by and with the advice and consent of the Insular Senate, and of the Commissioner of the Interior and the Amusements and Sports Commissioner." The governor would appoint the new commissioner to a term of four years. Furthermore, as indicated in Section 4, the new Public Amusements and Sports Commission (PASC) was entrusted with "all powers necessary to reorganize, direct, regulate, and control all professional sports, in the Island of Puerto Rico; provided that all duties, obligations, rights, funds, and belongings contracted or acquired by the extinguished Athletic Commission prior to the enactment of this Act, are hereby transferred to the Public Amusement and Sports Commission."[24]

The creation of this new commission incurred a governmental power grab to limit the FDPR's influence and gain absolute control over sport and recreation. With a new governor came a new government, and while Governor Beverley was in favor of an independent, centralized sporting regulator, Governor Gore thought differently. Gore was known for his heavy-handed approach in Puerto Rican politics that alienated local reformers and was even criticized for treating Puerto Ricans like children.[25] He probably appreciated that having control over sports meant having control over a popular activity, a method the new government used to regain its hold and control over Puerto Ricans. Gore was a supporter of U.S. statehood for Puerto Rico, and perhaps he believed that the existence of a Puerto Rican Olympic Committee was detrimental for eventual statehood and could fuel nationalist sentiment, as in fact it did. The COPR was replaced by an Insular Board in Section 22 of Law No.11:

All the powers, rights, duties, and obligations of the Olympic Committee of Puerto Rico created by Joint Resolution No. 8 approved April 7, 1933, entitled "Joint Resolution to create the Olympic Committee of Puerto Rico; to appropriate funds to send our selection of athletes to the Central American Olympic Games of 1934, and for other purposes," as well as the funds and appropriations belonging to, or in favor of, said Committee, are hereby transferred to the Public Amusement and Sports Commission which shall devote the funds, appropriation, and powers so transferred to the purposes provided for in said Joint Resolution No. 8, approved April 7, 1933, which are not incompatible with this Act; Provided, That the Public Amusement and Sports Commission shall appoint a special commission of which the Amusements and Sports Commissioner shall be the chairman, to be known as Insular Board on Central American Athletic Games, which shall be in charge of all matters in connection with the selection and registration of the athletes who shall represent Puerto Rico in the Central American Athletic Games; And provided further, That the Treasurer of Puerto Rico shall transfer the sum of five thousand (5,000) dollars to the Amusement and Sports Fund, which sum is hereby appropriated out of any funds in the Treasury not otherwise appropriated, with the object of carrying out the ends and purposes of this Act specified in Joint Resolution No. 8, or April 7, 1933.[26]

Several things happened with this resolution. First, the transfer of power from the COPR to an Insular Board on Central American Athletic Games was a downgrade in political and organizational status since, at least in this type of government, a board is usually under a commission and not the other way around. Second, by deleting the name "Puerto Rico," any relation to a "nation" instead became the generic "insular." Third, by using the term "Athletic Games" rather than "Olympic Games," the meanings behind Olympism, a movement that embodied nations at play, were erased. Fourth, despite all of this, the state acknowledged that sports were a powerful phenomenon and still wished to support it. The plans to send a delegation of "insular" athletes to the 1934 Central American Athletic Games were still in place, and the state was willing to support such an endeavor by approving the appropriation of $5,000 to the Amusement and Sports Fund.

From 1934 to 1948 the PASC was the official institution that regulated everything regarding sports and recreational facilities. The 1930s proved to be central to the early functions of the PASC mainly due to the leadership of Teófilo Maldonado. He was a member of the Comisión Atlética of 1933 that regulated all sports; he was the first president of the FDPR; he was one of the protagonists in the establishment of the first COPR; and after Justo Rivera Cabrera served as president of PASC between 1934 and 1938, Maldonado took office in 1938. Between 1938 and 1939, parallel to the emergence of the Partido Popular Democrático under the parameters of social justice, Maldonado aggressively asked for funds in order to build more and better sporting facilities.

Taking advantage of the work done by the Puerto Rican Reconstruction Administration (PRRA),[27] Maldonado wrote to Governor Blanton Winship to secure funding for local parks. Winship forwarded the memo to Ernest Gruening, director of the Division of Territories and Island Possessions, adding, "Sports and Amusements Commission will appreciate your support in securing definite appropriation for athletic parks from funds allotted to PRRA. Knowing your keen interest in developing sports in the island, feel sure we can count on your full cooperation."[28]

Gruening can be considered responsible for the extension of U.S. New Deal policies to Puerto Rico. As a committed progressive and outspoken liberal, he urged President Roosevelt to extend his economic reforms to the island, particularly because it could show U.S. goodwill to Latin America, advancing in turn the Good Neighbor policy. Gruening's progressive plan was well received at the beginning of his appointment, in 1934, yet his commitment to the Good Neighbor policy made him lose focus on the complexities of Puerto Rican politics. Instead he resorted to unidirectional top-down policies, which by 1936 gained him the distrust and disapproval of many of the Puerto Rican political leaders, including the conservative governor Blanton Winship.[29]

Gruening replied to Maldonado's letter by referring his request to Miles H. Fairbank at the Department of the Interior. However, this was not the end of Maldonado's quest for funding. He pulled strings and sent letters again in June, September, and October. His plea was that if there was not enough funding from PRRA, perhaps they could get funds from the Public Works Administration or the Works Progress Administration, two other New Deal programs.[30]

After many short cables back and forth among Maldonado, Winship, Gruening, and Ruth Hampton, the assistant director of the Division of Territories and Island Possessions, Maldonado wrote an extensive letter to Gruening on October 3, 1938, urging, "It is impossible, absolutely impossible, to work in the benefit of sports, without such athletic fields, playgrounds, gymnasium, courts and swimming pools as are needed." He asked, "Do you deem advisable for me to go to Washington and work for such an appropriation? I would make an effort if you believe that I should go, and I would only go if you promise me that you will help me in much the same way you did here in the PRRA and if you assure me that we will be successful in what we are working for."[31]

Despite Gruening's dismissal, Maldonado reached out again on February 3, 1939, this time asking for funds to build an indoor court for basketball and other indoor games.[32] Gruening's reply was uncharacteristically dismissive and evidenced the patronizing attitude of some U.S. officials toward Puerto Ricans: "Puerto Rico has unique assets in its sunlight and fresh air, and nothing would seem to me unwiser than to disregard them. There are relatively few days in the year when it is not possible to play out-of-doors. I think, therefore, that the emphasis should be on outdoor recreation."[33] Gruening's patronizing is somewhat contradictory, especially as some people claimed he was truly devoted to progressive and liberal ideals, sensitive to Latin American culture, and worked hard for Puerto Rican reforms. Not only was this a condescending letter, but it also showed the detachment of U.S. bureaucrats from Puerto Rico. Anyone who has lived for some months in a tropical island knows that in order to have lush flora and fauna there needs to be abundant rain. Gruening knew Puerto Rico due to his many travels to the island, so the dismissal of Maldonado's petition is strangely pointed. Perhaps he did not think highly of recreation for social benefits but only for athletic diplomacy abroad, with Puerto Rican athletes serving as ambassadors for the Good Neighbor policy.

Ironically that same year Gruening was quick to support a private project to build an indoor sports complex in the San Juan area. This project was the idea and design of Félix Benítez Rexach, a wealthy local engineer, who also designed and built the Hotel Normandie in the San Juan area. Governor Winship had contacted Gruening about this project, and the same day that Gruening wrote Maldonado saying that "out-of-door" sports were wiser, he wrote to Winship saying, "On the face of it, it would seem to me that this is an attractive proposal which would be helpful in promoting the Island's tourist program. It might be possible to stage some important sporting events there which would attract people from the mainland and from other countries."[34]

Why was an indoor court for the youth of San Juan not a good idea, yet an indoor stadium at the private Club of El Escambrón a magnificent concept? Was this double standard explained by the constraints of the 1930s or an elitist bias? Was Gruening trying to gain trust from the local political upper class that might have used the Escambrón facilities? Politics aside, the fact is that there was a need to build sports facilities. Also, Puerto Rican sports made progress regardless of the Depression, as evidenced by the upcoming performance in the Central American Games of the 1930s. However, that appearance was not devoid of political nuances that evidenced de facto colonialism on the one hand and the growth of a national identity on the other.

Puerto Rico at the Central American and Caribbean Games: 1930, 1935, 1938

The media may portray feelings of national unity during international sports competitions, yet national identity in sport is full of contradictions, artificial constructions of homogeneity, and foreign influences. That is, there is nothing natural or essential about nations, but much dealing with political projects, ideological battles, and local hegemony. Throughout the twentieth century sports contributed to the construction of nations and national identity.[35] The drama of sport competition that creates heroes and rivals for masses of followers has proven to be ideal for the development of imagined communities.[36] The historian Felix Rey Huertas González argues that Olympic sport in Puerto Rico has served as a "vehicle for national affirmation." He seeks to demonstrate that Puerto Rican Olympism has been a source of resistance against colonialism and has been able to unite diverse ideological, political, and even religious groups.[37] While this assertion might be true, Olympism, as national identity, is more complicated than that.[38]

The emergence of Puerto Rican representation at the Central American Games was not necessarily a result of passionate Puerto Ricans wanting to see their "nation" at play. As scholars of nationalism and sport maintain, there are expressions of national identity in international sports, but these are definitely not natural expressions of a collective national soul and an immemorial past. When we look closely at the dynamics of politics, economics, and culture that occurred behind the scenes of the Central American and Caribbean Games, we see a different portrait of the Puerto Rican national team, one that mixed different shades of colonialism, nationalism, and an ever-present desire to modernize.

Although Coubertin and the IOC had been interested in spreading Olympism to Latin America since 1917, even collaborating with the YMCA to support the Latin American Games of 1922 in Brazil,[39] stable Olympism in Latin America was actually achieved with the Central American Games after 1926. The Central American Olympic Games were envisioned and designed in Paris in 1924 at the Conference of the International Olympic Committee with representatives from Mexico, Cuba, and Guatemala. The Olympic Charter was approved on July 4, 1924, stating that Cuba, Colombia, Mexico, Venezuela, and the Central American and Caribbean republics would organize the games every four years, beginning in Mexico City, making the Central American and Caribbean Games the oldest regional Olympic Games sanctioned by the IOC.[40] The games were approved by IOC president Henry Boilet Latour, who also accepted the position as their honorary president. On October 16, 1925, twelve national delegations met in Mexico to continue planning the events. The countries represented were Mexico, Cuba, Costa Rica, Colombia, El Salvador, Guatemala, Haiti, Honduras, Jamaica, Nicaragua, Panama, and the Dominican Republic.

Although twelve countries participated in the 1925 meeting, only three (Mexico, Cuba, and Guatemala) participated in the 1926 CACG. Two hundred sixty-nine athletes participated in seven sports. To the disappointment of many, the games actually became a sort of dual meet between Mexico and Cuba, due to Guatemala's limited participation in only four events. In Puerto Rico these games did not attract major attention. Instead the focus was on organizing sports locally. This changed in 1930 when Puerto Rico participated in the CACG in Havana.

Puerto Rico's First International Games: Havana, 1930

What is seldom recognized about Puerto Rico's participation at the second Central American Games of 1930 is that it did not come about as a result of local initiative but rather from the U.S. ambassador in Havana, Harry Guggenheim. The organizing committee sent an invitation to the Puerto Rican commissioner of education, Juan B. Huyke, a pro-annexation member of the Puerto Rican Republican Party, but it appears that he did not respond. An invitation committee, headed by a Cuban, Miguel Ángel Moenck, traveled throughout the region to officially invite delegations, but this commission never arrived in Puerto Rico.[41] Therefore Puerto Rico's first participation at an IOC-sponsored games was a result of external initiative.

It is clear that Huyke did not initiate the process to send a Puerto Rican delegation to Havana because of his pro-annexation beliefs. Yet why did a U.S. diplomat, knowledgeable about Puerto Rico's unincorporated territorial status, want to include the island in a tournament for countries of Central America and the Caribbean? It is doubtful Guggenheim desired Puerto Ricans to exert their national pride and athletic ability. To the contrary, he wanted to send U.S. citizens to participate in IOC-sanctioned games and reap the benefits of Olympic diplomacy. Most probably Ambassador Guggenheim, knowing the enthusiasm for sports in the United States, did not want to miss the opportunity for a delegation of "U.S. athletes" to participate in these regional games. If Great Britain was represented through its crown colony Jamaica, the United States needed to send its own Caribbean colony. Acknowledging U.S. interest in strengthening its relations with Latin America, a Puerto Rican–U.S. delegation seemed desirable. In this regard Puerto Rico's participation at the Central American Games in Havana in 1930, in El Salvador in 1935, and in Panama in 1938 predates by a decade future attempts at Olympic diplomacy between the United States and Latin America, as evidenced in the Pan-American Games since 1942.[42]

As part of the international movement to bring back the Greek Olympic Games in the late 1890s, the United States could not miss an opportunity to participate in the games in Central America, an area it considered of great economic and political interest.[43] Although the specific reasons for their decision are unknown, Ambassador Guggenheim and Governor Theodore Roosevelt Jr. may have thought that a valid option existed for the United States to participate and foster the Good Neighbor policy. This is not to say that the Americans believed the Hispanic, dark, Catholic, poor Puerto Ricans were equal to them. Many Americans thought of Puerto Ricans as colonial others, and represented them in this way in World Fairs.[44] However, the U.S. hegemonic project was carried out in such a way that it would create a sense of inclusion and domesticity alongside practices of exclusion and foreignness.[45]

In 1929 Governor Roosevelt used the recently created Athletic Commission to raise funds to send a Puerto Rican athletic delegation to Havana. Heading the Athletic Commission's Olympic commission were Miguel A. Muñoz, Antonio R. Silva, and Teófilo Maldonado. While some scholars think it is "interesting" that the Puerto Rican delegation used the U.S. flag and national anthem as their symbols, it is completely understandable since those participating at this event were U.S. citizens from a U.S. territory, just as Jamaica used the British flag and anthem.[46] To compound the dubious meaning of the first Puerto Rican "national" delegation, their first head coach was George Keelan, the U.S. teacher from the University High School in Río Piedras. Some Puerto Rican athletes at the 1930 Games said they participated without any political motivations, but for the love of sports and as university students.[47] Of course, this does not mean that all Puerto Ricans were apathetic to the idea of the Puerto Rican nation at play. Other athletes were known for being supporters of Puerto Rican independence and sovereignty.

Two such nationalists were Manuel Luciano Gómez and Juan Juarbe Juarbe, ironically the U.S. flag bearer in Havana. Although the Partido Nacionalista and its leader, Pedro Albizu Campos, did not make official statements in regard to Puerto Rico's Olympic delegation during the 1930s, young nationalists did make their presence known at the games. Albizu Campos, who had been seeking transnational Latin American support for Puerto Rico's independence, believed that young nationalists should not be distracted by the adult struggle for independence, but should stay in school and learn as much as possible in order to become part of an educated leadership that would defend the nation with knowledge.[48] Juarbe Juarbe was a college student at the University of Puerto Rico and a talented athlete. He participated for Puerto Rico at the 1930 and 1935 CACGS and would make controversial pro-independence statements in future editions of the games, then as a journalist and the PN's foreign relations secretary. By the 1950s the FBI kept tabs on Juarbe Juarbe as part of a systematic surveillance project of all Puerto Ricans who expressed support for Puerto Rican independence.[49] (Juarbe Juarbe was inducted into the Puerto Rican Sports Hall of Fame in 1985.) Thus Puerto Rican participation in CACGS comprised multiple meanings and points of view, ranging from adherence to particular political ideologies to simply playing for the love of athletic competition.

Another athlete with nationalist leanings was Eugenio Guerra, who later became a staunch supporter of the Partido Popular Democrático. Known as "Trinitario," Guerra participated at these games for both political reasons and love of sport. He was probably the best overall athlete in Puerto Rican history. Born in Vieques in 1904, Guerra was a student at the Central High School from 1923 to 1926, dominating multiple sports. After high school he worked as a teacher in the towns of Ponce and Naguabo from 1926 to 1930 and later studied and taught at the UPR until 1969. While at the UPR he participated in the CACG in 1930, 1935, and 1938 and later became the trainer of the delegation in future CACG and Summer Olympic Games. He also became a sports journalist and radio commentator. Guerra dominated in track and field (for which he was named best college athlete in 1936), volleyball (as a member of the gold medal team of 1938), softball (he was the first pitcher in Puerto Rico to throw a perfect game), and basketball. For his achievements in the Olympic movement, he was awarded the Olympic Order medal by the IOC in 1994 and was awarded an honorary doctorate by the Universidad del

Sagrado Corazón in Santurce, Puerto Rico. Later in life he organized the Public Housing Olympics and the Municipal Olympiads with support from the Association of Commonwealth Employees.[50] Imbued with a populist (and PPD) mentality, both games were destined to provide healthy activity for the people and foster values of sportsmanship.

Traveling to Havana by way of Pan American Airlines (the only delegation to fly to the games),[51] Puerto Rican athletes did well in their first CACG. Guerra won silver in the 200-meter race and finished fifth in the 100 meter; Manuel Luciano Gómez won silver in the pole vault; Andrés Rosado finished fourth in the 110 meter with hurdles and fifth in the 200 meter. In the 4x100 meters the Puerto Rican team of Guerra, Luciano, Rosado, and Calderón finished fourth. Manuel Ángel Rodríguez and Jorge Juliá Pasareli participated in tennis, and a Puerto Rican delegation from the 65th Infantry of the U.S. Army participated in the shooting competition, winning a silver medal. Though it was a small delegation, the Puerto Rican team demonstrated athletic quality. Despite deep economic constraints, the 1930 CACG was the first time that Puerto Ricans showcased their athletic abilities at an Olympic competition and exhibited their place in the world of athletics.

While Puerto Rico was not originally expected to participate, the lackluster first edition of the games in 1926 forced Olympic authorities to agree with Guggenheim and allowed Puerto Rico to participate in 1930. Unfortunately there are few records available to trace the process of Puerto Rico's invitation to these games. However, there are abundant records for the third and fourth editions in 1935 and 1938, respectively. Taken together they evidence the complexities in the negotiation of Puerto Rican colonialism and identity.

On December 24, 1931, George Graves, on behalf of Avery Brundage, president of the American Olympic Association (AOA), thanked Governor Roosevelt for his "whole-hearted assistance in the interest of the 1932 American Olympic Team," which was to participate in the

Summer Olympics in Los Angeles. (Brundage was later president of the IOC from 1952 to 1972.) Specifically, Graves thanked Roosevelt for his "gracious acceptance of the position of Honorary Chairman of the Porto Rico Olympic Committee and your Kindness in making a splendid talk officially opening the American Olympic Team Fund Drive."[52]

It is clear that the AOA thought of Puerto Rico as part of the United States, at least for Olympic participation. As a matter of fact, the AOA planned to have "similar committees in the various territories and possessions of the United States apart from the North American Continent." They had already gained the support of the governors of Hawaii and Alaska for their governors' Olympic committees and encouraged Roosevelt to create such a committee in Puerto Rico. Future governor James Beverley replied, indicating that their office will cooperate with the AOA, but did not state a definite decision on the matter.[53] However, the message was clear: the AOA wanted Puerto Rico to join its organization.

Governor Roosevelt left office in 1931 and Governor Beverley assumed his first of two short terms as governor. It was under Beverley's leadership in 1933 that a Puerto Rican "national" Olympic committee, the COPR, was formed. On July 20, 1932, COPR secretary Rafael Santiago Sosa wrote to Beverly detailing the preparations for sending a delegation to the games in El Salvador in 1935. He stated that they needed the support of the Department of Education in order to celebrate local Olympic Games and other athletic meets to select athletes. Santiago Sosa referred to Puerto Rico's participation at these games in terms of economic benefits, stressing the publicity for the island that would potentially increase tourism, and added his hope that "these contests will increase our friendly relations with the republics of Central America."[54] It should be noted that tourism is a vital component in Latin American history, in its relation to culture, diplomacy, and local and international politics.[55] Dennis Merrill argues that tourism, particularly in Puerto Rico, was a "colonial project" partaking in a "soft power relation involving the U.S., Puerto Ricans, and the region as a whole."[56]

Part of Puerto Rico's role as a U.S. colony was to showcase the virtues and benefits of the U.S. government, and in the 1930s the Good Neighbor policy. Ernest Gruening was deeply involved in this process, particularly after 1934. One of Gruening's close allies, former governor Roosevelt, thought that the island could "serve as the connecting link between the two great divisions," assisting in lessening the "wide misunderstanding and antagonism between the two cultures."[57] According to this view, Puerto Rico served as a bridge between Anglo and Latin America that evidenced peaceful and successful coexistence. To some extent Puerto Rico became for the United States a response to the Uruguayan essayist José Enrique Rodó, whose essay "Ariel" exemplified the generational distrust of the United States as materialistic, superficial, and oppressive. By participating in these games, Puerto Rico would show that the United States was a positive presence in the area and a source of progress. U.S. officials and Puerto Ricans embraced this. In an official memorandum to Governor Gore, honorary president of COPR, Justo Rivera Cabrera requested additional monetary support from the U.S. government so that they could send a bigger and better delegation to El Salvador: "We could ask from the United States government its support and good wishes so that our emissaries to El Salvador next year, who are U.S. citizens and who in addition to representing Puerto Rico carry the representation of the great American Republic, be granted free tickets from San Juan to Panama in one of the national shipping lines, to the members of the Puerto Rican delegation. This would be, in addition to tightening the bonds of fellowship between Puerto Rico, Central America, and the United States, a means of abating the traveling expenses of our countrymen."[58]

This view of Puerto Rico as the bridge between two worlds and a potential tool for diplomacy was present every time the island participated abroad. Everyone involved in the selection and organization of the delegation shared this view, at least at the top level. For example, in 1934 the president of the Public Amusement and Sports Commission, Justo Rivera Cabrera, wrote to the director of the U.S. Division of Territories and Island Possessions for financial support for the games in El Salvador. Rivera Cabrera thought this would be a great opportunity for the United States to engage in goodwill relations with Latin America. He wrote, "Such aid as might be afforded by Federal Government to participate in said Games, where a spirit of international brotherhood will prevail, would further purposes of good neighbor policy."[59] The characterization of Puerto Rico's participation at these games as beneficial for tourism and publicity, as a bridge between two cultures, and to promote the Good Neighbor policy is abundant in the records and internal memos. Both U.S. officials and Puerto Rican Olympic leaders echoed it. This is not strange since at stake was the showcase not of colonialism but of a level of progress evidenced in athletic competition. Both the U.S. and the Puerto Rican government benefited from Puerto Rican participation. Not only were Puerto Ricans willing to compete, but they also managed to raise funds and send a delegation despite the Depression.

A Nation Is Born: El Salvador, 1935

Despite the benefits of having a delegation at these games, Puerto Rico's colonial status was evident, particularly during the invitation and acceptance process. Even though the 1930 invitation occurred almost by diplomatic improvisation, the 1935 and 1938 invitations occurred in an official, yet nonfluid, manner. Given that Puerto Rico is a territory without control over its international relations, how and to whom did the organizing committees send the official invitation? The actual invitation process involved many individuals and lots of bureaucracy. The organizing committee in El Salvador, headed by Ángel Soler Serra, sent invitations to the FDPR, the governor of Puerto Rico, and U.S. secretary of state.[60] Both the FDPR and Secretary of State Cordell Hull sent letters to Governor Blanton Winship.[61] The White House was also informed of Puerto Rico's invitation when Resident Commissioner Santiago Iglesias Pantín forwarded to Marvin H. McIntire, President Roosevelt's secretary, a cable he received from Justo Rivera Cabrera.[62] All of the communications made reference to the Good Neighbor policy and the benefits of tourism.

After the Sports Commission obtained permission from all authorities, Puerto Rico sent its delegation to the games in El Salvador, held between March 16 and April 5, 1935. The thirty-one-member delegation departed from San Juan's Dock 1 aboard the *Juan Sebastián El Cano* before a multitude that had gathered to send them off.[63] These games marked the first time Puerto Rico brought home a gold medal, when Fernando Torres Collac won in shot put. In the pole vault José O. Sabater broke the previous regional record held by Humberto Villa, jumping 12 feet 3 inches (3.73m). Out of a total of nine participating countries, the Puerto Rican delegation ended with fifteen medals (five of each color) for third place, behind Mexico and Cuba. In the end the Puerto Rican squad proved that with a bigger delegation they could bring home more medals and take their rightful place as a regional athletic contender.

Yet these games are known for more than athletic success. The 1935 games marked the first time that the Puerto Rican flag was used to represent the nation, when Manuel Luciano led the delegation in the opening parade (see fig. 5). This use of the Puerto Rican flag was significant for Puerto Rican culture and politics; it represented pro-independence leanings and nationalist affinities and points to the regional solidarity for Puerto Rico's Nationalist Party, a solidarity sought by Pedro Albizu Campos and other leaders of the NP during the 1920s and 1930s.[64] The Puerto Rican flag was used throughout the games, not only during the opening procession. It was raised when Puerto Rico won gold, an achievement not expected by the event organizers, who did not have on hand Puerto Rico's flag or anthem. Cosme Beitía of the UPR, who served as trainer of the delegation,

Fig. 5. The Puerto Rican delegation at the third Central American and Caribbean Games of 1935 in El Salvador. Source: *III Juegos Deportivos Centro-Americanos y del Caribe* (San Salvador, 1935), 44.

had brought with him a Puerto Rican flag; he gave it to the organizers every time Puerto Rico won a medal.[65] Then, to the surprise of many, when Fernando Torres Collac (shot put) won the first gold medal for Puerto Rico the organizers raised the Puerto Rican flag and played the Salvadoran national anthem. The Salvadoran people cheered in celebration of their anthem and for the Puerto Rican delegation in Central American and Caribbean solidarity. Manuel Ángel Rodríguez, a member of the Puerto Rican volleyball team, was another athlete who, in nationalistic fervor, raised a Puerto Rican flag during the awards ceremonies.[66]

For Salvadorans, especially the regime in power, these games and Puerto Rico's flag gesture were particularly special. Between 1931 and 1944 El Salvador was ruled by Gen. Maximiliano Hernández Martínez, who came to power in reaction to a failing liberal political system mainly concerned with the interests of the elite and U.S. businesses. Seizing power with a coup in 1931, his regime pushed the image of a "benevolent dictator" with a populist plan, though he

Fig. 6. The flag of Puerto Rico. GiannRiveraPR, Wikimedia Commons.

became brutally repressive. Nationalism, anti-U.S. imperialism, and resentment over foreign companies characterized his regime, even though Hernández Martínez kept a close alliance with and protected the coffee plantation owners. Under his regime, sport received considerable state support, aiding the establishment of the Salvadoran National Olympic Committee in 1934, developing physical education in all schools, and building the national stadium.[67]

The act of Puerto Rican nationalism got the attention of the U.S. diplomatic community in El Salvador. The head of the U.S. Legation in El Salvador, Frank P. Corrigan, communicated to the U.S. Department of State that the flag used by the Puerto Rican delegation was not the U.S. flag, although, trying to mitigate the political discomfort around the anthem incident, he asserted, incorrectly, that Puerto Rico had actually used "The Star-Spangled Banner," not the Salvadoran anthem. Although bothered by the act, he nonetheless accepted it because Capt. Harold D. Woolley (a member of the Puerto Rican rifle team) and Frank Campos (manager of the team) told him that that was the "territorial" Puerto Rican flag as approved by the island's legislature.[68] This is significant because the only time the Puerto Rican flag was adopted as an official flag was with the establishment of the commonwealth in 1952. Throughout the 1920s, 1930s, and 1940s the Puerto Rican flag was the flag for the Nationalist Party and other pro-independence movements. The flag was actually prohibited and criminalized under the "Gag Law" of 1948.[69]

Even before the games in El Salvador, there was confusion at the U.S. Department of State when the Salvadoran authorities asked for a Puerto Rican anthem. Corrigan wrote in 1934 to Cordell Hull, "While it is doubtful whether there is such a thing as a Puerto Rican National Anthem, since that island is a possession of the United States, it is thought that the United States Army or Navy Department might possibly be in position to supply some Puerto Rican music which would be appropriate for the Presidential Band to Play."[70] Ernest Gruening received the request and forwarded it to the Army and Navy Departments, as well as to Governor Winship in Puerto Rico, requesting an update with final decision.[71] Sports Commissioner Justo Rivera Cabrera wrote to all saying that he had sent "music" directly to the Salvadoran organizing committee.[72]

Whether there was confusion or manipulation of national, territorial, or even foreign identity symbols, the fact is that these symbols were powerful enough to produce different reactions. The Salvadoran media praised the Puerto Rican delegation for using their anthem, claiming that a nation was born. The Nicaraguan writer Juan Ramón Avilés wrote the following for La Prensa while in El Salvador:

Cuba, today a republic, is more fortunate than Puerto Rico, without being either a state of the North American Union or an independent republic. But in the Central American Olympics Puerto Rico has been a nation. Olympically speaking, in San Salvador we have witnessed the birth of a nation: Puerto Rico. Its small flag with its single star, like a younger sister of the other flags, has been raised for the first time on the common flagstaff of the Central American standards. This took place on Salvadoran ground, the free ground of a self-governing people. The firm ground of a people who have declared their independence. And we shall never forget it.[73]

Corrigan claimed that this was one of only two letters challenging Puerto Rico's status and supporting its independence. Thus it appears that he was pleased that there were no more subversive events in El Salvador. However, the damage was done. Puerto Ricans had made it public that they identified as a Latin American nation, separate from the United States. The delegation returned home on April 22, 1935, to another cheering crowd. All the major island dignitaries were present, and hundreds of Puerto Rican flags flew above the sea of people. A private plane flew over the crowd towing the Puerto Rican flag, while the crowd sang the popular *danza* "La Borinqueña,"[74] a song known for its nationalistic meanings that became Puerto Rico's official national anthem in 1952. Loudspeakers played the song "¿Cómo te cae?" by the Puerto Rican composer Rafael Hernández, whose music, while romantic and popular, also exalted Puerto Rican national identity and criticized colonialism.[75] Other bands that participated at the carnivalesque reception were the Puerto Rico Emergency Relief Administration, the 65th Infantry Regiment, and the band of the Children's Asylum. Some journalists regretted that the Puerto Rican anthem was not played during the medal ceremony, while others pointed to the Hispanic quality of Puerto Ricans as the premier reason to receive an invitation to the games in the first place.[76] Arturo Gigante wrote the following for the newspaper *El Mundo*:

That's Puerto Rico! That's Puerto Rico embodied in Figueroa, throwing itself on the ground after breaking the Olympic record by 1 centimeter, and in Luyanda, making a superhuman effort to defeat Bello, from Cuba, in the triple jump, by just another centimeter! That's Puerto Rico absent, overflowing with the hearts of its sons, that against drawbacks and vicissitudes have managed to have the name of our small island be repeated with admiration and respect by all the nations, which, forming an enormous heart on the map, are the nucleus of the Hispanic republics, spine and marrow of our race![77]

Adding to this euphoria for national Olympic representation, Fernando Rodil, a sports writer for *El Mundo*, took the initiative of writing to the Organizing Committee of the 1936 Olympic Games in Berlin, asking to include Puerto Rico among the competing nations. Rodil, aware of the Philippines's participation at Olympic Games, thought that Puerto Rico should also participate as its own country.[78] He took this unprecedented initiative after receiving discreet news that the Organizing Committee in Berlin had written to Rivera Cabrera inviting Puerto Rico to the Games, to no effect.[79] The details of this invitation and the inaction of the Puerto Rican authorities are unclear, but we do know that Rodil managed to send a few Puerto Rican athletes to the AOA's Olympic tryouts in the United States,[80] with the full support of Blanton Winship, Justo Rivera Cabrera, and other officials. In other words, Puerto Rico's chance to participate for the first time in the Olympic Games was silenced by the authorities, who instead supported Puerto Ricans trying out with the AOA.

Negotiating Identities and Authority: Blanton Winship and the Games in Panama City, 1938

It was ironic, if not contradictory, that Puerto Rican Olympic participation could rely on the unequivocal support of Governor Winship, who is considered one of the most repressive U.S. governors in Puerto Rican history. A veteran of the Spanish-American War and World War I and a military judge, Maj. Gen. Blanton C. Winship was considered responsible for the Masacre de Ponce in 1937, in which twenty Puerto Rican nationalists were killed and nearly two hundred were wounded while marching in commemoration of the abolition of slavery and also to claim Puerto Rico's independence.[81]

However, when it comes to sports, we see a different side to this governor. He always supported local sports and actively helped to send Puerto Rican delegations to both the 1935 CACG in El Salvador and the 1938 CACG in Panama City. Responding to a letter from Teófilo Maldonado, Governor Winship said that even though the island was facing dire economic conditions, he was interested in sending a delegation, and for this reason he had called a meeting of sports leaders to discuss funding to send a delegation to El Salvador.[82]

Perhaps due to his love of athletics or following Good Neighbor policy, Winship was constantly interceding with Gruening on behalf of Maldonado and Rivera Cabrera. Once the games began in El Salvador, he kept in touch with the delegation and congratulated them on their success. A cable to Frank Campos read, "Extend on my behalf effusive congratulations [to] our athletes. Puerto Rico proud of your triumph. Keep it up!"[83] After the games, Winship officially proclaimed July 17 to 26 the week of the "Puerto Rican Olympic Games" in preparation for the 1938 CACG in Panama. A portion of the proclamation stated, "Puerto Rico has always been a sport-loving country, for which reason it is our duty to maintain alive, to the highest degree, this spirit which animates our people. . . . For the first time in our history as a sporting country, Puerto Rican Olympic Games will officially be held, at which our most outstanding values in the field of sports will have an opportunity to distinguish themselves."[84]

Before the Puerto Rican delegation departed for the Games in Panama City, Governor Winship gave a public radio address on December 16, 1937, explaining in detail his view of sports in Puerto Rico:

Did you know that: We have in Puerto Rico some of the most promising athletes in the world, and that the interest shown in this subject by the youth of our island is most encouraging? . . . It is not at all difficult for me to wax enthusiastic over good, clean, wholesome sports and recreation. I have always considered it my duty to myself and to my country, to keep my body in good physical trim. . . . Taking into consideration the fact that certain countries are spending many thousands of dollars to train and equip their teams for the Pan-American Olympics next month, we in Puerto Rico feel that it is only right to give our excellent athletes an opportunity to participate in those games.[85]

The transcription of the address continues for four pages, as he discusses specific sports and analyzes Puerto Rico's chances of winning. He credits the PASC for its tireless work and even expresses his desire to bring the CACG to Puerto Rico in 1942. It is particularly revealing that Winship constantly refers to Puerto Rico as a sport-loving "country" and to "our" athletes. This might seem contradictory, since he was there to assert control over social instability and suppress political insurgents as a result of the volatile 1930s.[86]

It is true that Winship loved sports and recreation for their wholesomeness and physical health, yet in regards to Puerto Rican athletes at international competition, he responded to political pressure. While leading a repressive regime, he also needed to govern and keep the masses content, especially during the years of the New Deal and the Good Neighbor policy. Sport provided a good opportunity to show benevolence. Knowing the appeal of sport and recreation and the popularity of Olympic competition, Winship proactively gave them his support. Rivera Cabrera and Maldonado repeatedly requested his support for the Olympic delegation, while diplomats abroad extended invitations to the Puerto Rican delegation.[87]

Giving in to this pressure, Winship sent the Puerto Rican delegation to the 1938 CACG, securing appropriations of $7,500 and $15,000 to cover all necessary expenses.[88] Still, he was unambiguous about his job: suppressing any manifestation of Puerto Rican nationalism. This meant there would be no display of the Puerto

Rican flag during the 1938 games; instead the Puerto Rican delegation carried the U.S. flag and played the U.S. anthem. Rivera Cabrera
understood this, and he made sure that all involved understood it as
well. In a letter of recruitment to the Puerto Rican athlete Gilberto
Juliá González, a student at Columbia University, Rivera Cabrera
avoided any mention of patriotic duty or Puerto Rican pride and
kept his letter focused on athletic achievement.[89] In a letter to Winship, Rivera Cabrera assured him that Puerto Rican symbols would
not be displayed in Panama: "Due to the fact that Puerto Ricans are
citizens of the United States, our team will be carrying to the Central American Olympic Games the national flag, as it will represent
a part of the United States in said games."[90] According to Rivera
Cabrera, because Puerto Ricans were U.S. citizens he was expecting full support from the federal authorities in order to have a solid
representation. All nationalistic symbols were to be eliminated and
the focus kept on athletic competition and tourism. This suppression of nationalistic symbols also explains the silencing of the Berlin
Games Organizing Committee's invitation to Puerto Rico. There is a
significant difference in supporting a Puerto Rican athletic delegation to regional games representing the United States and a Puerto
Rican delegation to world Olympic Games. In an event where the
United States is already present, a Puerto Rican delegation signals
a different nation.

With the Puerto Rican delegation carrying the U.S. flag and playing the U.S. national anthem, the 1938 games in Panama reasserted
Puerto Rico's status as a U.S. territory. This is not to say that the 1935
games were an unambiguous expression of Puerto Rican national
identity. As mentioned, the games were seen as a venue for Puerto
Rico publicity and tourism, as a sporting stage to represent U.S. values, and as a political and cultural bridge between Anglo and Latin
America. Puerto Rico was a sort of mixed breed, neither totally Latin
American nor fully a part of the United States. At least that is how
many leaders, both American and Puerto Rican, saw the delegation.

However, for others, this mixed breed characterization of Puerto Rican Olympic participation was not so clear. Many in the United States regarded Puerto Rico as an independent country, not knowing that it was a U.S. unincorporated territory. For example, in 1937 Leslie Mann from Miami, Florida, who was vice president of the USA Baseball Congress and secretary of the International Baseball Congress, invited the Republic of Puerto Rico, via Blanton Winship, to participate in the International Olympic Baseball Congress. The invitation was sent at the suggestion of the Mexican Baseball Congress.[91] Justo Rivera, who received a copy of the invitation, accepted but clarified Puerto Rico's status by saying that although Puerto Ricans were of "Spanish origin," they were Americans due to the "American citizenship that was bestowed upon us by an Act of the National Congress." He acknowledged Puerto Rico's geographic position as the reason for inclusion in the Central American Games, yet upheld Puerto Rican alliance to the United States:

> Our local athletes will have the honor in February 1938 of upholding the national colors[.] We believe it is to be in order to ask your cooperation, if not materially, at least morally and spiritually, for our patriotic effort to put as high as possible and as security the sporting banner of Puerto Rico under the folds of the glorious stars and strypes [sic] as our token of love and respect for the institutions that have helped to bind our small island to the sisterhood of States with this spirit of human cooperation which animates to-day the relations between Puerto Rico and continental United States.[92]

There should be no doubt of Winship's support for sport, yet there should also be no doubt of his authoritarian administration. For this reason, Rivera Cabrera was eager to elaborate on Puerto Rico's alliance to the United States. After learning that Rivera Cabrera had responded to Mann without his permission, Winship reminded him that all communication sent to the Continental United States should pass through his office first.[93]

Once in Panama City, the Junta General de Delegados (General Board of Delegates) met to discuss and approve the new Central American and Caribbean Olympic Charter of Fundaments. At the meeting Rivera Cabrera actively participated in defining the terms of regional Olympism. However, he presented an amendment to the first article of the Charter to eliminate the mention of Puerto Rico as a cosigner and member of the Charter. While he did not think Puerto Rico should be counted as a "country," his Olympic colleagues disagreed. The delegates from Venezuela, Costa Rica, Nicaragua, Colombia, and Mexico supported Puerto Rico's inclusion in the Charter and, despite Rivera Cabrera's insistence to the contrary, insisted that Puerto Rico continue to belong in the "sporting community of Central American nations."[94] The amendment failed by a vote of ten to one, and Puerto Rico was ratified by its regional peers as an Olympic nation.

For Puerto Rico the 1938 CACG in Panama was unforgettable. With their largest delegation to date, eighty-nine men and nine women, they won first place in the coveted track and field competition. It was also the first time Puerto Rico sent women athletes. Participating in seven sports, the Olympic squad won thirty-eight medals (sixteen gold, eleven silver, and eleven bronze). Rebekah Colberg was the first Puerto Rican woman to win an Olympic medal, with a record-breaking performance in the discus. At the medal ceremony Colberg sang "La Borinqueña."[95] Puerto Rican women continued to contribute to Puerto Rico's athletic success and also promoted the national self abroad.

Once the games were over and the athletes had returned home, their reception was fit for champions. Just as in the 1935 reception, newspapers reported an immense crowd and great joy at the port of arrival. News reporters for *El Mundo*, *El Imparcial*, and *La Democracia* covered the events. The vessel carrying the athletes was received by private and navy planes, which gave them an honorary escort to the dock. Thousands of followers accompanied the athletes through the streets of San Juan to a platform at the Capitol steps. This time there was no singing of "La Borinqueña" nor waving of Puerto Rican flags; rather the national anthem of the United States was sung.[96]

The Puerto Rican Olympic delegation's reception and following might be taken as an undeniable sign of national identity. Expressions of Puerto Rican pride and identity were clear. However, for many, the success of the Puerto Rican delegation was not necessarily that of a nation. For some, Puerto Rico's participation in the CACG was a matter of proving athletic progress in the region. Additionally, the competition was, for many athletes, the main reason to attend the games, coupled with an interest in testing their skills against other college students of Central America and the Caribbean. For U.S. officials in Washington, Havana, San Salvador, and Panama City, the Puerto Rican delegation was a group of "U.S. American" ambassadors of goodwill and progress.

Yet the Puerto Rican sport leadership was divided in its view of these regional games. For some, a sole Puerto Rican nation played at the Games, yet for others, Puerto Ricans were a perfect blend of Spanish culture and Anglo-Saxon progressive values, embedded in harmony and seen in the Puerto Rican athletic body. Let's not forget that Puerto Ricans were separated from their Spanish years by only one generation, and many Puerto Ricans living in the 1930s and born before 1898 were Spanish citizens.

Furthermore, while the 1930s were a decade of social, economic, and political instability, they were also a decade of gradual athletic conscience and expansion. Athletic programs in the schools began to grow and sports began to reach different corners of the island. This produced high-caliber athletes fit for international competition.

The colonial relationship that tied Puerto Rico to the United States was obviously present once Puerto Rico began attending the CACG. However, this bond was not as strong as some had hoped.

After one generation under U.S. rule, Americans and some Puerto Ricans hoped that Puerto Ricans had left behind their Spanish past and accepted Americanization. However, while Puerto Ricans welcomed some U.S. progressive values, such as Olympism and sports, many upheld their Spanish Caribbean traditions and values. This reaffirmation of national identity merged perfectly with developing ideas of nationalism on the island, as in the Olympic movement overall. For this reason the Puerto Rican Olympic team symbolized the Puerto Rican nation not only for Puerto Ricans but also for the international audience. Yet the incongruence of a colonial relationship kept gazing from every corner. Why was Puerto Rico a sporting nation while being a territory of the United States? At stake was the appellative "best of both worlds," or the political agenda of the Good Neighbor policy that tried to make U.S. diplomats out of Puerto Rican athletes. Also at stake was a desire for athletic progress that would accelerate in the decades to come. In sum, Puerto Rican Olympism in the 1930s was just the beginning of a tradition in Puerto Rican sports that reflected a general impetus for nationhood embedded in colonial Olympism.

3 / Legitimizing Colonial Olympism in a Colonial Nation, 1940s

In *Soccer Empire: The World Cup and the Future of France*, Laurent Dubois skillfully traces the ways soccer has been the glue that binds the notion of French people in its transcontinental ethnic, racial, cultural, and ideological diversities. Regarding the French *départements d'outre-mer* in the Caribbean, Dubois argues that soccer, while introduced and developed under the tenets of French sport and under French parameters, became a source for Martiniqueans and Guadeloupeans to claim a separate identity. Nonetheless this identity was immersed within an imperial hegemonic relation that allowed for dual identities, as Caribbean and French nationals. French Caribbeans "sought to conform to French metropolitan models of sport and find recognition within the French sports world, and at the same time they used sports as a way of seeing full emancipation and a recognition of their difference."[1] When the French Caribbean reached departmental status in 1948, with political rights equal to other departments of metropolitan France, they still faced unequal and subordinated treatment, as evidenced in the development of the French soccer league.

This process of dual identities in sport and culture in the French Caribbean can be used to comprehend the process of Olympic participation in Puerto Rico. In the 1930s Puerto Ricans embodied the dualisms of U.S. and Puerto Rican sport identities in the regional Central American and Caribbean Games. This process extended to the world stage in the 1940s, when Puerto Ricans participated for the first time at the 1948 Olympic Games in London. Although Puerto Rico participated under the U.S. flag at the 1946 CACG, in 1948 the

Puerto Rican team experimented with the creation of a sport and national identity by using a flag depicting their centuries-old Spanish-granted coat of arms. While this flag might indicate yet another symbol of colonialism, it can also be seen as a symbol of the autonomist tradition. Autonomy had been growing since the nineteenth century and continued into the twentieth. By Puerto Rico's first Olympic Games, this ideal was very much present. But the symbol that represented autonomists was still to be negotiated, and delegates struggled over which flag to use. Legally they were all U.S. citizens, yet to the world they were Puerto Ricans. This complex process of identity and colonialism is similar to the experience of other Caribbean peoples, yet it is unique for the larger Latin American region. Moreover Puerto Rico did not cease to be, at least locally, the bastion of the Good Neighbor policy, the distinctive link that united the Anglo-Saxon American to the Latin American world.

During this decade Puerto Ricans also experienced a dramatic sport boom, led by the new sport commissioner Julio Enrique Monagas. Numerous athletic fields and courts were built all over the island as part of a government program known as Un parque para cada pueblo. Under Monagas's leadership (1942–66), the Public Amusement and Sport Commission became a key institution of the emerging Partido Popular Democrático (established in 1938) and its populist project, a process common in other parts of Latin America.[2] The values of social justice and progress combined with sport and athletics were viewed as the basis for a healthy and modernized society, all under the auspices of the United States. Monagas was given a special place among public leaders loyal to the PPD, which included its president, Luis Muñoz Marín (who became the first popularly elected governor); Teodoro Moscoso, director of the Puerto Rican Industrial Development Company; University of Puerto Rico chancellor Jaime Benítez; Ricardo Alegría, director of the Institute of Puerto Rican Culture; Rafael Picó, director of the Puerto Rico Planning Board; and Secretary of State Roberto Sánchez Vilella.

The plan to build an athletic infrastructure was achieved as a result of World War II. Puerto Rico experienced an economic boost due to its strategic position in Caribbean waters. The United States invested heavily in strengthening its military bases and built their largest base outside the Continental United States in Ceiba and Vieques, both part of Puerto Rico.[3] Spinning off New Deal policies of the 1930s while fully anchored in a war, the United States spent $1.2 billion between 1939 and 1950 on programs that included provisions for a healthy citizenry and potential soldiers;[4] however, this was also an investment in developing Puerto Rico as an island symbol of U.S. democracy and progressive values. Taking into account the ways international and Olympic sport is the scenario for athletic diplomacy and geopolitics,[5] it is easy to understand the U.S. investment in sport in this strategically situated colony. In this chapter I explore the intricate ways the local government sought to implement this pro-U.S. populist ideology in Puerto Rico's international sporting participation, while at the same time struggling to define its status as a nation-colony.

In a decade of growing industrialization of the developing world, increasing awareness of democratic policies, and planning postwar recovery, Puerto Rico became a key piece in the world diplomatic puzzle. The result was that Puerto Ricans began to cement a Latin American identity separate from the United States while at the same time establishing the bases to consolidate a colonial relationship. This chapter shows how international participation by the Puerto Rican Olympic squad was used in the negotiation of a colonial national identity, the supremacy of a rising global superpower, and the legitimation of the Olympic Games.

Julio Enrique Monagas, Olympism, and the Central American and Caribbean Games of 1946

Julio Enrique Monagas Sánchez was born on October 17, 1903, in Santo Domingo, Dominican Republic, to Puerto Rican parents from the city of Mayagüez. His father was a representative for the Singer sewing machine company in Santo Domingo, but in 1906 the family moved back to Puerto Rico and established a residence in the city of Ponce. There Monagas went to primary and secondary school during the 1910s and 1920s. At the prestigious Ponce High School, he participated in the competitive athletics program of Charles Terry, an American who had taken Ponce High athletics to the highest standards on the island. Monagas became a sports leader in Ponce and, along with a group of other Ponce sport leaders, founded the Federación Deportiva del Sur (Southern Sports Federation).[6]

Monagas was identified as a patron of sport and was included as a nonathlete in the Puerto Rican Olympic delegation at the 1938 CACG in Panama. This experience sparked a profound interest in Olympic competition for Monagas.[7] Yet he was first and foremost a follower and ally of the PPD, having personal communication with Luis Muñoz Marín since at least 1941.[8] Monagas had been a PPD activist and leader in Ponce when he was identified by Muñoz Marín soon after 1941 to lead the sport program of the newly industrialized and modernized Puerto Rico.[9] As a loyal PPD follower, Monagas would follow the PPD's adherence to development by focusing his attention on the United States rather than actively pursuing international competition. Initially he did not want Puerto Rico to participate at the 1948 Olympics in London.

During World War II the 1942 CACG and the 1940 and 1944 Olympic Games were canceled. A resurgence of global sport occurred in 1946 with the CACG and in 1948 with the Olympic Games. During Puerto Rico's first World Olympics participation in 1948, Monagas became a sort of hero, and would later become known as the father of Puerto Rico's Olympism. Yet what is seldom remembered of Monagas is that his vision for the development of sport was inward, that is, locally focused with little emphasis on international competition. If Puerto Rico was to compete internationally, the focus would be to compete with the United States rather than with other countries.

Why would Monagas, so interested in international competition, adhere to a rather limiting and inward program of Olympic participation? Because he was following the PPD's U.S.-centered program of development. He recognized that the ultimate goal of his agency was to aid the PPD's modernization program, which relied heavily on U.S. sponsorship. This intra-empire sport program was not uncommon, since the French Caribbean *départements d'outre-mer* had been mainly competing with France and other colonial French possessions through the 1930s and 1940s.[10] The intra-empire athletic competition was made clear when Monagas laid out the program Un parque para cada pueblo, as reported in *El Mundo* on May 29, 1945, where he stated, "I have the firm belief that Puerto Rico must channel its plans of international competition towards the United States because it is with this country that we are presently mostly attached and from whom we received most publicity in any activity, apart from the sporting similarities that we have been lately observing in the island."[11]

For Monagas, Puerto Rican Olympism was to be, to some degree, an extension of the United States. His argument was based on a historical sport reality; as a colony of the United States, Puerto Rico experienced an intense sport revitalization that revolved around U.S.-style sports such as basketball, baseball, volleyball, and softball. Nonetheless in this statement Monagas was arguing for the relationship between sport and publicity, which had a direct effect on tourism and other economic activities. This was also considered a matter of importance by previous Puerto Rican Olympic leaders such as Teófilo Maldonado and Juan Maldonado. However, they were more interested in the direct benefits of the Good Neighbor policy that included a regional approach to Central America and the Caribbean. For Monagas publicity was needed only from the United States, the country to which Puerto Rico was "mostly attached." Regardless of Puerto Rico's importance to hemispheric relations, Monagas was openly proposing to direct sport activity to the United States.

He did say later in the article that Puerto Rico was not going to stop participation with other countries, but that the island was going to channel its athletic competitions to the United States. In a 1947 interview with José Seda for the magazine *Puerto Rico Ilustrado*, Monagas again stated that "intra-island" sport needed to be more important than "extra-island" sport, arguing that the latter was the result of the first.[12] He repeated that he was not against international competition with "brotherly countries" but that successfully playing in the United States would be the fulfillment of the main goal of developing sports. This could be interpreted as an attempt by Monagas to not allow the euphoria of international competition to jeopardize the special relationship of Puerto Rico to the United States. It was fine to feel a brotherly connection to other countries, so long as people remembered that the most important relation to pursue, keep, and strengthen was the one with the United States. Monagas did view the United States as different from Puerto Rico and from countries with "international" status. To some extent the subtext of his plan still upheld the idea of a separate Puerto Rico while the United States was a foreign, albeit closely related country.

For Monagas the model of sport development was the United States, as seen in his explicit reference to the White House Conference on Child Health and Protection.[13] Different facets of Puerto Rico's modernization during the mid-twentieth century can be said to have been on a one-way street, from the United States to the island. Even the populist and modernist features of Luis Muñoz Marín sought to maintain amicable and close political and economic relations with the United States,[14] contrasting with the often anti-U.S. populism prevalent in certain parts of Latin America. For the United States, Puerto Ricans were expected to follow U.S. models of development.

However, Puerto Rico's Olympic development occurred somewhat differently than in the United States, where sport development was highly decentralized. While there were conferences at the federal level, the bulk of nationally organized sport was left to independent, private institutions. The U.S. Olympic Association was organized as a nonprofit association in November 1921. Its official report from 1948 states that the association's purpose was to "promote and to encourage the physical, moral, and cultural education of the youth of the nation to the end that their health, patriotism, character and good citizenship may be fully developed." In addition, the association would "select, finance, and control" the delegation to participate in Olympic tournaments, and also "maintain the highest ideals of amateurism, and . . . promote general interest therein." Its membership was taken from national sport associations that included the Amateur Athletic Union and the National Collegiate Athletic Association and national organizations of a "patriotic, educational, cultural, or civic character" wishing to support Olympism, such as the U.S. Army and Navy, the German-American Athletic Union, and the Knights of Columbus.[15]

The USOA (previously AOA) made clear that it was separate from politics and avoided political propaganda and economic profit. The 1948 report states that "neither the Association nor the Committee disseminates any partisan propaganda, engages in any lobbying, or in any other way attempts to influence legislation." Most of its funding came from admission tickets to Olympic tryout events, fundraisers, and donations from colleges and athletic organizations. Nevertheless, although the USOA was organized independently and did not seek federal money for its works, it was associated with the government. For the 1948 Olympic Games in London, it made "President Truman honorary president and Secretaries [of State George C.] Marshall and [of Defense James V.] Forrestal honorary vice presidents."[16] This is in addition to allowing the support and active membership of the armed forces.

This was the model familiar to Monagas when he reorganized Puerto Rico's Olympic Committee, one that some Puerto Ricans aspired to yet were not able (and some did not want) to implement. The lack of independent financially capable nonprofit organizations to fund the COPR made this option nonexistent. Furthermore the history of centralized and authoritative political control shaped COPR's symbiotic attachment to the central government. Still Olympism in Puerto Rico at least had to appear to follow the U.S. model, since it went along not only with the pro-U.S. populism of the PPD but also with the political colonial reality.

Muñoz Marín understood this. He saw that the United States would never concede independence and that their colonial relationship should stand strong. This is why, even though he created the PPD in 1938 as a social justice party with visions of independence (as seen in their motto, "Pan, Tierra y Libertad," Bread, Land, and Freedom), by 1945 he had renounced this political option, replacing it with an ideology that placed social needs before political ones, while dismissing independence as being against the best interests of the new nation.[17] His shift in ideology was beginning to show as early as 1943–44 and became evident in 1946 after he observed the conditions by which the Philippines got its independence from the United States.[18] For Muñoz Marín economic conditions would improve in close association with the United States and its capital power, providing a degree of social justice.[19] As a result of his shift in political ideology, dissenters from the PPD were expelled from the party and banded together to establish a new pro-independence party known as the Partido Independentista Puertorriqueño in 1946.

Knowing the close relationship between Monagas and Muñoz Marín, it would make sense that Monagas also looked to the United States for solutions to Puerto Rico's problems and development. Monagas stayed a close ally to Muñoz Marín's PPD government throughout his life, yet this relationship actually got him in trouble more than once. In 1950, looking to favor the governor and government officials, he conditioned the leasing of the Sixto Escobar Park to the Baseball Federation upon setting aside box seats for the governor and his associates. Upset about this matter, a private citizen sent a letter to Monagas and to Roberto Sánchez Vilella, then secretary to the governor, stating that in a "free country such as ours" he could not abide these political favors.[20] Monagas, who had gotten into political scandals before over box seats in the Sixto Escobar Park,[21] was more than a loyal follower of political ideals and the PPD; he was also an able politician involved in patronage circles.

Monagas's involvement in patronage and preference for the United States did not damage his legacy. Under Monagas, Puerto Rico participated in all CACGs since 1946 and in all Olympics after 1948. But he did have his share of critics, who would become opponents in the 1950s. Many of these critics based their comments on Puerto Rico's participation at international competitions. Writing for *El Mundo* in 1945, José Seda, the same journalist who interviewed him in 1947, complained that sports and athletics were not progressing as they should. His frame of reference, more than a review of sport infrastructure, was Puerto Rico's standing since the 1938 games in Panama. He asserted that while Puerto Rico's progress could be seen in basketball and volleyball, there was none in softball, baseball, or even track and field. His complaint regarding baseball was not against the professional level but rather the amateur one, especially trainers. Seda's vision, contrary to Monagas's, was not a one-sided dependence on U.S. trainers but based on a group of local experienced coaches who would become part of local teams.[22] His comparisons were not to the United States but to other Caribbean countries. He mentioned the case of Cuba, where the Cubans were in charge of the development of their sports rather than U.S.-imported trainers.

Felicio Torregrosa made a similar observation in 1946. Torregrosa, who was born in Guayama, Puerto Rico, obtained his bachelor's and master's degrees in physical education from Syracuse University in 1938. He left Syracuse in the 1940s as a doctoral candidate with an unfinished dissertation entitled "The Legal Status of Physical Education in Latin America."[23] He stated in *El Mundo* that the height of Puerto Rican sport was 1938 in Panama, but since then there had been a decline in the quality of sport, with no access to equipment or facilities and little interest in representing Puerto Rico internationally. He argued for full-time athletes, those who did not have to worry about their jobs or volunteering in wars or who were committed to colleges and universities in the United States.[24] He acknowledged the improvements in facilities but stated that more needed to be done. Torregrosa knew what he was arguing about; not only was he the coach of the Puerto Rican basketball team at the 1946 CACG in Colombia, but he had also been involved since the 1930s with athletics at the Polytechnic Institute of San Germán, where he established the legendary basketball team Atléticos de San Germán in 1939. He was also director of the Athletic Department at the UPR and had been director of the Golden Gloves program at the Public Amusement and Sport Commission with Monagas since 1943.

Torregrosa's public complaint in 1946 was specifically referring to Puerto Rico's participation at the fifth CACG in Barranquilla, Colombia, that year. Puerto Rico, although sending its biggest delegation to date, experienced a sharp decline in its medal tally. In 1938 a delegation of eighty-nine athletes won thirty-eight medals; in 1946 134 athletes won twenty-four medals.[25] The 1946 team finished in fourth place, failing to win the overall medal count as they had in Panama in 1938. Many sport leaders viewed this as a clear regression, disregarding the advances in sport infrastructure. However, this sentiment was not replicated by the masses in rural areas, who evidently enjoyed their new athletic and recreational facilities. This feeling of contentment resulted in wholehearted support for the PPD program, not only locally but also in its relationship with the United States. In this sense Monagas's work in the Public Amusement and Parks Commission (PAPC) was exactly what the PPD leaders wanted and what Monagas himself was aiming for. That is, in relation to Olympism, Monagas and the PPD mainly looked inward, while other sport leaders sought to direct it outward.

This did not mean that Monagas was not involved in the international non-U.S. competition and Olympism. He had arranged in

1944 with Cuba and the Dominican Republic to establish the Unión Gubernamental Deportiva Interamericana, which forced those two countries to adopt the amateur rules established in Puerto Rico.[26] Monagas was named vice president of this union and began to establish himself as a regional leader in sports. Moreover he was the leader of the delegation at the CACG in Colombia in 1946, where Puerto Rico again used the U.S. flag at all official ceremonies, including the opening and closing ceremonies. Nonetheless to establish a separate identity from the United States, the name Puerto Rico was displayed on the uniforms, along with the coat of arms granted by the Spanish monarchs in 1511. While many political and sport leaders saw Puerto Rico as part of the United States, there was a parallel movement that viewed Puerto Ricans as a distinct people. This feeling of distinctiveness had been developing since the nineteenth century under Spain and was (re)produced in the 1930s with the intellectual work of the Generación del 30, a group of Puerto Rican intellectuals who defined Puerto Rican identity during the 1930s.[27]

The display of colonial images did not impede athletes and teams from individually showing different national identity emblems. Puerto Rico's soccer uniform carried Puerto Rico's coat of arms, but a Puerto Rican flag was placed in the background of the team picture. (The Puerto Rican flag had been used by pro-independence parties throughout the twentieth century, including the radical Nationalist Party.) The soccer squad performed poorly in Barranquilla, losing all six games and being outscored 52–2.

Negotiations of an Empire and a Colonial Nation

During the 1940s Monagas evidenced two different yet cohesive programs: one that developed athletic facilities and another that represented Puerto Rico at international competitions. Though his sport expansion mission was intra-island, he did take national delegations to compete abroad in the CACGs. Yet the biggest step taken by Monagas, the PAPC, and the Puerto Rican government was to send a delegation to the 1948 Olympic Games in London. The process by which Puerto Rico participated at these Games was complex, including not only local concerns but also critical international politics.

Puerto Rico had been participating at the CACG since 1930 as a U.S. territory and a U.S. diplomatic initiative. However, as Olympic scholar John MacAloon correctly points out, with the United States participating at the World Olympics, Puerto Rico could not participate as a separate U.S. delegation with the same flag.[28] The problem and historical process of Puerto Rico's participation at the Olympic Games in London unfolded after Monagas and the PAPC, ignorant of international Olympic protocols and procedures, sent a letter on July 16, 1947, to request participation to the organizing committee in London rather than the IOC. After learning that permission must come from the IOC, Monagas sent another letter, dated September 17, 1947, to the IOC stating that Puerto Rico's National Olympic Committee (NOC) was composed of local government officials including Jesús T. Piñero, governor and chair of the Committee, and Julio E. Monagas, president of the PAPC and vice chair.[29] It is not clear whether Monagas knew that national committees could not be attached to governments, but he specifically indicated that Puerto Rico's NOC was a de facto governmental institution. What is clear is that Monagas was first and foremost a government representative who happened to be in charge of sports.

The IOC noted the governmental nature of Puerto Rico's NOC (the COPR) and sent a letter to Monagas on September 25, 1947, explaining that in order for Puerto Rico to participate and be recognized as a legitimate NOC it needed to gather the presidents of all athletic federations and select an executive board and president, and these local associations needed to be associated with international associations.[30] In this letter Otto Mayer, chancellor of the IOC, made clear that no governmental association would be allowed. Monagas also sent a petition to the International Association of Athletics

Federations (IAAF) on September 17, asking for acceptance of the PAPC by the organization.[31] The fact that Monagas made no efforts to present the COPR as independent from the government and still wanted to affiliate it with the IAAF reveals his priority as a government official. Ernest J. H. Holt, the IAAF's secretary and director of organization for the Games, replied to Monagas on October 1, stating, "It is not the practice of the Federation to affiliate government departments, but rather national associations of independent formation; it would therefore appear that the correct body to affiliate on behalf of Puerto Rico is the insular Track and Field association of Puerto Rico, and the same regulation is applicable to your National Olympic Committee." Holt included a copy of the rules and regulations of the IAAF and an application form for admission to the IAAF with a declaration as to amateur status. At its meeting in Lausanne on January 27–28, 1948, the IOC agenda included this item: "New NOC: Applications for Syria and Puerto Rico will be offered with favorable notice."[32] Puerto Rico's new NOC had been recognized by the IOC.

However, opposition to Puerto Rico's NOC persisted. In a local newspaper article written on February 13, 1948, U.S. amateur athletics leader Dan Ferris stated that "there will be no exception for Puerto Rico" and "there has been no official recognition."[33] The basis for this opposition is unclear, but the opposition did not have enough support. On February 14, at its meeting during the Winter Games in St. Moritz, Switzerland, the IOC welcomed the COPR to the "Olympic family with the hope of a successful work of your Committee in favor of our ideals."[34] Present at this meeting were the top leaders of the Olympic movement, including IOC president Sigfrid Edström, the Marquis of Polignac, Count Bonacossa, and IOC vice president Avery Brundage. Brundage, who had been president of both the Amateur Athletics Union and the U.S. Olympic Committee, would become president of the IOC in 1952 and establish a close relationship with Monagas.

The Organizing Committee of the London Games sent an invitation to "the National Olympic Association, Puerto Rico, Parks and Recreation Commission," which was received in San Juan on March 25, 1948.[35] As such, the IOC recognized Puerto Rico's NOC under the Public Amusement and Parks Commission of Monagas and did not uphold its rule of nongovernmental association. In this regard the IOC was a major player in recognizing a blatantly political NOC that was also a colonial territory. This presented a problem because the IOC was, to some extent, interfering in a colonial project of the United States. On the other hand, the IOC was aiding the development of a nationalist project by allowing the colony to participate at the Games as a separate nation.

The IOC had its own political reasons for inviting Puerto Rico to the Olympic Games in London. The 1936 Games in Berlin had been an extravagant and nationalist spectacle by Nazi Germany to show off the power of the regime. Then the Games were canceled in 1940 and 1944 as a result of the war. Hence the IOC needed to reclaim the purity and wholesomeness of the Games. For that reason it needed to schedule successful events with as many participating countries as possible. This is exactly what Joaquín Martínez-Rousset, a journalist at the time and eventually a Puerto Rican sport leader, thinks are the reasons the IOC allowed Puerto Rico to participate in London.[36]

Moreover the IOC knew of the stability and success of the CACG, which renewed competition after the war, in 1946. Puerto Rico had been a constant participant since 1930 and garnered enough respect to receive an invitation from the IOC. For the second time Puerto Rico was invited to the 1948 Olympic Games along with Venezuela, Guatemala, and Panama and the crown colonies of Jamaica, British Guyana, and Trinidad and Tobago also received invitations. The British Caribbean colonies received their invitation from their colonial metropolis and present somewhat similar yet contextually different problems of politics and Olympic sport. In addition to these delegations, the newly independent countries of Burma and Ceylon were invited, as were the recently established nation-states of Syria and Lebanon, among others. The IOC project of Olympic legitimation, consolidation, and expansion was well under way.

When the organizing committee in London sent an invitation to Puerto Rico, the United States was placed in the difficult position of either denying or permitting Puerto Rican participation in the Olympics as a separate country. Allowing Puerto Rico to compete could strengthen nationalist sentiment. A comparable case was the Philippines, which had been fighting U.S. occupation since 1898. The IOC recognized the Philippines' NOC in 1929, and independence was achieved in 1946. While there is certainly no causality between recognition of the Philippine NOC and independence (as Puerto Rico clearly demonstrates), some in the U.S. government might have perceived IOC recognition as a window to allow nationalist pro-independence sentiments to develop.

The Partido Nationalista kept pressuring at different venues. The former Olympic athlete Juan Juarbe Juarbe, now living in exile and continuing Latin American solidarity work for the nationalists, confronted Byron Price, auxiliary secretary of the United Nations and a guest at the fourth Congress on Pan-American Press in Bogotá on March 30, 1948, about Puerto Rican independence. Representing both the Lima and San Juan press, Juarbe Juarbe asked Price (who was also a former director of the U.S. Censorship Office), if his country would give independence to Puerto Rico. Taking attention away from Price, another American journalist, Jules Dupois, from the *Chicago Tribune* and chairman of the Inter-American Press Association's Freedom Committee, challenged Juarbe Juarbe to a fist fight.[37] While the incident did not go beyond an exchange of words, it showed the indirect ways in which Juarbe Juarbe and the nationalists exerted pressure on Puerto Rico's colonial status at international events.[38]

The immediate solution of the U.S. authorities was to go against the IOC's request and deny Puerto Rico's participation at the 1948

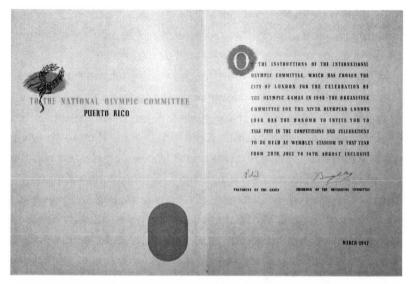

Fig. 7. Invitation by the Organizing Committee, Summer Olympic Games in London, to the Puerto Rican National Olympic Committee, 1947, Box 963, RG 126, Office of Territories Classified Files, 1907–51, File 9887, Recreation and Sports, General, National Archives and Records Administration, Washington DC. Photograph by the author.

Olympic Games. A note written on April 15, 1948, on the original invitation, now at the National Archives in Washington DC (see fig. 7), reads, "Invitation not transmitted because after discussion Davis, Barr, and Derrickson decided Puerto Rican participation should be on the United States Team. State Dept. advised by telephone."[39] The note did not explain the reasons for the decision, but the U.S. State Department clearly agreed with it.

However, U.S. officials changed their mind and did allow Puerto Rico to participate at the London Games. Although we do not know the official reasons for their reversal, the pressure of postwar humanitarianism and human rights movements may have proven too strong. England had been allowing its colonies to participate at the CACG since the 1930s,[40] and Jamaica would participate in its first Olympic Games in London in 1948.

The PAPC, led by Monagas, supported House project No. 822, which requested the government to approve $10,000 to send a small Puerto Rican delegation to London. The law was approved in the legislature but was vetoed by Governor Piñero. This veto sparked a public debate in the press, in which Piñero favored the completion of local construction of athletic fields and recreation areas before spending money to send a delegation to the Olympic Games. Regardless of Monagas's support of project No. 822, and in spite of numerous conversations, he eventually sided with Piñero in the veto and defended the view that the PAPC should be for building athletic facilities and providing "gloves, balls, bats, etc." for the "smaller communities in Puerto Rico." Monagas's backing of Piñero's government was in light of the legislature approving the Commission's biggest budget yet, $525,000, destined for local sport. This large budget was in addition to the staggering $1,129,000 used in 1948 by the sport program of the PAPC. By the end of the next fiscal year the Commission had approved a historic $1,263,500 for sports.[41] Monagas believed the money allotted to PAPC proved the success of his sport program. Sending a Puerto Rican delegation to London could have been a great success for Olympism, but building sport infrastructure was his and the PPD's first and foremost goal.

But the popularity of sport, and of Puerto Rico's international participation, was stronger than the political and economic ideologies of a group of individuals in government. Reacting to indications that a popular movement was being organized to raise funds for the delegation,[42] all government officials, including Piñero and Monagas, supported Puerto Rico's participation in London and funds were made available to send the delegation. A so-called populist government could not appear to be unsupportive of a highly popular activity.

Locally the problems were not only economic but also political. Athletes knew the politics behind Puerto Rico's participating at the Olympics in London. José "Fofó" Vicente, a track and field athlete, stated in a 2007 interview that the controversy was due to "political and economic" reasons.[43] Yet, as he put it, he was an athlete and would not get involved. Other athletes were not as neutral. Regarding the controversy of Puerto Rico's participation as a separate country, José Celso Barbosa (not to be confused with his grandfather of the same name), a pole vaulter, stated in an interview in 2007, "The American Olympic Committee could have vetoed it by stating: 'they are American citizens. If they are going to compete, they must compete with us.'"[44] Although affirming that he was not into politics at that time, he was aware of the political dilemma. More so than today, Puerto Ricans were aware of the colonial situation. Being able to participate in the Olympic Games separate from the United States was, for some, a great feat.

The press was all over the event; numerous articles in *El Mundo* traced the departure, participation, results, and return of the athletes. Needless to say, it was a historical moment and many were aware of it. Puerto Ricans were finally recognized as legitimate members of the international community. For the first time in more than four hundred years of colonial existence, they were seen as equals, at least in the athletic arena. And this was not any athletic event; these were the Olympic Games, the epitome of a modern and truly global politico-cultural ritual. Moreover the Games in London were not typical Olympic Games; they represented hope for European recovery and that of Western civilization. The Games were hosted by a place ravaged by war and violent destruction; it would be a resurrection for both England and the Olympic Games.

The Colonial Nation at Play, 1948

Puerto Rico sent a small delegation of only twelve men to London that included Julio E. Monagas as head and Eugenio Guerra as trainer. Members of the track and field team included José "Fofó" Vicente and José Celso Barbosa (pole vault), Julio E. Sabater (110-meter hurdles), and Benjamín Casado (high jump). Two athletes, George Johnson and Miguel A. Barasorda, represented Puerto Rico

PUERTO RICO

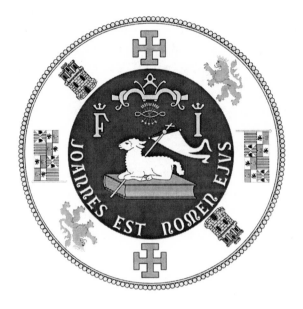

Fig. 8. The Puerto Rican flag displayed during the opening procession of the 1948 Summer Olympic Games in London. Malarz pl, Wikimedia Commons.

in target shooting, and Clotilde Colón Santiago, Israel Quitcón, and Juan Evangelista Venegas in boxing. The smallness of the squad signaled a high improbability it would win medals. The Puerto Rican sport historian Emilio Huyke believes the small delegation was more of a symbol; "más bien como un gesto de estar presente [more of a gesture of being present]."[45] The idea was to perform as a nation on equal terms with the Olympic community, not necessarily to win.

When the delegation was set to depart for London, it carried the flag that was to represent Puerto Rico at the Olympic Games, the coat of arms on a white background (see fig. 8), the same symbol used on uniforms throughout the 1930s and 1940s. However, once in London and with the delegation ready to march at the opening ceremony, the flag bearer Miguel A. Barasorda changed plans at the last minute and insisted on the Puerto Rican flag. This caused a brief but intense confrontation; Monagas firmly denied the request, saying that that flag was not allowed according to instructions from Luis Muñoz Marín. Barasorda then was replaced as flag bearer by José Vicente, who recalled the incident in a 2007 interview with Jaime Partsch McMillan:

> JP: I understand you were the flag bearer, true?
> JV: Yes.
> JP: Talk to me about that.
> JV: (Laughs) Barasorda was actually the one to be the flag bearer. Well, then, there was a conflict with the flag. Muñoz did not want us to use the Puerto Rican flag because in those years it was a nationalist symbol.
> JP: That was Muñoz?
> JV: Muñoz. He had told Monagas not to use the Puerto Rican flag because it had nationalist connotations that harmed us. So we took the Puerto Rican shield. There was a discussion in which I did not participate. I only know that Monagas was the one who told me "Fofó, since you had been a soldier, you know how to march, you are the one to carry the flag. Period." Hence it was me by a fluke. (Laughs.)
> JP: And what happened with Barasorda? They did not give it to him, why?
> JV: I don't know. They told me that he wanted to use the Puerto Rican flag and wasn't allowed.[46]

Monagas's loyalty to Muñoz Marín was vehement and without question (fig. 9). Puerto Rico, even though performing as a nation among nations, was not to be confused with an independent nation-state. Displaying the prohibited Puerto Rican flag at the Olympic Games would connect Puerto Rico's participation with the nationalists and pro-independence movement, which was criminalized in 1948. Influenced by McCarthyism, which persecuted Americans for alleged sympathy with leftist or communist ideas, the Puerto Rican legislature approved Law No. 53, popularly known as "Ley de la Mordaza" or Gag Law. This Gag Law prohibited any display of pro-independence nationalist symbols, including the Puerto Rican flag, as well as prohibiting meetings, songs, and art with nationalist connotations, claiming they were communist plots to overthrow the government. The Gag Law, which was supported by Muñoz Marín, lasted from 1948 to 1956; many Puerto Ricans were placed under surveillance, persecuted, and arrested for speaking or expressing their sympathy for the nationalists.[47]

Attempting to use the Puerto Rican flag at the Olympic Games in London was a big dare by Barasorda. While Miguel Barasorda, Eugenio Guerra, and even José Celso Barbosa were patriotic athletes who believed in the Puerto Rican nation, not all athletes and delegates believed in these same ideals. Monagas, while acknowledging Puerto Rico as a separate cultural entity from the United States, still upheld the PPD's ideology of association and autonomy over independence. In his interview Vicente does not imply there was much political importance at that time to Puerto Rico's participation in London, indirectly evidencing his disinterest in the political-colonial issue. He did indicate that Puerto Rico's Olympic Committee was a roadblock to eventual statehood but that the "common people" did not see the political implications.[48] In reality there was a controversy with political implications, as reflected in the numerous articles in *El Mundo*. This contradiction suggests that Vicente was not interested in the politics of the Games, a vision shared then and today by many Puerto Ricans. These seemingly opposing visions of the Olympics and politics imply that while the connections between Olympic sport and politics are real, there are also people who see sport only as Coubertin did, as an apolitical healthy activity to celebrate the body and the spirit of goodwill.

Fig. 9. Julio Enrique Monagas as represented by the Puerto Rican cartoonist Carmelo Filardi. Source: *El Mundo*, February 1, 1949.

Juan Evangelista Venegas won the first Olympic medal for Puerto Rico, a bronze in boxing, bantamweight class. He was considered to be one of the best boxers of his division at the time, expected by many to win the gold medal in London. Venegas quickly became a hero. Vicente and Barbosa also had good performances in pole vault, finishing in ninth and tenth place, respectively. Overall Puerto Rico achieved four points, which placed them thirty-seventh out of a record fifty-nine participating countries.

Venegas's bronze medal is not a small detail. Although this book, for lack of space, does not dwell on specific sports, it is appropriate to provide some context. Venegas's achievement was not Puerto Rico's first international boxing victory. Once boxing became regulated in 1927 with the creation of the first governmental sport commission, Puerto Rican boxers, at least professionally, quickly began attaining success locally and abroad, producing a total of twenty-four world champions in different categories from 1934 to 1990, although there was a considerable winless gap between 1939 and 1959. The first Puerto Rican world champion was Sixto Escobar, who beat the Mexican Rodolfo "Baby" Casanova on June 26, 1934, to win the bantamweight class. The hiatus of Puerto Rican professional boxing champions began on the date of Escobar's retirement and ended when Carlos Ortiz beat Michigan native Kenny Lane to win the junior welterweight class.[49] Professional boxing has been a powerful sport to foment Puerto Rican national identity.[50]

At the amateur and Olympic level, Puerto Ricans had also been successful before 1948. At the 1938 CACG in Panama City, Puerto Ricans won four medals in boxing and weightlifting, two in volleyball and golf, one each in shooting and aquatic polo, and twenty-four in track and field. In 1946 Puerto Rican boxers won three gold medals for the CACG in Barranquilla, with Orlando Reverón winning the light heavyweight class, Evaristo Reyes winning the heavyweight class, and Juan Evangelista Venegas winning the bantamweight class.[51] Puerto Ricans not only wanted to participate at the London Olympiad but had hopes of winning in the sport of boxing.

After the London Games were over and the athletes had returned home (or, in the case of Barbosa, back to college in the United States), government officials recognized the popularity and importance people gave to Puerto Rico participating at the games. Governor Piñero publicly congratulated Monagas and the PAPC, stating the need to secure Puerto Rico's future participation at CACG and the Olympic Games. Referring to Puerto Rico as a "country," Piñero went on to say, "It is a source of satisfaction for our island that Puerto Rico has been recognized by the most important international federations and that they have approved the right of genuine participation at international competitions." Thus Piñero acknowledged that sport had intersecting local and international components and that to support it was a good political move. Regardless, the PPD administration was a de facto government since Piñero was leaving office that same year; the newly elected governor, Luis Muñoz Marín, would then be in charge. As a government the party recognized that it was better to support Puerto Rico's international participation alongside the local Un parque para cada pueblo project. Piñero continued, "It is fair to make clear that all of these arrangements and achievements have been reached since July 1st, 1947 until today and that proper credit for its success is due to the Amusement and Parks Commission of Puerto Rico." Relating Puerto Rico's international sporting presence and success with the government's PAPC, Piñero listed some of the local achievements of the Commission: the construction of dozens of rural athletic parks and state-of-the-art playing fields in Ponce, Mayagüez and Caguas and even the screening of movies in urban and rural neighborhoods, all part of the recreation project of the PAPC. He concluded by honoring the work of Monagas, who had undertaken this "governmental program" with "intelligence and a firm hand."[52]

The local media and sport leaders also congratulated Monagas and the PAPC. In fact the work of Monagas, as mentioned before, had been reaching the attention of sport leaders in other countries of the region. This is what Antonio Lutz reported from his interview in 1948 with Luisín Rosario, Puerto Rican director of sport of the PAPC and vice president of the International Federation of Amateur Baseball, while at an international meeting in Caracas, Venezuela, to plan the World Series of Amateur Baseball in Nicaragua. Rosario expressed the rising enthusiasm for the success and achievements of Puerto Rico in all aspects of sport, particularly in baseball.

He attributed this to the PAPC and Monagas and stated that Puerto Rican achievement in sport was because "for the first time in history we have a Government that believes in the practice of sport." His concluding paragraph succinctly summarizes the general feeling regarding sport: "In a few words, it could be said that we have put on long pants in sports. We sent a team of nine men to the Olympics, and achieved four points. We have professional baseball players in the minor and Colored Leagues and our Golden Gloves have won the U.S. national amateur boxing championship. With a population of two and a half million inhabitants, Puerto Rico without a doubt is giving a lesson in sports to many countries with larger number of inhabitants."[53] Though Rosario mentioned the local sport initiatives that Monagas and the PAPC were undertaking, his concluding paragraphs were directed at an international level. Puerto Rico was not only competing successfully in the United States but also at the Olympic Games. It would seem that Monagas's emphasis on participation with only the United States was being left behind (albeit not fully) as many locals pushed for further international competition.

The result of this international participation actually worked against political groups looking for decolonization. As the PPD and Muñoz Marín's government accepted and supported Puerto Rico's participation in the Olympic Games and other international sporting tournaments, and as this participation was allowed by U.S. political and sport groups, Puerto Rico's colonial status began to be cemented. Having a venue to perform the nation in international sporting events while still a colonial territory allowed Puerto Ricans to foster a national identity without the need to have political sovereignty. Moreover having this sporting nation join other cultural performances and competitions, such as Miss Puerto Rico Universe since 1952 and musicians in different genres throughout the twentieth century, significantly fostered the existence of a nation without the need of having political independence. This is not to undermine the effects of systematic persecution and repression against pro-independence groups, as seen in the Gag Law and the thousands of *carpetas* or dossiers on individuals gathered by the Puerto Rican and federal authorities documenting subversive and pro-independence activities.[54] But the Puerto Rican Olympic Committee became a popular way to channel expressions of nationhood in an apolitical, unthreatening way, or so they thought.

Puerto Ricans still participated in their nation-building process by displaying the symbols of their nationhood internationally without being an independent nation-state. This might seem contradictory, but it is not. The goal of the PPD government was to lift Puerto Ricans from poverty and to place Puerto Rico on the international map, not necessarily to create an independent nation-state, but to instill in the populace a sense of progress, of belonging to a wider world. The role of sport was to aid in this populist project, locally and internationally. The impediment of colonial obscurity appeared to have been overcome by being present at the Olympic Games. The context of the war and postwar world allowed Puerto Rico and other nonsovereign countries to participate at the Olympic Games, and thus be recognized as sovereign, at least in sports.

This recognition did not mean that local repression against independence had waned. Growing repression targeted at pro-independence groups coupled with a sporting national identity made independence unattractive. Puerto Rico was not the Philippines, and no sustained widespread violent resistance for independence threatened U.S. rule. While the nationalists were still radically opposed to U.S. occupation, the fact is that the majority of Puerto Ricans supported it. The majority of Puerto Ricans approved the establishment of the commonwealth in 1952; the nationalists abstained.[55]

The PPD's program of social justice, evidenced in the governmental program Un parque para cada pueblo, fulfilled the immediate basic needs of a healthy body, a healthy mind, and a healthy workforce. In this way the PPD's development program, which included sport and recreation, became a powerful tool to help Puerto Ricans and to consent to the PPD's agenda. The future enactment of the common-wealth of 1952 represented political reform, which allowed the per-ception of autonomy, making international sport crucial. Yet during these years other problems relating to sport and politics, both local and international, arose with reverberating consequences.

4 / The Commonwealth and the Search for Colonial Sovereignty through Olympism

The Estado Libre Asociado, or commonwealth, was established on July 25, 1952, as a result of U.S. Public Law 600 of July 3, 1950, which allowed Puerto Ricans to draft a constitution for the first time since 1898.[1] Becoming a commonwealth allowed for a degree of self-rule on local matters, but within the overarching rule of the U.S. government. Puerto Ricans were still U.S. citizens; the economy was still fully integrated with the United States; and all U.S. federal laws still applied on the island and trumped local ones. Since then the supporters of the commonwealth and a majority of the members of the PPD (including Monagas) have been on a constant campaign to explain the autonomous basis of the formula and underscore the noncolonial nature of the compact between the United States and Puerto Rico.[2]

If the legitimation of commonwealth status during the 1950s was a vital endeavor for the Sport Commission (now organized as the Public Recreation and Parks Administration, PRPA) and the PPD government, it was equally important to legitimate this political arrangement abroad. Conveying commonwealth status was a political formula to mitigate growing concerns over imperialism and colonialism after World War II.[3] Struggles over decolonization were present in other islands of the Caribbean and in other parts of the developing world.[4] The renewal of the Olympic Games in 1948 was not only an event for the legitimation of the Games as such but also a way to celebrate goodwill among nations in a process of athletic diplomacy.[5] Commonwealth leaders understood the importance of the Olympic movement and used these events as a platform to legitimate two goals of the new status: sovereignty in association and cultural uniqueness. In this regard the commonwealth tried to put away questions over colonialism by continuing to participate in mega sporting events such as the Central American and Caribbean, Pan-American, and Olympic Games. Puerto Rico was a now a legitimate member of the community of nations, as seen in their participation at Olympic Games.

More important, the result of this participation was that it legitimized and consolidated colonialism. Creating the commonwealth did not alter the basic colonial structure of the unincorporated territorial status, as stated in the Insular Cases of the early twentieth century. Puerto Ricans still had no official international political presence, could not establish trade with other countries, and were still subjected to Congress's plenary powers. They still could not be fully represented in the U.S. Congress or vote for the U.S. president. However, by being U.S. citizens they were under U.S. jurisdiction. Therefore the COPR and the commonwealth status provided Puerto Ricans with an international presence, while still having the benefits and responsibilities of being U.S. citizens. International Olympic participation filtered the aspirations of independence followers because it gave the island a chance to play as a sovereign nation, hoist the Puerto Rican flag, and sing the national anthem, "La Borinqueña." At the same time it calmed pro-U.S. statehood followers by declaring Puerto Rico's permanent and voluntary association with the United States despite Olympic participation. This process has been so powerful and its impact so deep that today, a decade into the twenty-first century, the commonwealth and the COPR have endured amid political challenges. The end result was colonial Olympism, the construction of a colonial Puerto Rican national identity based on the performance of Olympic sport. This national identity relates more to a sense of cultural distinctiveness than a political project of independence, reminiscent, for example, of the case of Galicia in Spain or soccer in Scotland or early twentieth-century Ireland.[6]

That is, cultural nationalism has been more prevalent than political nationalism in Puerto Rico.[7]

The problems over colonialism during the 1950s in Puerto Rico occurred in times of rapid progress, industrialization, and modernization. Under the economic project known as Operation Bootstrap, foreign companies (mainly in manufacturing) were invited to settle in Puerto Rico in exchange for tax incentives and cheap labor with the hope that industrialization would trickle down to all areas of society. Between 1950 and 1960 per capita income more than doubled (from $342 to $716), with an economic average annual growth of 8.3 percent,[8] as Puerto Rico was dubbed the "showcase" of the Caribbean. This economic model became so successful that later it became the basis for NAFTA.[9]

However, contrary to these numbers, the Puerto Rican economy grew more dependent on the United States. Unemployment was still a problem (12.9 percent in 1950 and 13.3 percent in 1960) and poverty still a major source of concern.[10] Sugarcane fields were abandoned for work at factories; rather than adding jobs, factories mainly replaced the source of employment. More money meant more consumption; rather than saving, Puerto Ricans actually fell deeper in debt (from $18.9 million in personal savings in 1952 to $–64.1 million in 1960).[11] A series of governmental reorganizations aimed at centralizing power under the figure of Muñoz Marín created some discomfort among a segment of the population.[12] For example, in 1950 the Public Amusement and Parks Commission became the Public Recreation and Parks Administration,[13] to be headed by Julio E. Monagas. Sport historian Emilio Huyke thought this centralized form of government allowed a single administrator too much control, similar to a communist state. He argued instead for the development of sport free from governmental interference, such as in the United States.[14] But these complaints did not alter the course of local sport development. During the 1950s the PRPA developed a sort of "Operation Sport" that provided sport as a source of relief for workers from the stresses of rapid industrialization.[15]

This chapter features the ways the commonwealth and Olympic sport interacted in the 1950s to turn a de facto colonial territory into a sovereign sporting nation. It was not easy; the political dynamics of a continuing centralist and patronage-oriented government permeated political structures. Along the way the commonwealth's claims of autonomy were put to the test not only at the local level but also internationally. These effects reverberated throughout Latin America, the United States, and even the IOC. Indeed the so-called case of Puerto Rico demonstrated its imminent and constant role in politics, regardless of the IOC's claim to the contrary.

Revolution, the Commonwealth, and the Puerto Rican Nation

Governor Luis Muñoz Marín opened his 1950 Report of the Governor by noting the level of economic expansion and progress of the previous decade under the sponsorship of the United States. Politically he expressed his rejection of communism by saying that it was a "threat to human freedom and progress," yet he also acknowledged that communist societies did not harbor ill will but were poor and desperate. In all, and loyal to a decades-old ideology, he thought that Puerto Rico's role in world affairs was still that of a cultural mediator: "The people of Puerto Rico, being American citizens with the unique advantage of training and tradition in both the Latin-American and Anglo-American cultures, understand both cultures and can thus help to interpret both, the one to the other. The importance of such a function at this time can hardly be over-estimated."[16]

Muñoz Marín was active in spreading the ideology of Puerto Rico as the bridge between two worlds not only on the island but also in the United States. On November 19, 1953, for the 460th anniversary of Columbus landing on the island and roughly one and a half years after the establishment of the commonwealth, Muñoz Marín appeared on a nationally broadcast show for CBS. Titled "Puerto Rico Since Columbus," his talk praised the Hispanic culture of Puerto Rico, saying that Spain had given them a "modern spiritual democracy," while celebrating the island's modernization under the United States. Puerto Rico as a commonwealth was now in a "favored position to interpret to the world the true meaning of liberty and democracy as lived in association by a western Latin people with the greatest western democracy."[17]

Not everyone shared this harmonious vision of the Puerto Rico–U.S. relationship. In 1950, between late October and early November, a group of armed Puerto Rican nationalists attacked different municipalities in the island and Blair House in Washington DC, reacting against U.S. colonialism in Puerto Rico.[18] On October 24, 1954, four nationalists, led by Dolores "Lolita" Lebrón Sotomayor, opened fire on the U.S. Congress, demanding attention to the still unresolved colonial status of Puerto Rico.[19] In Puerto Rico insurgents took the town of Jayuya, as Blanca Canales hoisted the then illegal Puerto Rican flag and declared the establishment of the Republic of Puerto Rico. The governor's mansion, La Fortaleza, was also attacked. Local police, aided by U.S. P-47 Thunderbolt fighter planes, defeated the insurrection, which lasted from October 27 to November 7. Albizu Campos and the nationalists were also adamant believers of *Hispanismo* and *Hispanidad*, discussed in chapter 2.

In addition to the PPD's U.S.-association platform and the nationalists' vehement pro-independence stance, there was (and still is) a third political ideology: those who favor full U.S. statehood for Puerto Rico, referred to as *estadistas*. It is pertinent to outline the three major political-ideological currents in order to fully understand the stakes for each in light of Puerto Rico's growing Olympic participation. Puerto Rican admiration for U.S. liberalism and democracy has been present since the late nineteenth century and throughout the first decades of the twentieth. After the establishment of the commonwealth, the aspirations of the *estadistas* mainly resided in Luis A. Ferré. In 1968 Ferré became the first *estadista* governor of Puerto Rico under his newly established Partido Nuevo Progresista. Ferré represented the growing movement for Puerto Rican statehood, a movement that to this day has not been able to undermine the power of Olympism in Puerto Rican culture.

The growing Estadista movement is well represented in Ferré's politico-cultural ideology. The movement in the 1950s was known for urging statehood while at the same time upholding Puerto Ricans' cultural uniqueness as Latin and Spanish Americans. In his work on the cultural nationalism of *estadistas*, Mario Ramos Méndez argues that they sought a sort of "annexed independence," meaning that Puerto Rico's statehood would be a true and dignified independence, a recognition of Puerto Rico's progress within the federation of the sovereign U.S. states.[20] Ferré believed that Puerto Rican representatives in the U.S. Congress would be representatives of Latin America, seeking to bridge the gaps between the Anglo and Latin American civilizations for better political and economic collaborations.

The three conflictive political ideologies were evident at the Central American and Caribbean Games. With the United States absent from the 1950 competition, Puerto Rico used the U.S. flag just as it had in the games of 1930, 1938, and 1946. However, due to a populist and "spiritual socialist" government in Guatemala led by Juan José Arévalo,[21] these games were highly politicized. The conflictive Central American politics, in the postwar context of decolonization and anti-imperial movements, made the U.S. flag a despised symbol of oppression.

The procession of the Puerto Rican delegation during the opening ceremony on February 25, 1950, was used to show different political ideologies. Under the motto "For the good of sport, fraternity and greatness of the peoples of the Americas," the ceremony was described by the Puerto Rican journalist Joaquín Martínez-Rousset as being "one of the most impressive ceremonies held in this capital and like nothing we have seen in our lives."[22] Yet when the Puerto Rican del-

Fig. 10. The Puerto Rican delegation during the opening ceremonies at the Central American and Caribbean Games, 1950. Photograph by Rafael Morales S.

egation, led by its flag bearer Fernando Torres Collac, paraded at the Estadio de la Revolución carrying the U.S. flag (see fig. 10), the Guatemalan band played "La Borinqueña" instead of "The Star-Spangled Banner." Someone announced over the loudspeaker, "Guatemala does not recognize colony, we are against colonialism in America." Some argue that the nationalist athlete Juan Juarbe Juarbe was responsible for this act.[23] By 1950 Juarbe Juarbe, now recognized as an important nationalist figure, was living in exile in Cuba and serving as foreign secretary of the Partido Nacionalista; in 1954 he was suspected of leading another uprising in Puerto Rico.[24] Present at the CACG ceremony were U.S. Ambassador to Guatemala Richard Patterson and Monagas, who quickly protested to the Guatemalan authorities and demanded that this insult not be repeated during the medal ceremonies.

This event was covered by the *New York Times*, the *New York Herald*, and the *Chicago Tribune* and reached worldwide audiences. The U.S. and Puerto Rican governments' attempt to use the games to foster goodwill among the Anglo and Latin American worlds failed; it became evident that their colonial political arrangement was running out of time and acceptance. In 1935 there had been symbolic protests, the use of the Puerto Rican flag, and use of the anthem "La Borinqueña," but this occurred during the interwar period that had not fully faced the atrocities of European fascism. At stake in 1950 was not the fight against fascism but the beginnings of the cold war and the fight against communism, while democracy and freedom spread and acquired new meanings. Furthermore, having participated at the 1948 Olympic Games in London as a separate nation, Puerto Rico's presence with the U.S. flag at the CACG in Guatemala seemed a sort of political reversal.

After this episode the games took place with no other major distractions. The Puerto Rican delegation, composed of seventy-five athletes, all men, achieved third place overall. Although not able to win a medal in basketball, the delegation did achieve success in track and field. Coached by Eugenio Guerra and Rafael Mangual, the team dramatically beat the esteemed Cuban delegation by a score of 120 to 82,[25] proclaiming themselves once again athletic champions of Central America and the Caribbean. Puerto Rico also won medals in weight lifting, shooting, tennis, and volleyball, for a total of twenty-nine medals, behind Mexico (ninety-three) and Cuba (seventy-nine). On their return to the island, the delegation was welcomed with an effusive celebration. The journalist Rafael Pont Flores describes the moment: "It was tremendous, hundreds and hundreds of automobiles, thousands and thousands of enthusiasts, by foot, on the sidewalks, in the balconies of their houses clapped and cheered for our champions. . . . The triumphal procession took place on Fernández Juncos Avenue and then on Ponce de León Avenue, it did not appear to have an end in sight, the band from the Colegio de Agricultura y Artes Mecánicas (CAAM) played 'La Borinqueña' and also the 'Star Bangled [sic] Banner,' to avoid problems."[26]

More significant than the point position of the delegation or how many medals they won, Puerto Rico had once again achieved its place in the cultural life of Central America and the Caribbean. But the games highlighted Puerto Rico's colonial problem once again, pressuring U.S. and Puerto Rican authorities already working toward a new association that later became the commonwealth of 1952. The nationalist revolt later that year could be considered the final catalyst for political change, regardless of the lack of mobilizing support for the nationalists.

Despite the political embarrassment at the opening ceremony in Guatemala, the U.S. Department of State saw no problem with Puerto Rico's participation at the newly organized Pan-American Games, to be held in 1951 in Buenos Aires. The possible problem with a Puerto Rican delegation at the Pan-American Games was the same as that for the Olympic Games: the presence of two delegations using the U.S. flag and national anthem. Nonetheless U.S. General Rose, a member of the organizing committee, indicated that the Philippines and some British territories had previously participated in the Olympic Games and did not foresee any problem with Puerto Rico doing the same.[27] Avery Brundage, then president of the Pan-American Sports Committee and of the USOC, also desired the presence of Puerto Rico separate from the United States.[28] On November 25, 1950, Brundage wrote to Forney Rankin at the State Department, stating his intent to present the issue at the next USOC meeting. He also stated his desire for Puerto Rico to participate in the next Olympic Games, to be held in Finland, although this, he acknowledged, would be a harder task.[29]

Avery Brundage was an up-and-coming world leader in Olympic sport, becoming vice president of the IOC in 1942 and eventually becoming the third longest serving president of the IOC, from 1952 to

1972. Although he fervently opposed the intrusion of politics in the Olympic movement, his actions say otherwise. He is partly responsible for Puerto Rico's continuing participation in Olympic events, managing to do so against opposition from the U.S. Department of State. According to officials at the Department of State, the Department of the Interior, and the Department of Defense, since Puerto Ricans were U.S. citizens, like Alaskans and Hawaiians, they had to comply with the same rules and could not send separate Olympic delegations. This was the conclusion communicated to Brundage in a letter dated December 14, 1950.[30] The letter added that this applied not only to the Pan-American Games but also to the Olympic Games and that Puerto Rican athletes needed to attend U.S. tryouts if they wanted to participate at any of these games.

Brundage acknowledged the conclusion of the U.S. government but indicated the unlikelihood that Puerto Ricans would win in U.S. tryouts. In an effort to send Puerto Ricans to the Pan-American Games, Brundage thought of inviting Puerto Rican athletes to the games along with the USOC but carrying their own flag. He added, "This, of course, is a special concession but is warranted by the fact that they have been competing for many years in the Central American Games."[31] By February 1951 Brundage was still looking for ways to admit the Puerto Rican team at the Pan-American Games to be held that month in Buenos Aires.[32] Puerto Rico did not attend the first Pan-American Games of 1951. However, the British Crown Colonies of Trinidad and Tobago and Jamaica did participate, the first winning a gold and three silver medals, and Jamaica winning three bronze medals.

Brundage's acknowledgment that Puerto Rico had a long history of participation in the IOC-sanctioned CACG reflects a larger point of view in the Olympic world. The CACG, although small and regional, were the oldest of the regional games. In a world with increasing awareness of the importance of sports and Olympic Games, having a history of participation was meaningful. The fact that other colonies and territories were also consistently participating in these international events facilitated a common cause for colonial Olympic participation. This external influence merged with internal desires for Olympic participation and national identity to keep Puerto Rico in the Olympic cycle.

This is exactly what occurred for the 1952 Olympic Games in Helsinki. When it seemed as if Puerto Rico's participation at the Olympic Games and Pan-American Games was over, news came from the director of the Department of the Interior, James P. Davis, who wrote to Governor Muñoz Marín on September 19, 1951, stating that he had received a letter from the State Department forwarding a communication from the Finnish Legation, which had invited the National Olympic Committee of Puerto Rico to participate in the 1952 Olympic Games. The Finnish Legation said, "The Finnish Government, as well as the people of Finland, would highly appreciate it if Puerto Rico might be represented at said international contest by sending participants thereto."[33] As in Puerto Rico's first participation in the CACG in 1930, and regardless of inherent local desire to participate, the initiative for Puerto Rican participation came from outside the island.

The COPR managed to find government money to fund the delegation of twenty-one male athletes (nine in track and field, three in boxing, four in weight lifting, and five in shooting) to the Helsinki Olympic Games, which were held from July 19 to August 3, 1952. Although they did not win any medals, they did achieve a crucial feat: by participating once again in the Summer Olympics, and as a commonwealth after July 25, they asserted Puerto Rico's existence as a nation while simultaneously making the United States appear as a sponsor of freedom and a champion of decolonization. The Olympiad of 1952 was also noteworthy, for the Soviet Union participated for the first time, beginning a long-term fierce competition of East versus West that defined the cold war.[34] Puerto Rico was fully immersed in the significance of the cold war because the island was considered a showcase of capitalism, democracy, and progress. This became clear at the 1966 CACG in San Juan, but in 1952 the Olympic Games marked a shift in the political context of the second half of the twentieth century with the debut of Israel, China, Vietnam, Gold Coast (now Ghana), Guatemala, Hong Kong, Bahamas, Indonesia, Netherlands Antilles, Nigeria, and Thailand. In addition, Japan was allowed to participate again after being prohibited from attending the 1948 Games in London, and after the division of Germany into two different states, West Germany was allowed to send a delegation, while East Germany refused to participate in a joint German squad.

The Commonwealth of Puerto Rico was established on July 25, 1952, and according to historian María Margarita Flores Collazo, July 25 is a day of celebration for Puerto Ricans under Spain, under the United States, and as a commonwealth. This day celebrates Spain's patron saint, Santiago, the driving figure behind the centuries of the Reconquista, and thus a special date of celebration in Spanish Puerto Rico. U.S. leaders knew of the importance of this day to Puerto Ricans and used it as the day for the invasion in 1898, hoping that its celebratory air would transfer to the new alliance, as it did. PPD leaders continued this hegemonic tradition and used it to inaugurate the commonwealth.[35] It is therefore not surprising that on this day as well the Puerto Rican delegation in Helsinki hoisted their flag for the first time, without opposition and alongside other national flags.

The Games opened on July 19, 1952. For the initial parade, as well as in the Olympic Village, Puerto Rico used the U.S. flag. For six days Puerto Rico was represented by this flag, for many the symbol of Puerto Rico's association with the United States, and for others the symbol of imperialism and colonialism. Yet when hoisted on July 25 the new Puerto Rican flag, revealed for the first time by Puerto Rican patriots in New York City in 1895, represented the new Puerto Rican national imagined community (see table 2).

Table 2. Flags of the Comité Olímpico de Puerto Rico

EVENT	PLACE	DATE	FLAG
Central American Games	Havana, Cuba	1930	U.S.
Central American and Caribbean Games	San Salvador, El Salvador	1935	Puerto Rican
Central American and Caribbean Games	Panama City, Panama	1938	U.S.
Central American and Caribbean Games	Barranquilla, Colombia	1946	U.S.
Summer Olympic Games	London, England	1948	Puerto Rican Coat of Arms
Central American and Caribbean Games	Guatemala City, Guatemala	1950	U.S.
Summer Olympic Games	Helsinki, Finland	1952	U.S.; Commonwealth of Puerto Rico

However, there is a major difference between the flag ceremony to inaugurate the commonwealth in San Juan and raising the flag in Helsinki: the Puerto Rican flag flew alone in Finland. This is not a minor difference, since the Constitution of Puerto Rico, approved by the U.S. Congress and president, allowed the Puerto Rican flag to fly only with the U.S. flag next to it. That is, the flag of the Commonwealth of Puerto Rico cannot fly alone in any official building or official event. The only time it can be hoisted alone in an official representation of the commonwealth is at Olympic sporting events.[36]

For many, flying the flag by itself in Helsinki was of extraordinary importance. It was the first time this symbol of the Puerto Rican nation, created by patriots against Spain and used by the nationalist and independence parties in the twentieth century, was able to fly on its own. Many members of the delegation were aware of this fact and observed the moment in its historical significance. One was Eugenio "El Trinitario" Guerra, a Puerto Rican sport hero since the

1930s, who was entering legendary status in 1952. He would capture the moment in an almost poetic tone:

> The Puerto Rican delegation in perfect formation and placing their hands on their chest, must have heard La Borinqueña at a distance, before a shinning sun, shinier than ever in the Finnish sky, when seeing for the first time the flag of the lone star being raised on the pole of the Olympic Village. . . . It was eleven in the morning and, from where I'm writing, I see and do not get tired of looking at our flag, floating proudly and majestically alongside the other flags of the world . . . the beginning of more dignity for our people among the world family of sports.[37]

Even though many Puerto Ricans, like Guerra, were proud and satisfied with the political achievements of the PPD in the establishment of the commonwealth, the nationalists, on the contrary, were aware that the commonwealth did not alter the colonial relationship of Puerto Rico to the United States. For this reason the nationalists did not celebrate the Olympic delegation. After the 1950s independence activity dramatically decreased and the PIP's electoral support progressively waned. Although some people point to repression (such as the Gag Law, in effect from 1948 to 1956) to explain the decrease in *independentismo*, another explanation lies in the effects of the PPD's pro-U.S. populist project and discourse, which proved highly effective.[38] A crucial part of this populist project included the adoption of the Puerto Rican flag and Olympic participation.

Puerto Rico participated in its third Olympic Games in Melbourne in 1956; it was there that local sport leaders grew more confident in their unique national identity. Although the road to Melbourne proved to be highly problematic and full of political battles, Puerto Ricans managed to send a small delegation of nine male athletes, seven in track and field and two in shooting. None of the athletes won medals, but the mere presence of a separate Puerto Rican delegation carrying the Puerto Rican national flag was enough to call the trip successful. It was successful from the standpoint of performing the nation, but it was also a victory in terms of athletic diplomacy.

By the time of the Melbourne Games, Monagas had soundly left behind his initial intentions of having Puerto Rico participate in Olympic competitions between Puerto Rico and the United States or making Puerto Rican athletes participate as part of the U.S. delegation. Nor was he against the delegation's carrying the Puerto Rican flag in the Olympic ceremony. On the contrary, in 1956 Monagas fully embraced Puerto Rico's national symbols and joyfully wrote to Muñoz Marín that in Melbourne Puerto Rico "hoisted its flag and played its national anthem in the middle of the lavish and imposing opening ceremony of the Sixteenth World Games."[39] Before 1952 PPD leaders did not refer to Puerto Rico as a nation. After the creation of the commonwealth, however, reference to Puerto Ricans as having a nation became more accepted, although the common (and politically safe) way to refer to Puerto Ricans was as having a distinct personality or culture.[40] To refer to Puerto Rico as a nation might imply association with the criminalized nationalist movement.

Nonetheless Monagas used this reference to nationhood freely as he continued to bring Muñoz Marín good news of Puerto Rico's achievements in Melbourne: "It is now in Melbourne, Australia, that Puerto Rico returns to the scenario of the greatest international representation of sports, to confirm once again the recognition of its national personality before the representation of the select world youth and the highest ranking dignitaries of international sport." He analyzed Puerto Rico's progress in the world of sport, which he equated with politics, in contrast to colonial times: "When we went to London, Puerto Rico had not yet emancipated itself from the colonial features that still prevailed in its political and governmental relations." In spite of this, Monagas said, the nations of the world had recognized Puerto Rico's personality by allowing them to send to London a separate delegation of a national nature. Once in

Fig. 11. Julio Enrique Monagas holding the flag of Puerto Rico during the seventh Central American and Caribbean Games of 1954 in Mexico City. Courtesy of Carlos Uriarte González.

Helsinki (1952), Monagas continued, Puerto Rico had the "glory" of hoisting its flag and listening to its anthem thanks to the inauguration of the commonwealth. Monagas noted the vital distinction of Puerto Rico's participation at the Pan-American Games of 1955 in Mexico, when, for the first time and in an official manner, Puerto Rico and the United States participated as two separate nations. His own words captured the significance of the moment: "But this glory was more eloquent and fundamental when before our flag and under the melody of our anthem the entire United States delegation paraded, led by its Ambassador and its flag to pay then and there the salutation and acknowledgment and cordial affection of that distinguished North American representation to the national representation of our people."[41]

Although the U.S. media does not give much attention or importance to the Pan-American Games, in Latin America and in Puerto

Rico these games are relevant. These are the games where the Americas meet in competitive play to test the strength of their athletes and the strength of their nations and cultures. For more than a century the United States has left a deep mark on Latin American history, and its dominant influence extends from the economic and political to the cultural and social. The Pan-American Games offers a chance to level the playing field and try to defeat the "colossus of the north." This same meaning can be attributed to Puerto Rico when it participates at the Pan-American Games separate from the United States. On one level there is the excitement of competition as a nation against other Latin American nations, but against the United States the competition is special; it is a competition between U.S. citizens, albeit from different nations. More critically it is a deep and transcendental realization that although Puerto Ricans are U.S. citizens, they are a different nation, one that is Latin American and Caribbean.

Melbourne's Olympic Games represented the culmination of this realization. For the third time in a row, Puerto Ricans paraded in the opening games as a separate nation. In this regard they consolidated their international Olympic participation and, as Monagas said, received a "friendly recognition of the Puerto Rican personality amid the admiration and applause of more than 110,000 foreign spectators." Monagas understood the implications of Olympic participation in terms of nationhood, as well as the political benefits this participation offered. This Olympic participation helped to appease pro-independence activism by the performance of the Puerto Rican nation, and in this way helped the PPD win sympathy over this segment of the electorate. The commonwealth could now claim to have allowed for the blossoming of the nation and its international presence, a government Monagas asserted was always at its "service."[42] To some extent it also pleased the *estadistas*, or at least it was not politically threatening, because this happened in a close association with the United States and with their U.S. citizenship protected and untouched.

In 1957, during an official trip to Washington, Monagas thought he had achieved official recognition of Puerto Rico's athletic sovereignty. Despite the IOC's recognition of COPR, Puerto Ricans needed the recognition of both the Athletic Amateur Union and the American Olympic Committee, which Monagas finally obtained during his trip. According to Monagas, these two institutions recognized Puerto Rico's "magnificent Olympic record" and the "prestige that the Commonwealth status has in Latin America." Once again he declared that "Puerto Rico's own personality has been established and its right to participate separate from the United States delegations."[43]

In addition to being a vital aid to the commonwealth, Monagas and his PRPA/COPR was acquiring international relevance as a Latin American sports leader. This leadership became official in 1955, when, soon after the end of the Pan-American Games in Mexico, leaders of the Pan-American Sports Organization (PASO) and their newly elected president, José de J. Clark Flores, met in Mexico City and elected Monagas to the presidency of the Statutes Committee of the Pan-American Games. This was not just any committee; this was PASO's "most important committee," as Clark Flores declared to Teófilo Maldonado, now a reporter for El Mundo newspaper.[44] Monagas was now in charge of the "study and writing of the Charter of Rules and other regulations that govern these sporting events." Moreover it was decided that Puerto Rico, under the leadership of Monagas, would have the honor and responsibility of coordinating the next Pan-American Games, to be held in Cleveland, Ohio (later Chicago, Illinois), in 1959.[45] Monagas was not only leading Puerto Rico's national sporting presence internationally; he was also becoming the key participant in this movement, a guardian of the rules of Pan-American Olympism.

There Can Be Only One: The Future of the Olympic Committee

The 1950s witnessed the consolidation of Puerto Rican Olympism. This consolidation set the basis for a stronger sense of national identity, but the process was by no means smooth or easy. As we have seen, Puerto Rican participation in the 1951 Pan-American Games was curtailed by pressure from the U.S. government, and its participation at the 1952 Olympic Games in Helsinki was aided by the Finnish Legation. Puerto Rican agency in Olympic participation nonetheless cannot be negated or dismissed. As previously indicated, the Olympic movement and the desire for international competition had been active on the island since the 1930s and throughout the 1940s. After Puerto Rico's participation in the 1952 Olympics, denying Puerto Rican participation in future IOC games could have been seen as oppressive and damaged the U.S. image abroad. However, there were persistent problems in Puerto Rican Olympism (as was the case in other Latin American countries): direct government interference and patronage.

With the Soviet Union and other communist countries having IOC-recognized NOCs, the IOC set out to clarify and reinforce the protection of amateurism and the separation of the Olympic movement from politics. The sudden awareness of government-run NOCs was actually a result of cold war conflicts, as evidenced in the article "Of Greeks and Russians," published in *Sports Illustrated*. For this article, Robert Cramer interviewed IOC president Avery Brundage about the Soviet government's role in its NOC and possible conflicts with the Olympic ideal.[46] The debut of the Soviet Union in the 1952 Olympic Games placed the cold war and the spread of communism dead center in the Olympic movement. As a result the IOC adopted Olympic Rule No. 25 at its general session in Athens in May 1954, which stated that "National Olympic Committees must be completely independent and autonomous and entirely removed from political, religious or commercial influence."[47] Many Latin American countries were openly violating this rule and faced being banned from IOC-backed events. Cuba was one such country, yet between 1954 and 1955 it managed to reorganize its NOC according to Rule No. 25 under the leadership of Miguel A. Moenck.[48]

Monagas had been a friend and close ally of Muñoz Marín since the early 1940s, helping him in party organization, campaigns, and publicity. As the head of sport he was another right hand of the PPD in its populist agenda with the project Un parque para cada pueblo, and as the government became more centralized Monagas acquired even more control of the PRPA. As a close ally and leader of the PPD, he was vital in the legitimation of the commonwealth, showing Puerto Rico's autonomy and cultural sovereignty performed in Olympic events. Given his close connection to the PPD and his role as administrator of the PRPA he had been breaking Olympic Rule No. 25 for quite some time.

Whether it was the introduction of communist countries into the Olympic cycle, the debacles of World War II, or the IOC's gradual influence, the IOC believed it played an increasingly influential role in Olympism. Following the Games in 1948 and 1952, the Olympic movement gained new force and proved to be a resilient, growing, and powerful concept. The IOC could now uphold its rules, and actually did so, when Argentina was banned from the 1956 Games in Melbourne due to government appointments of Olympic officials.[49] Because of "communist threats," the Argentinean ban, and Monagas's position as head of the PRPA, Puerto Rican Olympic leaders, led by Fred Guillermety, feared that a similar ban might be imposed on Puerto Rico. Guillermety, along with other respected local sports leaders, including Ramiro Ortiz, Emilio E. Huyke, and Eliseo Combas Guerra, decided to end Monagas's long tenure in Puerto Rico's government-run COPR. What they did not foresee was that their Olympic coup d'état placed not only the COPR but also the IOC on a tightrope between Olympism and politics.

Although Moenck and Brundage suspected that Puerto Rico's NOC was breaking Rule No. 25 since early 1955, the controversy on the island began in March 1956, when Guillermety asked IOC chancellor Otto Mayer for the IOC's book of rules, claiming that the COPR was breaking the rule on governmental interference.[50] The situation was made public, and Monagas was forced to contact Mayer for a clarification of government support for COPR. In a letter sent on August 23, 1956, Mayer warned Monagas, "If your government is conceding funds to your organization, there is a great danger that it will control them, and finally also will control your Committee. This would not be admitted."[51] Mayer made it clear that Monagas, as the government-appointed administrator of the PRPA, was in open violation of Rule No. 25. Five days later Guillermety publicly confronted the COPR in his newspaper column "Bullseye," asking, "Who are the members of this committee?" According to Guillermety, Monagas led the COPR as a committee of one, selecting athletes and coaches and administering money from the government. Quoting Rule No. 25, he wrote that COPR needed to "include within its organization representatives of all sports" and that "it must recognize only one association for each sport." He also insisted that the NOC "must be completely independent and autonomous as well as being entirely separated from political, religious, and commercial influence." Finally, Guillermety asked Monagas to help organize an independent COPR and to please "not permit the Puerto Rican Olympic Flame to be extinguished."[52]

Monagas would not relinquish power without a fight. He attempted to reorganize COPR and sent news to Lausanne that a new COPR had been elected, with him (president of the Athletic Association of Puerto Rico) as the new president, Pablo Vargas Badillo (Golden Gloves) as vice president, Luis Mejía (Cyclist Federation) as secretary-treasurer, and Luis Vigoreaux (a captain in the Puerto Rico Police and head of the Shooting Counseling Board) and Néstor Figarella (an employee of Puerto Rico's Port Authority and president of the Weightlifting Federation) as members at large. Describing the reorganization as illegitimate, Guillermety labeled the new COPR a "fiasco" and sent a cablegram on to the IOC and to Brundage declaring that the "New Olympic Committee of Puerto Rico was not, repeat, not selected by local sports federations" and that Monagas was the "self-appointed new president." He pointed out that the Federación de Tiro de Puerto Rico, presided over by him and affiliated with the IOC's International Shooting Federation, had been totally ignored. He ended by asserting that "article twenty-five [was] still flagrantly violated" and requested an immediate investigation.[53]

Mayer, although acknowledging Monagas's new COPR, wrote confidentially to Brundage, "As you see Monagas seems to have done something. It went so quickly that I presume he has put some of his friends in the Committee representing: Golden Gloves (!), Cyclism, Tiro al Blanco (?) and Levantamiento de Pesas (probably Weight Lifting?) and himself for Athletics. We better give him a lesson next year when he comes to Evian." Mayer did not need to see the cablegram from Guillermety to realize that Monagas was engaging in patronage practices in the COPR. The IOC was willing to let it pass, recognizing the new COPR on September 10 and, with a patronizing attitude, give Monagas "a lesson."[54]

After investigating and proving Monagas's corrupt power grab with the COPR, Guillermety requested a delay for submitting Puerto Rico's application to the Olympic Games in Melbourne. Not willing to risk Puerto Rico's chance at a third Olympics, Monagas stepped down to allow inclusive and fair elections for the new COPR. This happened at an emergency meeting in San Juan on the night of October 4, where COPR's Executive Board selected Jaime Annexy as president, Néstor Figarella as vice president, and Luis A. Mejía as secretary-treasurer. The fact that two of the three officials had been on Monagas's handpicked COPR suggests that the coup was directed at Monagas himself and his dictatorial ways rather than at other well-known sport leaders.

Meanwhile the IOC leadership discussed the Puerto Rican case in an executive meeting on October 3 and 4 and once again provisionally recognized the COPR and Puerto Rico, allowing them to participate in the 1956 Games.[55] As a result of this intense and public Olympic coup Puerto Rico consolidated its status as an Olympic nation and legitimized the aspirations of commonwealth leaders of cultural autonomy. Unlike Argentina, Puerto Rico was able to overcome its patronage issues, in doing so proving its institutional maturity.

Deciding which countries are allowed to participate makes the IOC the arbiter of local Olympic politics. The IOC was willing to overlook Monagas's role as an appointed government official, obviously violating its own rules. But Monagas was different from other cases; he was preeminent in the Olympic movement in the Americas, which in 1955 had given him the presidency of the Pan-American Games' Charter of Rules. As such he was granted the benefit of the doubt when he handpicked the COPR in September 1956. It was only after public reaction to Guillermety's article reflecting cold war conflicts and communist threats that the IOC was forced to uphold its rules. It is not known what the IOC meeting in October concluded, but the fact is that the IOC was saved from public embarrassment when Monagas stepped down and a legitimate COPR was elected.

To make matters worse, when the Puerto Rican delegation returned from Melbourne, COPR president Jaime Annexy suddenly died. Néstor Figarella became the interim president while the controversy and instability of Puerto Rican Olympism continued. As a result of Annexy's death, Guillermety created the Olympic Association of Puerto Rico (OAPR) on July 14, 1957, to follow the government-free style of the USOC.[56] Faced with two Puerto Rican NOCs, the IOC decided to appoint member Miguel A. Moenck (Cuba) to handle Puerto Rico's NOC reorganization. An architect by trade, Moenck was a graduate of Tulane University, a cofounder of the CACG, and a past president of the Cuban Olympic team during the 1926 CACG in Mexico. Under Moenck's supervision Monagas was reinstated as president of COPR. Monagas gladly received this appointment and gave Brundage his "word of honor" that the COPR would be strictly organized according to Rule No. 25.[57]

But if Monagas was going to follow the rules, he would apply them to the competing OAPR. On July 18, 1957, Monagas wrote to Mayer in Lausanne complaining that Guillermety's OAPR was also violating Rule No. 25. Referring to Guillermety and Ramiro Ortiz as Mayer's friends, he denounced the OAPR's leadership as composed of professionals: the president was a lawyer, the vice president was a coach of the Polytechnic Institute, and other members were also professionals. Moreover, Monagas wrote, Puerto Rico's national federations did not have voting powers and were treated as "minorities," that is, disregarded.[58] In response Mayer kept a neutral position, waiting to hear back from Brundage and Moenck.[59] The conflict over Puerto Rican Olympism grabbed the attention of Lord David Burghley, sixth Marquess of Exeter and president of the International Amateur Athletic Association, who asked Moenck about the situation.[60] Although we don't have Moenck's reply to Burghley, his interest shows the reach of Puerto Rico's Olympic case.

In August 1957 it appeared that the conflict over COPR was finally resolved when Monagas wrote to Brundage informing him that the COPR was now organized "in accordance with the rules and regulations of the IOC" and with the participation of the presidents and delegates of all sport federations.[61] The supervision and direct involvement of the USOC and the Amateur Athletic Union in the reorganization of the COPR went through 1958. Max Ritter of the USOC wrote to Monagas on April 24, 1958, that "progress has been made." However, after more meetings in San Juan to finalize the new organization, new problems surfaced that involved accusations by Guillermety that Monagas was forging letters to portray a sense of harmony to the IOC, and by Manuel Alsina Capó, who claimed that Monagas was running a personal Olympic athletics club in addition to violating the Olympics/politics divide.[62]

This new round of conflict revolved around the consolidation of several sports federations. In order to elect COPR's new leadership, several Puerto Rican federations had to be recognized by the international federations and the IOC. In Puerto Rico there were various federations and associations for the same sport (including swimming, athletics, and shooting), which curtailed COPR's organization and centralization. By the summer of 1958 Monagas, now serving as the secretary,[63] was still the unofficial leader and head of these efforts, much to the dismay of Guillermety, who had an almost personal vendetta against Monagas's power, control, and ties to the government.

In a letter to Mayer dated May 13, 1958, Guillermety demanded a final answer to the legitimacy of Monagas as president, vice president, secretary, or even member of the COPR given his position as a government official.[64] Lt. Col. H. R. Brewerton of the Puerto Rico Swimming Association also attacked Monagas, complaining to Brundage of Monagas's "unorthodox and undemocratic" ways. Brewerton pointed to Monagas's alleged "block" to his federation's recognition by falsely alleging racism within the swimming federation.[65]

Once again Olympic politics was central in the resolution of this conflict. Mayer told Moenck that he was not going to answer Guillermety's demands regarding Monagas's eligibility as a government official and instead would wait to hear back from Brundage and Moenck.[66] Mayer did seem to agree with Guillermety that the IOC had not issued a "FINAL recognition" to COPR. Yet the Olympic legacy and preeminence of Monagas, his years of contact and relationship with Brundage and the IOC, and his position as a leader in Pan-American Olympism was enough for the IOC to overlook his blatant political affiliations. After failed attempts to reorganize the COPR,[67] a meeting was held on June 6, 1958. Under the guidance of Moenck and with Puerto Rican sport leaders from all factions in attendance, a new leadership of COPR was democratically elected and all Puerto Rican Olympic institutions were consolidated.[68] The new, or rather reinstated COPR president was Julio E. Monagas, still administrator of PRPA. The Olympic coup that deposed Monagas in 1956 worked only nominally for approximately two years, and Monagas was again both the official czar of sport and leader of Pan-American Olympism. The IOC's contradictions were exposed.

With Monagas's second presidential tenure, Puerto Rico's Olympic leadership and institutionalization were stabilized. Francisco Bueso became vice president, and Luis Mejía served as secretary. Guillermety, Monagas's archenemy, became the treasurer, and Emilio E. Huyke served as a member. After a fierce battle over the leadership of Olympism, Puerto Ricans had learned to solve their problems, showing Olympic judiciousness and institutional consolidation. From this moment on, COPR has been a stable institution for the promotion of Puerto Rican culture and identity.

Olympic Glories and Athletic Modernization in Caribbean Underdevelopment

The Central American and Caribbean Games, Pan-American Games, and Olympic Games proved to the world that the Puerto Rican nation was alive and vigorous. Yet the optimism of the 1950s also demanded a lot from Puerto Ricans, who were still very much a part of the developing world. For all the reforms in the economy, politics, and society, the reality was that Puerto Rico could not fully reach the achievements of athletic world powers such as the United States, the Soviet Union, and the European countries. Even though Puerto Ricans were legitimate contenders for top honors in Central America and the Caribbean, the nation's athletic underdevelopment was visible at the Pan-American Games.

By the 1950s Puerto Ricans had participated in three Olympiads, seven CACGs, and two Pan-American Games. Although Puerto Rico was supposed to organize the 1959 Pan-American Games, that privilege was lost due to the instability of the COPR and the change in venue from Cleveland to Chicago. In Chicago, Puerto Ricans finished fourteenth out of a total of seventeen countries. They won only six medals: two silver and four bronze. For an athletically proud and sport-loving country this was a great disappointment.

For Emilio E. Huyke the problem was clearly a lack of facilities. The sport facility boom during the 1940s and 1950s was a great populist project for the PPD and the commonwealth, using basic infrastructure as a message of social justice, and gave Puerto Ricans the means to practice in order to compete abroad. However, these reforms fell short. Huyke stated that despite all the athletic parks in Puerto Rico, they were surpassed in number, and perhaps even in quality, by Buenos Aires. Moreover, the British crown colonies trained their athletes in the best U.S. universities. Huyke made the point in a description of one of Puerto Rico's best athletes: "Rolando Cruz left here [for Chicago] with a wooden pole to challenge the championship of Don Bragg, who already had, for five years, a fiberglass pole that allowed him to reach a few more inches in his jump." He continued, "That is the reality and it is not hard to say, because that reality precisely enlarges even more our achievements in the past. In matters of sporting facilities, and of organization, we are in an infant stage and live in an infant innocence, and we have not reached the maturity that we think we have." Stopping short of labeling the PRPA's mass sport infrastructure a failure, Huyke made his point loud and clear. Yet in spite of these Olympic shortcomings, participation was what mattered: "The most essential thing is to compete and that is what we are doing. We comply with the mandate, the law and the Olympic spirit."[69] If a lack of victories at Olympic meets was an indicator of a lack of sport modernization, then at least Puerto Rico would be present, a rightful participant in these cultural festivals and therefore a bona fide Olympic nation.

Puerto Ricans would have to rely on individual or single-sport accomplishments if they were to prove their existence outside of an opening procession at sporting competitions. If the overall performance of Puerto Rico at the Pan-American Games in Chicago was below expectations, the performance of the basketball team was enough to fill Puerto Ricans' hearts with pride. With a record of four wins and two losses, the basketball squad ended in second place, winning, according to local press, the *subcampeonato* (second place).[70] The leading scorer of the tournament was a Puerto

Rican, Johnny Báez, and Juan "Pachín" Vicéns won the admiration of the U.S. press and basketball squad, which included future NBA legends Oscar Robertson and Jerry West.[71] Vicéns later became a Puerto Rican basketball hero and legend for his excellence in the local Baloncesto Superior Nacional league and with the national squad in other international tournaments. At the FIBA World Championships in Chile that year, he was named "Best Player in the World" by the international press in a tournament that included Robertson and West.[72]

Even though Puerto Ricans were actively representing the island at international events and had proven their ability to the international Olympic community, by 1959 there was still the idea (admittedly not false) that Puerto Rico's territorial status should not allow it international representation. The International Lawn Tennis Federation rejected Puerto Rico's membership application due to the opposition of the U.S. Lawn Tennis Association, which insisted that Puerto Rico was part of the United States and should not have independent international representation.[73] It did welcome Puerto Rico's membership in the USLTA, however.

Needless to say, Monagas vehemently challenged this ruling. In a formal letter to Asa S. Bushnell of the U.S. Olympic Association, Monagas began his argument by supporting the IOC and the USOC in eliminating "Nationalist [he meant to say Communist] China" from the Olympic family due to its imperial position toward Formosa (Taiwan). He then accused the USLTA of behaving in the same imperialist manner, but against Puerto Rico:

The colonial spirit informed by the gentlemen who integrate the American Federation of Tennis will clearly compel the Puerto Rico Olympic Committee to bring this case before the Nations of the World, so that once and for all the position of the Puerto Rican Federations be made clear. Evidently the United States Lawn Tennis Association has committed toward the Puerto Rican Tennis Federation the same outrage protested against by the American Olympic Committee in the case of Nationalist [Communist] China. The position of the United States is contradictory, and when this matter be [*sic*] brought before the Pan-American Congress no moral authority will support the United States in the pertinent exposition of the case.[74]

Monagas was not going to let this affront pass, not after the struggle to recognize the COPR, not after his own battle to hold onto power in the COPR, and definitely not given his integral role in the legitimation of sport autonomy in the commonwealth. The position of the USLTA was an indication that the commonwealth did not resolve Puerto Rico's colonial relation to the United States. Making the USLTA or the International Lawn Tennis Federation resolution official would have been politically disastrous to both the U.S. and Puerto Rican governments' claims of final decolonization. Moreover such a ruling would place the IOC and the UN in a difficult predicament because both had recognized Puerto Rico, the former as separate from the United States, the latter as a decolonized territory.[75]

Rejection of Puerto Rico's Olympic presence, and nationhood, was also internal. Estadista followers were quickly gaining ground in the 1950s, and one of them, Pedro Ramos Casellas, denounced the existence of COPR. In a letter sent to Brundage on September 23, 1959 (the ninety-first anniversary of the Puerto Rican pro-independence uprising against imperial Spain), he averred that Puerto Rico was "not a nation, never has been a nation and will never be an independent nation" because the "compact" of 1952 affirmed Puerto Ricans as U.S. citizens, as part of the United States.[76] He attacked Rolando Cruz's behavior at the Pan-American Games in Chicago for not accepting his bronze medal in the pole vault unless the Puerto Rican flag was hoisted and the Puerto Rican national anthem played. Ramos Casellas called this act "shameful" and demanded an investigation. Brundage responded that the IOC's recognition of a Puerto Rican

National Olympic Committee was given at Puerto Ricans' request, and he suggested that Ramos Casellas address the COPR directly.[77]

Still, under Monagas's leadership, the COPR was perceived by other Latin American NOCS as a separate and sovereign Olympic entity. After the Pan-American Games in 1959, Venezuela, Colombia, Ecuador, Peru, Chile, Uruguay, Brazil, and Argentina requested a visit from Monagas to evaluate their Olympic track and field programs.[78] (Even though Puerto Rico did not win the track and field meets, the team did place above many other Latin American teams.) More important, Monagas was praised as the key figure to help resolve difficulties between Latin American and U.S. delegations. Just as in the 1930s, Puerto Rico's Olympic delegation and leadership in the 1950s were still seen as the bridge between two cultures.

Puerto Rico's struggle for recognition of its sporting sovereignty was far from over. The fact that some viewed Puerto Rico's Olympic participation as unlawful while others viewed it as successful points to the island's pervasive colonial Olympism. As in other facets of daily life, colonialism permeated the island and resulted in its colonial sovereignty. Athletic modernization came with a cost: subjugation to an external metropole. Internal bureaucracy, patronage practices, and overarching centralization also hampered the development of institutions. Yet one successful outcome resulted from the development of Olympism in the 1950s: the consolidation of a sporting identity that fueled Puerto Rican national identity. The Puerto Rican nation could claim to belong to the community of nations by taking part in the Olympic Games, a progressive and prominent festival. But there was one more test that Puerto Ricans needed to pass in order to fully demonstrate their membership, and that was hosting a major Olympic tournament. This was the purpose of the CACG of 1966.

5 / A Cold War Playing Field in the 1966 Central American and Caribbean Games

The tenth Central American and Caribbean Games (X CACG) of 1966 in San Juan became for Puerto Ricans the event to showcase progress and the best indicator that Puerto Rico was a legitimate nation-member of a sporting international community, a stable and a vital member of Central American and Caribbean Olympism, having participated in all editions of the Games since the second in 1930. Puerto Rico's résumé in the region's Olympism left no doubt that this was a sporting powerhouse. Now, as hosts, Puerto Ricans opened their doors to their regional neighbors in order to show their national vitality, athletic prowess, modernization, and cultural uniqueness.

After the creation of the commonwealth in 1952, the consolidation of Olympic leadership in the 1950s, and continuing participation in the Pan-American and Summer Olympic Games, there was no doubt that Puerto Rico was a nation, at least culturally.[1] Granted, this nationhood was internationally visible and applicable only in sport, but it was a nation nonetheless. With the growing popularity and precedence given to Olympic competition worldwide, having such a presence equaled for many the status of nationhood. The X CACG of 1966 in San Juan became the climax of this journey.

The X CACG became not only a showcase of development and nationhood, but also, unwillingly, of its inherent colonial status. Faced with the problems of communist Cuba and the uncertainty of its participation, the games were a window through which to view colonial and regional politics, colonial Olympism, and the cold war conflict. In fact the dilemma of banning or inviting the Cubans to the games reflected cold war principles, bringing an air of hostility to the Caribbean once again. In the end these games demonstrated that while all parties involved tried to keep Olympism and politics separate, doing so ultimately proved impossible. Olympism became a political game, in which Puerto Ricans, U.S. Americans, Cubans, the IOC, and the Soviet bloc were directly involved.

Tie Game: Politics and Sport in Latin America

The X CACG of 1966 are special because an Olympic delegation was denied participation for political reasons. Puerto Rican authorities denied the invitation and opposed the issue of visas to the Cuban delegation, alleging that the presence of a delegation among approximately twenty thousand Cuban exiles in Puerto Rico constituted a threat to the stability and security of the island. The Cuban exiles and the Puerto Rican conservatives collaborated with the state, both Puerto Rican and U.S., in right-wing "colonial state terrorism."[2] From 1967 to 1986 Cuban exiles and the Puerto Rican right, condoned by the government, carried out 106 terrorist attacks that included destruction of property, usually with explosives, political assassinations, kidnappings and disappearances, and psychological warfare.[3] These attacks could be considered the start of a rightist alliance of anticommunist repression in Puerto Rico.

In this chapter I detail the process that led to the denial of Cuban visas and its diplomatic consequences. First, however, we need to recognize that Puerto Rican opposition to the visas was not the first time communist Cuba was denied visas to an athletic event in the area. Though it was unsuccessful, there had been a movement to deny visas to the Cuban delegation for the IX CACG of 1962 in Kingston, Jamaica; Cuban athletes were denied visas to the IOC-sponsored XVI World Cup of Baseball in Colombia in 1965; and they were denied visas by the Guatemalan government for the soccer finals of the IOC-sponsored Confederation of North, Central American, and Caribbean Association Football in 1965 and, as a result, were denied visas for the regional soccer competitions in Curaçao.[4] The politics of exclusion and denial affected others besides Cuba. Up to the 1910s Coubertin himself was against the inclusion of women in Olympism, and in 1948 the Soviet Union (still not a participant in the Olympic Games) made a condition before joining the IOC: to ban Franco's Spain due to its antagonism during World War II.[5] In 1962 Indonesian authorities hosting the fourth Asian Games denied visas to Israel and the Republic of China (Taiwan) due to religious and political objections from the People's Republic of China and Arab countries.[6] Visa denial occurred in nonsporting events as well. In the summer of 1966, the United States denied visas to a group of participants from Eastern and Western Europe to attend the 18th National Convention of the Communist Party of the USA in New York.[7] Nonetheless the Puerto Rican case was unique in that this was a U.S. territory or colony that had received approximately twenty thousand Cuban exiles, denying visas to communist Cuba, an ally of the Soviet Union. Regardless of their peripheral Caribbean condition, these two islands were unmistakably involved in a global conflict.

At the individual level, it is pertinent to highlight that Julio Enrique Monagas was not only the leader of Puerto Rican Olympism but also a leader in regional and hemispheric Olympism. Clearly Monagas was prominent in athletic diplomacy. To make official his preeminence, he was elected president of the newly established Organización Deportiva Centro Americana y del Caribe or Central American and Caribbean Sport Organization (CACSO) at a meeting held in Mexico City in February 1960. This organization, whose creation dates to a meeting of NOC leaders in Kingston, Jamaica, was part of a larger plan of the IOC to organize Olympism in the Americas. One IOC member, Gen. José de Jesús Clark Flores, considered it a fundamental step toward better world Olympic organization. The process to organize CACSO was full of closed-door conflicts and opposition, and the new organization was supposed to be led by a Mexican. Yet in order to eliminate an overpowering Mexico in hemispheric Olympism, the presidency was given to Monagas.[8]

As the head of PRPA, COPR, and CACSO, Monagas had achieved undisputed athletic leadership stature in the Olympic world. The X CACG in his home country could have been the final test that would place him among the immortal Olympic leaders. Yet when Puerto Rico was selected in 1962 as the site of the X CACG, Monagas was the first person to reject the proposition, stating, "Personally I am against this decision because I think we are going to come under major ridicule."[9] He was afraid that Puerto Rico did not have the infrastructure necessary to host the games regardless of the progress achieved in mass recreation facilities since the 1940s. He had also rejected a previous offer, to host the IX CACG in 1962.[10] After Jamaica hosted low-key games in 1962, however, Monagas became more receptive to the idea of Puerto Rico hosting future games.

Credit for the eventual siting of the 1966 CACG may be given to other sport leaders and the Puerto Rican secretary of state, who put enough pressure on Monagas to make him concede. The proposal was made just before the eighth edition of the games, in 1959 in Caracas, during a COPR meeting of Monagas's previous rivals, Fred Guillermety and Emilio Huyke.[11] The formal petition was made during the CACSO meeting in Kingston in 1962 by Monagas's brother, Héctor R. Monagas, and José Luis Purcell. During this meeting Julio Monagas reluctantly approved.

Despite Monagas's reluctance to support the games, there was a popular and elite coalition backing the proposal for Puerto Rico. In 1961 the Fraternidad de Escritores de Deportes de Puerto Rico (Brotherhood of Sport Writers of Puerto Rico), an organization of sport writers, petitioned support for the San Juan 1966 seat to a Comité de Ciudadanos (Citizens Committee). The membership of this committee was composed of two retired presidents of the Supreme Court of Puerto Rico, Roberto H. Todd Jr. and Martín Travieso; two preeminent lawyers, Marcos Rigau and Enrique Campos del Toro; and industrialist Bernardo Méndez.[12] The committee was appointed by Governor Luis Muñoz Marín and resulted in a positive recommendation and endorsement of a 1966 CACG bid. In 1962, as part of the third round of inductions to the Hall of Fame of Sport of Puerto Rico, attendees signed a petition to Governor Muñoz Marín asking his support.[13] Acknowledging the ample support for the games, the journalist José (Pepe) Seda reported that all three branches of government—executive, judicial, and legislative—had made their support public by making funding available for sport facilities year after year.[14]

The executive branch was particularly prominent in this affair because Secretary of State Roberto Sánchez Vilella (who would be elected governor in 1964) backed Guillermety, Huyke, and Felicio Torregrosa, the COPR leadership. Before attending the IX CACG in Kingston, they had requested a meeting with Muñoz Marín to seek final consent to host the games, saying that "the Olympic Committee of Puerto Rico understands that it does not correspond to the sport history of our island or to the giant stage of progress that Puerto Rico is currently living, to keep accepting invitations without us now inviting the other countries of the circuit to visit us."[15] The reference to Puerto Rico's progress was part of the reason to finally host these games.

In the end, and despite Monagas's wishes, this coalition of citizens managed to get the support of the governor and started planning the X CACG. As the czar of Puerto Rican sport, Monagas had to concede to the wishes of the majority. As president of CACSO he heard the petition of other NOCs, who declared Puerto Rico the ideal place to host the X CACG due to its successful athletic history, strategic geographical location, and tourist attractions.[16] These regional sport leaders wanted to come to the island even if it meant running competitions in the streets or swimming events in the ocean.[17] But the crux of the matter was that Puerto Rico should host the games to prove that its modernization had been fruitful. José Seda put it clearly by saying that Puerto Rico's mission for these games was to "demonstrate that it is true that our sport progress is such that [other countries] have to see our island and our men for orientation and guidance."[18]

The games were certainly a matter of economic and political legitimation. Puerto Rico's new political status as a "free associated state" with the United States provided the political stature to claim true sporting autonomy and athletic diplomacy. The secretary of the Organizing Committee, Joaquín Martínez-Rousset, thought so when he sent a letter to all members of the Puerto Rican Legislature inviting them to the activities of the X CACG because the leaders of other delegations wanted to "get to know us better."[19] In light of this, and knowing their limitations, there was great concern about not having proper facilities for the competitions and the Olympic Villa. Of particular concern was the reluctance of Governor Muñoz Marín to increase the budget for the games from $7 million to $11 million.[20] Huyke, Sánchez Vilella, and others concluded that they would hold the games with the existent facilities and with "possible improvements within the economic reality of Puerto Rico."[21] In order to prepare for the games, and taking account of economic limitations, COPR leaders consulted with local engineers and accountants as early as 1962 to determine cost and infrastructure.[22] The organizing committee went to Tokyo, host of the Olympic Games of 1964, to inspect, get inspired, and be influenced by their facilities. José Luis Nieto brought back millions of feet of film of Japanese sport installations.[23]

The other major hurdle Puerto Ricans faced was the Cuban problem. All groups involved in the politics of these games claimed to be protecting the Olympic ideal from political intervention. Yet all involved definitely took political stances that mirrored cold war and regional political conflicts. Although discussions over communist Cuban athletes were held, it became an official internal government matter in early 1964. Monagas asked Sánchez Vilella whether Puerto Rican authorities planned to ask the U.S. Department of State to issue visas for the Cuban delegation. Sánchez Vilella, who would be elected the second governor of the commonwealth after replacing Muñoz Marín later that year, wrote to Muñoz Marín regarding the Cuban visas. He aligned himself with a broad sentiment that hoped Cuba would be banned from the games: "This Government decidedly opposes that a Cuban team come to Puerto Rico to participate in said games as long as the present Cuban regime governs that island. We do not think that their presence can be of any service but, to the contrary, it will create a difficult and intolerable situation in the country."[24]

His main reason for this ban was the "18,000 Cuban refugees" that had escaped Fidel Castro's "totalitarian and Communist regime." He thought it would be almost impossible to prevent clashes between the exiles and the Cuban athletes because of "the demonstrated aggressive attitude in Jamaica as well as in Brazil and other places of the hemisphere where they have participated." These reasons addressed internal conflict between two groups of Cubans, but Sánchez Vilella also listed direct affronts by the Cuban government toward Puerto Rico. He cited the Cuban Ramón Calcinas of the Partido Unido de la Revolución Socialista: "Puerto Rico will be free by the struggle of their people and the solidarity of all countries of this continent and of the world. . . . Puerto Rico will be free like South Vietnam will be, who is fighting against North American imperialism, just like Angola and Venezuela."[25]

Sánchez's conclusions were based on a commission that studied the case and determined that since 1959 Castro's government had "developed, sponsored, and directed" an interventionist policy throughout the continent to establish communist regimes. The commonwealth government thought these were "acts of political aggression," as were other acts, such as calling the Puerto Rican governor a "satrap" and "insignificant traitor" (*traidorzuelo*) and expressing support for a Puerto Rican "war of national liberation." And the quotation from Calcinas pointed to Puerto Rico's colonial situation. These accusations were most despised by the commonwealth leaders, who were trying to present their new political status as a decolonized country. Indeed having a Cuban delegation in Puerto Rico attacking their autonomy went against the athletic diplomatic mission of presenting a decolonized Puerto Rican Olympic delegation. Simply put, Puerto Rico's presence as a sporting nation best represented the commonwealth's autonomy to the world. Having this autonomy mocked and attacked by communist Cubans was considered a political affront.

Sánchez Vilella thought it better not to have any sort of relation with the Cubans, "not even in the field of sports." He did acknowledge that the United States had revised its policy and now accepted the Soviet Union and other communist countries in the Olympic Games, but the Puerto Rican case was different. According to Sánchez Vilella, the Soviet Union had abandoned its support of other "wars of national liberation" and instead assumed a policy of political coexistence, something different from the Cuban case. As such, and most gravely, the commonwealth government's decision was "definite" and "will actively combat any measure before the United States government intended to allow the entry of the Cuban delegation to Puerto Rico."[26] Despite the fact that the United States maintained sovereignty over the commonwealth's borders, customs, and migration, Puerto Rican leaders were willing to defend their alleged sovereignty against U.S. authority on this point. It was rare during the commonwealth period for Puerto Rican statesmen to openly and defiantly confront the United States in external political matters. At stake in Puerto Rican-U.S. relations was the legal meaning of political association and the pragmatic security concern of a perceived threat from revolutionary communist Cubans and Cuban exiles in the island. Thus Puerto Ricans sought to exert their autonomy to protect their country.

The Cubans had touched a sensitive political nerve by accusing Puerto Ricans of being colonials. The accusation was even more threatening because it came from a communist, formerly Caribbean brother country and because the games were held in Puerto

Rico. More than an attack on Puerto Rico's international credibility, it was an attack on the nature of the commonwealth's association with the United States.

When the news was released in early 1965 that the commonwealth government, now led by Governor Sánchez Vilella, would oppose the granting of visas to the Cubans, it became the talk of the country and even international forums. In his newspaper column "Desde el Dugout," Martínez-Rousset pointed to the Olympic-political dilemma by indicating that Avery Brundage, as president of the IOC, could take away Puerto Rico's games due to the interference of political issues into Olympic competition.[27] The problems with the Cubans, coupled with the pressure of appropriate infrastructure for the games and his overall work with sports, proved too much for Monagas, who suffered a heart attack in late 1964. Nonetheless he was back at work in February 1965 after a few months' rest.[28]

By early 1965 Monagas had written to Brundage communicating the commonwealth's position with regard to Cuba and the volatile situation of the Cuban exiles. To this Martínez-Rousset asked, "What will happen if Cuba sends some two hundred athletes to the X Games and here they confront some 20,000 countrymen exiled and willing to send them to the firing squad?" While he acknowledged Brundage's earlier resolution of taking the World Championship of Basketball away from Manila because the Philippines had denied visas to some communist countries, he pointed out that there were not twenty thousand exiles in Manila. The X CACG in San Juan was a "problem of government against government," an "anticommunist" government against one "painted red." He concluded, "It is possible that this is the most explosive situation that the IOC has ever stumbled against in all of its history."[29]

There is no direct reference to the Cuban missile crisis in Martínez-Rousset's article; however, there was cold war language: "firing squad," "explosive," "anticommunist," "painted red." The issue was highly problematic for the IOC, which is known to have had a strong antipolitical position under Brundage's presidency.[30] Yet the Puerto Rican case was special, and this is precisely what Monagas told Brundage in a private cable. Although the commonwealth government was willing to go against the United States if necessary, Monagas publicly presented the situation as if Puerto Rico were following U.S. mandates when he stated that the commonwealth would not intervene since the United States had no diplomatic relations with Cuba. Furthermore, Monagas continued, the presence of twenty thousand Cuban exiles "can be the cause of a tragedy in an activity that is supposed to foster goodwill amongst the different countries of the world."[31] The new Puerto Rican secretary of state, Carlos Lastra, told the press that his government would maintain its decision to deny visas for the Cubans and that its decision was "in harmony" with the U.S. Department of State.[32] This latter statement was not necessarily true. Indeed during this period there was a confidential yet constant search for diplomacy between the United States and Cuba.[33] The Puerto Rican authorities used their colonial relationship to appear innocent in relation to the Cuban visas, making the United States appear the culprit.

When Monagas called Brundage to inquire about the IOC's position, Brundage claimed to comprehend the complexity of the problem and said that he would need to study the circumstances further.[34] The situation was definitely complicated because if Puerto Rico lost its seat on grounds of political interference, other options were equally problematic. Guatemala might be chosen to host the games, except it had neither the funds nor the infrastructure to do so and had declared that it too would deny visas to the Cubans. Alternatives were Colombia and El Salvador, but they had also broken diplomatic relations with Cuba.

Brundage stood his ground and told the international press that the IOC "strongly opposed political interference in sport" and that if Puerto Rico failed to invite all nation-members in the area, it risked losing the opportunity to host the Summer Olympic Games in the future. Monagas, dismissing Brundage's comments, said, "Puerto Rico neither wants nor has applied to be seat of the world Olympic Games."[35] According to Monagas, the COPR was innocent of mixing politics and sport and had not intervened with commonwealth authorities regarding the visas.[36] He said the decision to deny the visas was "entirely governmental" and was not related to COPR whatsoever; hence he did not see anything wrong.

The problem of the Cuban visas began to spread throughout the Olympic world. Martínez-Rousset reported that the Central American and Caribbean nations were attentive to the situation, and even in Colombia there were rumors that Puerto Rico had relinquished its seat.[37] News of the conflict reached California, where Brundage lived and where the newspaper reported that the IOC president opposed the decision to ban Cubans from the games, though he said that the matter was in the hands of CACSO.[38] Brundage also stated that the topic would be brought up in the next IOC meeting in Madrid. To some extent it can be concluded that Brundage was hoping that CACSO would follow the IOC's stance against political interference and argue for the visas to be issued. The problem had also reached European Olympic circles; Juan Cepero reported in *El Mundo* that Monagas called the general secretary of the International Federation of Amateur Athletics, D. T. Pain, in London to explain the situation. Pain promised to study the case and to help resolve the issue.[39]

Resolving the Caracas Resolution

In the meantime the CACSO meeting in Caracas produced an unprecedented decision, called the "Caracas Resolution." Brundage's hopes of seeing CACSO oppose political intervention in Olympism vanished when the organization, presided over by Monagas, officially passed a resolution banning the Cuban delegation from the X CACG in San Juan.[40] Citing "security concerns," CACSO claimed that the resolution upheld the IOC's nondiscrimination statute on race, religion, or politics. The alternate host countries (Colombia, Guatemala, and

El Salvador) indicated they could not be hosts and could not guarantee that their governments would grant the Cuban visas due to international agreements they had signed as members of the Organization of American States.[41]

The Caracas Resolution was signed on March 16, 1965, by Monagas as president of CACSO (Puerto Rico); Anibal Illueca S., vice president (Panama); José Beracasa, treasurer (Venezuela); Manuel de J. Rivas Rodríguez (El Salvador); Víctor Luque Salanueva (Mexico); and George Abrahams (Jamaica). Also present at the meeting were Gen. José de J. Clark Flores, honorary president of CACSO and member of the IOC's Executive Board, and Julio Bustamante, an IOC member. However, the meeting in Caracas was far from cohesive. In fact it was a political showdown, demonstrating the weight of Monagas in international sport and the politics of athletic diplomacy. An anonymous "confidential" letter to Brundage provides details:

The attitude of Julio Enrique Monagas has not changed in the last ten years. He is swayed entirely by the domestic political winds in Puerto Rico for the sake of strengthening his political position with the new Commonwealth in power in Puerto Rico since the resignation of Mr. Muñoz Marín.

The Executive Committee of the CACSO came prepared to its Caracas meeting, with the exception of Víctor Luque Salanueva of Mexico, to exclude Cuba from the Puerto Rican Games, ignoring not only the principles and rules of the IOC, but also those of its own Constitution. Their arguments were definite: 1. Impossible to cope with 26,000 Cuban exiles in Puerto Rico; 2. The U.S. Government will not issue visas; 3. The State Department of PR will not request the visas from the State Department in Washington.

Obviously, the theme was fully prepared with the previous assurance that Guatemala, Colombia, and El Salvador would also deny the visas and with other subterfuges, they invited to the meeting the Latin American members of the IOC, only Bustamante and

Clark being present, whose hands were tied, so that with the public and newsmen attending, they should approve the proceedings—which I called "the hold-up of Caracas." We rebelled against such actions and forced them to appoint a sub-committee to present a resolution on which they had not been agreed and we would not allow them to present in public and to the press.

This resolution [the Caracas Resolution] was approved the following day, despite my efforts to prevent it. The motives were definite, lack of discipline toward the IOC, which was called an old, archaic organization which works so slowly that it would reach a decision after the Games were held without Cuba, (sic. Illueca of Panamá [sic] and Illescas of Guatemala). However, once approved, they demanded my complicity in silence so that resolution No. 1 would not be publicized for the time being.[42] My reply was that they should publicize it now as I would do it with plenty of supplementary details. This caused a commotion, second thoughts and recess. In an aside with Monagas I asked him to abandon this stupid farse [sic], cited the consequences as in other similar cases.[43] I urged him that since they had expressed their feelings against the Olympic movement, against yourself personally and others, it would be better to leave the Movement, to stage their games without official title and without the recognition of the IOC, and then I would guarantee that there would be at least one country, Mexico, that with [sic] withdraw. Again, loud words, discussions, until they gave in to approve unanimously the Caracas Resolution. . . . They sugared the pill for the press by granting Puerto Rico 45 days to ask for visas and then make a definite decision. In reality, this pause was meant to give you and the Executive Board in Lausanne, time to analyze the matter and express your viewpoints, which I know will be concrete and which Mexico upholds and will uphold. Then, the meeting was adjourned.

Before my visit to Caracas, Enrique and I interviewed the U.S. Ambassador to Mexico, Mr. Fulton Freeman, who assured us that the State Department had neither granted nor denied visas for the Cubans for the simple reason they had not been requested, but that he personally would recommend our point of view so as to grant the visas for the athletes going to Puerto Rico, accepting our arguments specially in view, at this time, of the international policy of the United States toward countries far away from the Americas.[44]

The Caracas Resolution was a political struggle involving cold war ideologies and Puerto Rico's leading position in regional politics at the time. By setting the tone and content of the resolution to ban communist Cuba from the games, Monagas made the commonwealth's policy in regard to communism and set the parameters of how the games, and the region's politics, for that matter, would unfold. It was clear that CACSO, under Monagas's leadership, was willing to go against the "old and archaic" IOC in a position relatively similar to Sánchez Vilella's willingness to go against the U.S. Department of State.

News of the CACSO resolution reached Brundage shortly after it was made public in March 1965. As indicated in the confidential letter, Gen. José de J. Clark was strongly opposed to the Caracas Resolution; in protest he asked Brundage and the IOC to cancel his earlier petition for IOC sponsorship of the games.[45] After a meeting of the IOC's Executive Board on April 12, 1965, in Lausanne, Brundage agreed with Clark and communicated to CACSO that it needed to apply for IOC recognition of the games. This recognition was contingent upon the Organizing Committee agreeing to invite all regional members of the IOC to the X CACG, including Cuba, as the IOC had "an inflexible policy against political interference in sport, for any reason whatsoever." The meeting in Lausanne included all international amateur sport federations, which approved this policy "unanimously."[46] It seemed that Brundage's IOC and Monagas's CACSO were head-to-head in a confrontation of Olympic values inherently immersed in political ideologies. Brundage, though he regretted the situation, thought that Puerto Ricans had no excuse because Jamaica had weathered the same situation regarding Cuba's participation at the CACG in in 1962.

However, the two situations are hardly equivalent. First, angering twenty thousand Cuban exiles was a real threat. Because the Cuban delegation had openly proselytized their revolution at the 1962 Kingston games, provoking some clashes with a small group of Cuban exiles that had traveled to Kingston, security was a real concern for the Organizing Committee. It is true that thousands of anti-Castro Cubans had emigrated to Jamaica between 1959 and 1962, but their emigration was mostly temporary; some ten thousand Cuban exiles had gone to Jamaica, but 9,670 of them had received visas for the United States. Unlike in Puerto Rico, anti-Castro Cuban exiles in Jamaica did not intend to stay and develop a community; hence the conditions for sustained and organized demonstrations against the Cuban Revolution were not fully met. Second, although heavily influenced by U.S. Caribbean policy, Jamaica was at that time an independent and sovereign nation, with control over its ports, customs, and visa grants.[47] Puerto Rico was totally dependent on the United States regarding who could enter the island. Third, as an unincorporated territory of the United States, Puerto Rico had to follow U.S. policy in foreign relations, and at that time the United States had broken diplomatic relations with Cuba. The United States had just come out of the Cuban missile crisis. A potentially violent incident involving Cuban athletes in a U.S. territory with U.S. citizens and thousands of ardent Cuban exiles was a recipe for disaster and could renew the threat of war with the Soviets.

General Clark, despite being ignored at the Caracas meeting, still intended to work toward making the X CACG with Cuba possible. He met with Monagas in late July 1965, and talked over the phone with Germán Rieckehoff Sampayo, a member of the Organizing Committee who was a key person in the resolution of the "Cuban problem," to help resolve the situation. Born on February 5, 1915, on the island town of Vieques, Puerto Rico, and of German ancestry, Rieckehoff Sampayo had been active in the nationalist movement in New York and Puerto Rico before joining the PPD's populist movement. In his early school years in Río Piedras, he played basketball and baseball and eventually became a sports leader through his work with the early stages of the local professional basketball league (known today as the Baloncesto Superior Nacional), serving as president from 1942 to 1944. From 1947 to 1949 he worked at the Colegio de Agricultura y Artas Mecánicas in Mayagüez in the development of sport facilities, and in 1952 he graduated from Law School at the University of Puerto Rico. In 1963 he founded the Equestrian Federation of Puerto Rico, which marked his full and official introduction into COPR.[48] Rieckehoff Sampayo's greatest wish was that CACSO would "find its way" and not lose its "permanent recognition" within the IOC.[49] During the X CACG issue with Cuba, major changes were occurring within the leadership of Puerto Rican sport.

The pressure that Clark and the IOC exerted on Monagas may have been too strong, or he may have finally felt that he was over-exerting himself, because at some point in the fall of 1965 Monagas ceded his legendary control over Puerto Rican sport authority and resigned from his posts as president of COPR and administrator of PRPA. His effectiveness at these positions was definitely reduced by his heart attack, his old age, and the expiration of his comrade Muñoz Marín's term as governor. Nonetheless he still was in charge of CACSO, perhaps to tackle what came to be his last, and perhaps his most crucial, battle.

Not only was the X CACG at stake in 1966 but also the existence of CACSO and Central American and Caribbean Olympism. It seems that after the ultimatum by the IOC and Brundage, CACSO, COPR, the Organizing Committee, and even the PRPA reevaluated their positions and were now open to extending invitations to all IOC members of the area, including Cuba.[50] It now became a matter of dealing with Puerto Rican and U.S. authorities to issue the Cuban visas. This proved to be difficult, since the Puerto Rican government was still upholding its position of banning Cuba from the games. At least this can be inferred by Lastra's comments in the newspapers: "We will neither help them [the Organizing Committee] get the visas for the Cuban players nor will we oppose the granting of such visas."[51] With the broken diplomatic relations between the United States and Cuba, this might have meant the commonwealth government was relying on a refusal of the United States to grant the visas.

Because of the Puerto Rican government's refusal to request the visas, Clark was suspicious of the honesty of the Organizing Committee in assuring the participation of Cuba, and he told Brundage that Puerto Rico's reconsideration was all "a new farce." Consequently Clark now threatened the Puerto Ricans by declaring the CACG's site vacant and offering it to Guatemala or El Salvador.[52] At the same time that CACSO held an emergency meeting in Mérida, Mexico, on December 7 and 8, 1965, Martínez-Rousset of the Organizing Committee wrote to Brundage restating Puerto Rico's request to hold the games and promising that COPR would comply with IOC rules and regulations. Still there was no assurance from the commonwealth regarding the visas.[53]

Once again an outside element interceded in Puerto Rican Olympism: Brundage, in conversation with U.S. Ambassador C. Allan Stewart (who was director of Caribbean Affairs), managed to get the U.S. Department of State to issue visas for the Cuban delegation. On December 5, 1965, the U.S. secretary of state sent a cablegram to Felicio Torregrosa indicating that the Cuban visas would be processed.[54] Thus Brundage, as president of the IOC, committed the same fault he had been decrying throughout his presidency: political interference. By obtaining the Cuban visas from the U.S. State Department he had de facto interfered in a political matter to safeguard the participation of the Cuban delegation at the X CACG. Moreover he and Ambassador Stewart overrode and disregarded the policy of the Commonwealth of Puerto Rico, an act that exposed its colonial condition. It became evident that Puerto Rico, regardless of claiming sporting and even political autonomy, had failed to fully achieve either. This colonial dynamic distinguished the Puerto Rican from the Jamaican situation and is what makes Puerto Rico unique within Latin American politics and international sports.

With this move the IOC was again unmasked as a political actor. Ambassador Stewart clearly acknowledged this when he stated, "It would be very bad policy for the Government to refuse visas simply because they are Cubans, because then it would prevent any U.S. city from being considered for the Olympic Games."[55] Certainly the U.S. State Department was more than willing to deny visas to communists, from Cuba or other places, as they did in June 1966 when the United States denied visas to communists attending the 18th National Convention of the Communist Party of the USA.[56] But Olympic sports is different. Stewart knew the importance of athletic diplomacy in international competition, and he was not willing to risk it because of stubborn colonial subjects. Even though the United States was immersed in the cold war, it was more beneficial to play by the rules of the IOC if they wanted to win the war in the athletic field.

Only after Brundage himself was assured the Cuban visas would be issued did he finally give the IOC's patronage to the X CACG in San Juan.[57] Nonetheless, to safeguard the legitimacy of CACSO, as Clark had requested, he later communicated to Torregrosa and the Organizing Committee that they needed final official recognition from CACSO.[58] However, just because Brundage had obtained confirmation that the U.S. State Department would issue visas did not mean that the Puerto Rican government would accept; remember, Puerto Rico was willing to refuse any move by the United States to allow the entry of Cubans. This is what Clark noted in the Mérida meeting of December 7 and 8. He could not get assurance from COPR that the Puerto Rican government would accept the visas if granted. He was opposed to the manner in which Brundage had obtained the visas.

Declaring that Washington was working against IOC regulations, he indicated that it was a matter for the Puerto Rican government to affirm "its acceptance to the Cuban participation." Based on this, Clark gave another ultimatum to the Puerto Rican government that included a deadline of December 17, 1965, at 1:00 p.m. to "guarantee that the athletes, officials, and technicians in general [in other words, Cuba] will be accepted." This certification, he continued, should be addressed to CACSO with copies to IOC officials and to IOC members in Latin America. If such certification failed to be clear and to the satisfaction of CACSO, Puerto Rico then forfeited its rights to be the site of the X CACG.[59] The ball was back in Puerto Rico's court.

Meanwhile tensions continued to escalate when the Russians became involved in support of their Cuban allies. The games were nearing, and on December 31, 1965, Brundage replied to a letter from Konstantin Andrianov, president of the USSR's Olympic Committee and vice president of the International Olympic Committee, saying that for the past several months he and Clark had been "devoted to defending the right of your Cuban friends (although many claim they are not following Olympic regulations) to participate in the Central American Games, which are scheduled for Puerto Rico next year." Brundage wondered, "When are we going to be able to concentrate on sport and not be bothered with these unsolvable political problems that do not concern us?"[60] Cold war politics was a major concern for the IOC and Andrianov and was widely discussed in the 64th Session of the IOC in April 1966. In preparation for this meeting, Andrianov called on the IOC to "reaffirm the necessity to organize the official competitions and meetings only in those countries, which guarantee free entries for all participants and observe the prescribed rules and traditions of the international competitions."[61] Although he firmly believed in the separation of Olympics and politics, Andrianov was invested in solving the situation. One week before the games started, he sent another cablegram to Brundage, saying, "Consider the situation quite an emergency and ask your immediate intervention."[62]

Not only were the Russians paying more attention as the games drew closer, but another group of Puerto Ricans in favor of Cuba entered the conflict. This group, the Movimiento Pro Independencia (MPI), was founded in 1959 in Mayagüez under the leadership of Juan Mari Brás, who gathered discontented members from the Partido Independentista Puertorriqueño and the Partido Nacionalista. The MPI declared itself to be sympathetic to the Cuban Revolution and its methods of popular mobilization under anti-imperialist ideology to claim the independence of Puerto Rico.[63] The MPI had already expressed its solidarity, active support, and even protection for the Cuban delegation. An MPI "manifesto" was published in the Cuban newspaper *Granma* on March 24, 1966: "The Cuban athletes will not be alone. There will be the Puerto Rican sportsmen and *independentistas* to stop the provocation plans against Cuba that Yankee imperialism intends to pursue and to answer, along with the Cuban athletes if they are forced to do it as well, said provocations in the necessary manner. The people of Puerto Rico, certainly will not permit that those worms and lackeys usurp their representation or moreover stain our prestige and national dignity."[64] With this in mind, Monagas was visibly worried about the involvement of the MPI during the games, which, according to him, had set up an "embassy" in Cuba, and the possibility of student reinforcements brought from the Dominican Republic.[65] Moreover Monagas hoped that if Brundage were present during the games, peace, or at least composure, would be achieved. Yet Brundage declined the invitation because he needed to be present at the opening ceremony of a new museum in San Francisco that would hold his collection of Oriental art.[66]

The Cold Games of 1966: At Sea and on Land

With the Cuban visas approved, it appeared the games would be held without problems. The Puerto Rican government, though originally opposed to receiving the Cuban delegation even if the United

States issued the visas, now followed the U.S. mandates. This change in attitude by the Puerto Ricans was apparently a result of Germán Rieckehoff Sampayo, who negotiated with local authorities.[67] Thus the threat of a Puerto Rican–U.S. conflict was gone. Because the United States and Cuba had broken diplomatic relations, the visas were to be given to a third country, such as Mexico or Jamaica, where Cuban officials could pick them up. Once obtaining the visas, they would then fly a commercial plane to San Juan. However, the Cubans thought this extra step entailed an "act of aggression" by the United States because they wanted to enter Puerto Rico without impediment. Indeed Castro called the mandate "stupid, cynical blackmail."[68] The Cuban press also covered the problem of the visas, reporting that the Cuban officials wanted to have relations directly with COPR, though they understood this was impossible because Puerto Rico was an "Estado Libre Asociado" (Free Associated State commonwealth) and that "the associated part impedes them from being free."[69] It is not clear how, but the Cuban visas were later taken from Mexico City to Cuba, either by Mexican or Cuban officials.[70]

Brundage had already notified the Cuban Olympic Committee (COC) of the problems pertaining to their alleged political interference in sport.[71] In their defense Manuel González Guerra, president of the COC, wrote a seven-page letter dated March 30, 1966, indicating that the Cuban government did not interfere in Olympism and that they respected and strictly followed IOC rules. He identified countries that had violated Olympic rules regarding religious or political discrimination; for example, the Jamaican Olympic authorities had a Christian minister bless the 1962 Games and "spoke of God, spoke of politics, of democracy" in their opening ceremony. González Guerra wondered why there was no action taken against Cuban counterrevolutionaries when they "attack[ed]" the Cuban athletes with propaganda. He believed that there was a real "threat of attack" in Puerto Rico not only from their "enemies" but also from Monagas and even the mayor of San Juan, to which the IOC did not seem to give credence. The most recent form of aggression, he said, was that Cubans needed to go to Mexico or Jamaica to obtain their visas when the Swiss Embassy in Havana was usually in charge of U.S. matters.[72]

For months no one knew how, or even whether, the Cuban delegation would make its way to Puerto Rico. These were moments of great tension due to the unpredictability of the Cuban delegation and the meanings of a communist delegation in U.S. territory at the height of the cold war. The IOC Executive Board met in Rome on April 1966 and gave final recognition to the X CACG to be held in Puerto Rico, which they described as "an independent state under the protection of the United States with whom it had a custom union."[73] The unilateral and external approval of the Cuban visas by both the United States and the IOC was silenced, or unacknowledged, in the official minutes.

The Cubans had actually boarded a plane to fly into San Juan, but it was stopped in Santiago for further instructions. In response Castro told the head of the Cuban delegation to take the merchant sea vessel *Cerro Pelado* instead. During the thirty-six-hour trip from Santiago to San Juan (alongside the deepest part of the Atlantic Ocean; see map 2), the Cuban ship was followed by a U.S.-registered aircraft. Leaders inside the ship considered three ways they might enter San Juan: sailing the *Cerro Pelado* in without permission, rowing in by lifeboat, or swimming to shore. As they approached San Juan while still in Atlantic waters, a U.S. Coast Guard plane dropped a message inside a plastic tube: "Cuban vessel Cerro Pelado. Your entry in U.S. territorial waters, San Juan, or any other port in Puerto Rico is prohibited. Repeat prohibited. We are notifying you that your entry would result in the confiscation of your vessel. Territorial waters extend three nautical miles from the coast. Signed U.S. Coast Guard."[74]

The Cubans continued their voyage toward Puerto Rico but anchored at the edge of international waters on June 10, 1966, just one day before the opening ceremonies. A Cuban ship in interna-

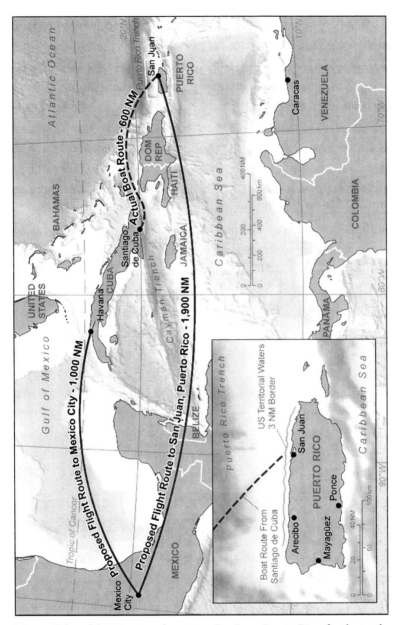

Map 2. Cuban delegation travel routes to San Juan, Puerto Rico, for the tenth Central American and Caribbean Games of 1966. Map by James V. Whitacre.

tional waters so close to U.S.-controlled ports and territory meant trouble. This audacious, provocative, and risky move by the Cubans placed all parties on immediate alert, including COPR and the Organizing Committee, the Puerto Rican and U.S. governments, the IOC, and different NOCs from the Soviet bloc. Facing what they thought was an affront against Olympism, Cuban leaders and athletes on board the vessel adamantly ratified the "Declaration of the *Cerro Pelado*," the last point stating, "I SWEAR, in the name of the martyrs of the 'Cerro Pelado' and of all who have made possible our commitment to sport, to defend it with our lives if needed."[75] This was another "crisis at sea" involving East versus West, without nuclear missiles this time yet fertile for conflict.

The leadership of the Cuban delegation had already contacted their Russian allies on June 8, saying that their "participation ed [*sic*] Puerto Rico under threet [*sic*] as the USA authorities not permitting Cuban team aircraft landing."[76] In response Andrianov once again cabled Brundage, insisting "upon your urgent actions" to mitigate the conflict. If the Cubans were not allowed to participate, he continued, the IOC must withdraw its patronage of the games, effectively canceling and delegitimizing the Central American and Caribbean Games of their regional status.[77] These were the most severe, dramatic, and punitive measures ever mentioned by an IOC member in the history of regional games. Taking away IOC patronage would effectively mean stripping the games from any association with Olympism or the IOC, thus terminating Central American and Caribbean Olympism.

While Andrianov's demands were considered diplomatic, they were extreme and grave. Only a few years after the Cuban missile crisis, this incident meant more to Soviet political leaders. The Cubans counted on the official support of the Soviets. In late May the Soviet news agency TASS published the following statement in its main newspapers, *Pravda* and *Izvestia*: "Soviet ruling circles are attentively watching developments in this area [the Caribbean] and consider it necessary to point out statements that have been made concerning support for heroic Cuba, which is fighting for its freedom and independence. Those who hatch aggressive plans against the Republic of Cuba should not forget that Cuba has loyal and reliable friends."[78]

Simultaneously, at the Congress of the Communist Party of Czechoslovakia, Leonid I. Brezhnev, general secretary of the Central Committee of the Communist Party of the Soviet Union, exclaimed, "Our Cuban brothers may be sure that the Soviet Union firmly supports revolutionary Cuba and its sacred right to freedom and independence. Our statements on this account are well known the world over."[79] It seems that the Cubans had also contacted their allies in Puerto Rico, the MPI, and informed them of their decision to travel by ship; on June 10 a boat carrying Juan Mari Brás, Norman Pietri, and Ángel Silén went out to receive the *Cerro Pelado* in open waters.[80] It appears as if the Cubans were lining up their chess pieces for protection. When local authorities were informed that the Cuban vessel was just outside international limits and threatening a political disaster, local officials once more contacted the Puerto Rican Olympic leader Rieckehoff Sampayo to intervene between the Puerto Rican government and the Cuban leadership.

Rieckehoff Sampayo, along with Secretary of State Lastra and the athletic legend Eugenio Guerra, boarded the U.S. Coast Guard ship *Peacock* to meet the *Cerro Pelado*. It was raining heavily and the sea was rough near the deepest point in the Atlantic. As they approached the merchant ship, the Cubans cheered the Puerto Rican delegation while playing the songs of Puerto Rican singer Tito Lara over the ship's speakers.[81] Once they reached the Cuban ship (considered Cuban territory), it took the Puerto Rican delegation, with passports in hand and on rough water, over an hour to board. Capt. Cornelio Pino Izquierdo received them, as Rieckehoff Sampayo discussed the situation with José Llanusa, González Guerra, and others.[82]

The instructions given to Rieckehoff Sampayo by Governor Sánchez Vilella were to allow the Cubans to land on the island with their visas, but not to allow the ship to cross into U.S waters. Discussions lasted for over an hour as Rieckehoff Sampayo encouraged the Cubans not to sail the ship into San Juan. His theory was bold: "This vessel is property of the Cuban government, which has seized the property of many Cubans who currently live in Puerto Rico, without proper legal procedure. If this vessel enters Puerto Rican waters and, under the Laws of Admiralty, a Cuban initiates action against the Cuban government, this ship gets detained in warranty and many years will pass in which it will stay in Puerto Rico under impoundment."[83]

The Cubans stopped negotiations and "scribbled something to the telegraphist." During this recess, the Puerto Ricans were served coffee and Cuban cigars. It is probable that the Cubans took this opportunity to relay their complaint to their Soviet allies; emergency telegrams were sent to Brundage from the leaders of the Hungarian, Bulgarian, Romanian, and USSR NOCs. Andrianov cabled, "Ask urgent IOC official assistance for Cuban teams [to] enter Puerto Rico."[84] As during the missile crises four years before, the Cubans were fully backed by their Soviet communist allies.

This stressful moment dissipated when the telegraphist returned with a piece of paper for Llanusa, who passed it to Georgie García; after reading it García said, "We are ready to get off and leave the ship here."[85] What that piece of paper said is not known, and it is not known what influence Brundage may have had, but at the end of this tense moment of athletic diplomacy the Cubans decided to leave the ship in international waters and transport the delegation to land by other means. The following statement is from the vice president of the COC, Armando Riva Patterson, from that afternoon: "The Cuban Olimpic [sic] Committee considers it a great victory for sports and the Olympic movement the entrance of the Cuban delegation in San Juan Puerto Rico. . . . Once again the ever so clear ideas the renewer of the Olimpic [sic] Games Baron Pierre de Coubertin have triumphed and have put in evidence all those who really intend in a permanent manner to mix politics with sports. . . . We expect great success from these ames [*sic*] that constitute part of the history of the nations located in Central America and the Caribe [*sic*]." In this way the Cuban delegation announced its peaceful attendance of the games, claiming they were protecting Olympism by overcoming political obstacles. Nonetheless they knew that political tension persisted and warned the Puerto Rican authorities and the members of the IOC that "different groups of Cuban exiles resident of voeitr [*sic*] hat [*sic*] have proclaimed their purpose to attack our delegation."[86]

The actual transportation of the delegates occurred the next day, June 11, the day of the opening ceremonies, beginning at 5:00 a.m. Under great public pressure and dramatically, several private boats sailed out to the *Cerro Pelado* to pick up the athletes, an ordeal that lasted more than four hours (see figs. 12 and 13). After going through customs and immigration, the Cubans were taken to the opening ceremony using buses from Puerto Rico's Autoridad Metropolitana de Autobuses. But the fact that the Cubans were able to land peacefully was not the end of the confrontations.

The reception of the Cubans in San Juan was full of different reactions. Some reporters described the Cuban athletes as cordial and talkative, though they would not discuss politics. The only Cuban representative who expressed his political dissatisfaction at the games was Minister of Education José Llanusa, who accused the United States of "interfering, obstructing, and delaying" Cuba's participation at the games.[87] During the bus trip to the opening ceremonies at Hiram Bithorn Stadium, the delegation was met by crowds lining the road: some (led by the MPI) held up signs of support that read "Fatherland or Death, We Will Win" and "Greetings Cuban Athletes";[88] others (led by the Cuban exiles) showed their hostility with signs that read, for example, "Russians Go Home" (see figs. 14 and 15).

Regardless of this political friction, the opening ceremony had no major problems before a crowd of 19,262 spectators.[89] The opening

Fig. 12. Returning to the *Cerro Pelado* from the San Juan port. Courtesy of Carlos Uriarte González.

included the hoisting of the flags of the CACG, IOC, and San Juan. A chorus of one hundred sang the official anthems of the games, including the popular song "En Mi Viejo San Juan," with which the audience sang along.[90] The CACG torch, known as Fuego Azteca, reached the stadium after arriving from Mexico on June 1 and being carried by runners across the island. Then George Keelan, the long-time educator and the first chief of delegation for Puerto Rico in 1930, led a symbolic run of the track.[91]

Despite the air of national and regional confraternity and the games' reputation today as peaceful and uneventful, there were anxious and charged moments. One of the most heavily covered incidents was the defection of Cuban athletes. Juan Pablo Vega Romero, a wrestler, defected at midnight on Sunday, June 12, protesting Castro's communism and the absence of racial equality in Cuba.[92] He was taken to the U.S. Immigration Services district office, where he declared that he wished to be taken to the United States.

There was another incident with a "defector." It started as a rumor when a newspaper report stated that an athlete nicknamed "Chiqui"

Cuban Landing Provides Pre-Game Show

MAIN ATTRACTION — The tugboat Peacock nears Isla Grande dock yesterday with first load of Cuban athletes from the freighter Cerro Pelado lying outside the three-mile limit.

Fig. 13. The *Peacock* with part of the Cuban delegation. Courtesy of Carlos Uriarte González.

was trying to defect and reunite with her exiled parents in Puerto Rico. The reporter claimed that she was being held prisoner in the Olympic Village.[93] This story was refuted by Llanusa, who declared that the athlete, María Cristina González, had been "rescued from unknown individuals" who tried to kidnap her. She was later taken to the *Cerro Pelado* "for her safety." Rumors of defection were constant; Llanusa dismissed one that alleged seventeen women athletes had tried to jump off a Puerto Rican bus to ask for asylum.[94]

Defecting can be said to have been a systematic project to attack Castro's communist government during the games in San Juan. In anticipation of defectors a Puerto Rican governmental plan was in place (that included the local police, Immigration Service, and the State Department) before the games started.[95] The Puerto Rican public, the media, and Cuban exiles put a lot of pressure on Cuban athletes to defect. In fact the majority of the Cuban delegation was said to have received some sort of monetary offer to defect and make declarations against Castro's regime.[96] According to COC president González Guerra, the Torres Velázquez show on radio station WIAC

Fig. 14. Pro-Cuban demonstrators. Courtesy of Carlos Uriarte González.

used "provocative and offensive" language exhorting Cuban athletes to defect, announcing phone numbers of individuals who would give food and shelter to up to twenty-five athletes for up to thirty days. The initiative was called Operation Jump the Freedom Fence (Operación Salto a la Verja de la Libertad). González Guerra claimed the hostility of the radio program reached the level of offending Cuban women by referring to Cuban men as "sons of such and such."[97] Calling them "communists," however, was not offensive to them.

It is difficult to ascertain how many Cuban athletes were tempted to defect in San Juan, since there was absolutely no conversation

Fig. 15. Anti-Cuban demonstrators. Courtesy of Carlos Uriarte González.

about it due to fear of G-2, the Cuban Secret Police, who had allegedly infiltrated the delegation.[98] Pressure to defect even came from police officers at the Olympic Village, who constantly invited the Cubans to "begin their flight to freedom." Leaflets, handouts, and newspapers were taken to the Village urging the Cuban athletes to defect. Even priests tried to persuade some delegates to leave communist Cuba and stay in Puerto Rico, and at some matches the loudspeakers announced (apparently falsely) that more Cuban athletes were defecting. During a bus trip from the Olympic Village to the pool, the bus driver made unplanned stops at the sport facilities of the University of Puerto Rico and at a private house on Ponce de León Avenue that displayed a sign announcing "Shelter" (Refugio).

The bus driver opened the door of the bus and asked the passengers, "Doesn't anybody get off here?"[99]

Invitations and pressure to defect were not the only "acts of aggression" against the Cuban delegation. There were also physically violent moments. A "paid agent" allegedly attacked Luis de Cárdenas, the COC treasurer, and when the police came they held de Cárdenas so that the "agent" could keep hitting him. During basketball practice at the Colegio Espíritu Santo coliseum, a group of "contrarrevolucionarios" provoked and attacked the Cuban team, "forcing" the Cubans to fight back. At the end of the incident, a local policeman confirmed that the attack was indeed provoked by "Cuban exiles."[100] At a soccer match in the Baldrich neighborhood the MPI fought a group of Cuban exiles.[101] When a car pulled into the Olympic Village and two passengers "threatened" some Cuban delegates, they made one of the aggressors drop a Mossberg "Brownie" gun.[102]

This was not the only incident involving firearms. Llanusa claimed that on two occasions four individuals attempted to murder him. On the first attempt, they were driving an Impala and held a rifle; on the second, the same individuals, now driving a Comet, were holding handguns. Llanusa denounced the attempts as "exclusively guided by the Central Intelligence Agency of the United States." He said that the Cuban exiles were "not directly responsible," implying that they were more likely puppets paid by the CIA. Worse than the violent attacks, Llanusa said, the constant provocations to defect constituted a "psychological war" against the Cuban delegation.[103]

The violence and hostility at the X CACG of 1966 were more than a simple reflection of cold war tensions; Cuba and Puerto Rico incarnated the cold war rivalries of the Soviet bloc and the United States on the athletic field and in the streets of San Juan. For Puerto Ricans the political and security concerns associated with the X CACG became an unwanted reason to exert their autonomy as a Caribbean people and confront Castro's government, the IOC, and even the United States. Yet the limits of their association, the precariousness of the commonwealth status, and the importance of Olympism in performing the nation ultimately prevented them from carrying out their ban of the Cuban athletes. In this sense these games proved the colonial condition of Puerto Rico. Despite being the protagonist and host of the games, Puerto Rico became a de facto subaltern to the U.S. Department of State and even the IOC due to the imposed granting of visas. Notwithstanding their intention to prove to their Latin American and Caribbean neighbors that they were modern enough to host these Games, it became evident that this included a heavy price: colonial sovereignty.

The MPI was clear about Puerto Rican colonialism; that is why they were so active during these games. At the same time, a growing sector of the Estadista movement for U.S. statehood also felt this blatant political subjugation and actively attacked the commonwealth. Puerto Rican senator Arturo Ortiz Toro openly declared that "Fidel Castro has ridiculed the Commonwealth government" at the X CACG: "The ridicule of the Puerto Rican people consists in that making claims of sovereignty, they invite the Cuban athletes with great fanfare, and when they get to barely 3 miles from our beaches, a simple order by a subaltern employee of the Coast Guard stops the Cuban vessel outside our shores. This is evidence that there is no Puerto Rican sovereignty."[104]

The Estadista movement actively sought to use the games to advance its political aspirations. The group Ciudadanos Pro Estado 51, led by a future governor, Carlos Romero Barceló, wrote to Secretary of State Carlos Lastra accusing the COPR and the commonwealth government of not properly (and legally) using the U.S. flag at the official ceremonies of the games. The letter, which was published in the newspapers, demanded that the U.S. flag and national anthem be used on all occasions along with the Puerto Rican versions.[105] Instead, COPR and the Organizing Committee decided to have two opening ceremonies: a preliminary ceremony to welcome the heads of state that displayed the Puerto Rican and

U.S. symbols, and a second Olympic ceremony using only Puerto Rican symbols.

When the X CACG were over, Puerto Rico had finished third overall, behind Mexico and Cuba (winning more medals than Cuba but fewer gold). This presented the Puerto Rican nation as still strong, competitive, and powerful in regional sport. This was the message given to all 270,251 people who officially attended the games and to the millions who followed the events throughout Central America and the Caribbean.[106] Though this nationhood was colonial and subordinated, it was real for many. Indeed the X CACG legitimized the progress of Puerto Rican Olympism since the 1930s. The obstacles to making Puerto Rico visible among the nations of the world had been conquered. There was no looking back, and Puerto Rican Olympism was officially consolidated. This feeling of progress and achievement was captured in the last page of the games' "Memorias":

> The sad task of "undressing" the Central Sport Village had begun. All had ended.
>
> They picked up the furnishings and they did the general cleaning. The Central Sport Village went back to the role that progress had granted it in the life of Puerto Rico: Public Urbanization Las Virtudes. . . .
>
> In the silence of a Puerto Rican sunset the men that finished the task of taking down those structures, the sporting garb with which it had been dressed up, cried like children.
>
> Like children who had been deprived of a toy. The best toy that sport could have offered to men like them. . . .
>
> The Tenth Central American and Caribbean Games.[107]

6 / The Eternal Overtime?

Monagas's Legacy

In the summer of 1967, a year after the tenth Central American and Caribbean Games, the sport leadership in Puerto Rico looked quite different. Monagas, now sixty-three, might not have been old enough to retire from sport leadership, but his constant political battles over the previous twenty-five years made him a veteran. He had been on the front lines of sport and recreation during Puerto Rico's strong push for modernization, and, like a true political soldier, his battles left a deep mark. He had been an ally of the Partido Popular Democrático and its program of social justice but had also dealt with pressing international politics. From his campaign work in the early 1940s to the development of Un parque para cada pueblo, the recreational programs of the 1950s, the centralization of the Administración de Parques y Recreo Públicos, the COPR, the Central American and Caribbean Sports Organization, and finally the coordination of the X CACG, Monagas's role in the infrastructural and programmatic growth of the PPD and Puerto Rican and Latin American sports was undeniably monumental.

Yet what is perhaps Monagas's greatest recognition came after his retirement from public office in 1967. Each year since the 1950s the COPR held an event to honor the previous year's best athletes. In 1967 COPR's new president, Felicio Torregrosa, organized the awards evening. Germán Rieckehoff Sampayo introduced Monagas on behalf of COPR, followed by Torregrosa's presentation of the night's keynote address from former governor Luis Muñoz Marín. Muñoz Marín's speech encapsulated all the ideological elements involved in Puerto

Rican modernization under his legendary administration and in equating sporting achievements with the good of the nation.

Saying that a tribute to Monagas was a tribute to Puerto Rico, Muñoz Marín also stated that sport's three main values—determination, patience, and honesty—were the same values that a country needed to prosper. In sport you need determination to achieve your goals, patience not to surrender to a loss, and honesty to compete fairly: "A country needs determination to decidedly and tirelessly fight for the betterment of the entire community. It needs patience because the problems we face do not get resolved just by approving a law, but require a collective effort, long term, from all citizens. Honesty— honor—because we must understand that there is not a nobler enterprise than service, without expecting a reward, for all our compatriots. Our people have fulfilled their responsibility to the fullest in both areas in recent years."[1]

Muñoz Marín said he had these values in mind while supporting Monagas's athletic and recreation proposals since 1941. He reminded the audience that in the twenty-five years that Monagas had led the sport institutions, Puerto Rico had gone from being "submerged in despair" to having a radically brighter future. All of this was due to Monagas, whose "contribution to sport and to the life of our country is great." The work that Monagas did for the betterment of sport and recreation in Puerto Rico was representative of the temperament, achievements, and hopes of the Puerto Rican people: "A tribute to Julio Enrique Monagas is a tribute to our people. A people that insists, as we have insisted, in working hard and well, in widening and deepening our values, our democratic way of living, in the opportunities to better ourselves for all as a people with worth. A people that deserve progress and do not deserve roadblocks, but if they encounter them will know how to overcome them with the same purity as they have done before."[2]

With this in mind, Muñoz Marín spoke about the recent X CACG in San Juan, describing them as the ideal way to show the world what Puerto Ricans were made of and their potential:

We can be proud of having been hosts. Regardless of the problems that we encountered, we sponsored Games, which if not better, certainly were equally comparable with the best hosted so far in its category. Independently of the good work we did in competitions, we demonstrated first of all, that we are a hospitable people, conscious of their tradition, serious, and dedicated. But what's more important is that we demonstrated that we are a people on the move, a people who live according to the noble exigency of the Olympic motto: "Higher, Further, Stronger." Let's keep honoring and making this motto a reality. Let's raise our sight higher and further in our sport horizons. Let's increase our international participation and let's receive with open arms other countries who come here to compete. Let's strengthen our youth, stimulating them to participate, not be mere spectators in sport and in the solutions of the problems we still need to resolve. Let's provide them with more facilities so they can develop physically and can understand what sport and their people are and mean. Moreover, that all of that energy, physical and mental, be channeled in favor of the well-being of all of our people.

Let's raise the standards of living in every category in Puerto Rico. Let's look decidedly at the difficult but certainly not impossible goal of a great civilization for our country. Let's strengthen our main institutions so that we can face better our future and in this way contribute, although modestly, to the happiness and well-being of others. If we achieve this we will have reached our purpose.[3]

For Muñoz Marín sports alone do not alleviate the ills of a developing country. Yet sports embody the progress of a nation that statesmen, political leaders, and the citizenry strive for. To some extent, athletic competition can be compared to society's development. The sweat and pain an athlete endures in the quest for victory mimics the hardship people bear in their daily work in search of a better life. At the national level, development is tested by hosting international mega-events, such as the Central American and Caribbean Games. Muñoz Marín was aware of this, and that is why he expressed his desire to increase Puerto Rico's local sport infrastructure and international participation. He was fully aware that success in staging regional Olympic Games was only half of the equation, the other half being a healthy and successful sport infrastructure. After twenty-five years of sport expansion led by Monagas, Muñoz Marín was proud to say that Puerto Ricans had been "determined, patient, and honest" in their quest.

However, he did acknowledge that "regardless of the problems they faced" they managed to host, if not better, at least comparable games in the region. This is the modernization that a Caribbean island strove for in the mid-twentieth century. Compared to models in the North Atlantic, Puerto Rico was being "honest" with itself in admitting that modernization was a long shot, or at least an uphill climb. Ultimately sport modernization was not necessarily about winning at any cost. The idea was to have a healthy sport and recreational culture while leaving behind the miserable conditions in which Puerto Ricans had lived for centuries. Playing in international competition gave Puerto Ricans a chance to partake in international politics. International athletics gives a developing country an opportunity to showcase its national strength and diplomatic capabilities and, in doing so, prove its relevance. For a decolonizing territory like the Commonwealth of Puerto Rico, this was most important. To some extent, the problems that Puerto Ricans faced in their process of modernization were similar to those of other places in the Caribbean, Latin America, and elsewhere in the developing world.

In 1967, after fifteen years of being a commonwealth and of Operation Bootstrap, Puerto Ricans still battled high unemployment. The once booming manufacturing sector began a sharp decline, poverty still dominated the lives of more than half the population, and political uncertainty permeated all facets of life. The commonwealth formula was still attacked by pro-independence groups, the rising *estadista* party Partido Nuevo Progresista (New Progressive Party, PNP),[4] and even communist Cuba as part of a larger cold war rivalry and an increasing regional rivalry. Locally, while the independence movement declined after the 1950s as a result of systematic repression and the social justice discourse of the PPD,[5] the Estadista movement began a steady growth, owing also to internal divisions within the PPD. In 1968 Luis A. Ferré, candidate for the PNP, won the governorship in the general elections. He had founded the party after branching off from the Partido Estadista Republicano of the old sugar barons. Muñoz Marín was right in saying there were problems within the party and the country, but little did he know that PPD hegemony would now have to fight for control against the Estadista movement.

Taking advantage of the continuing colonial paradigm of the commonwealth, the Estadista movement managed to hold a status plebiscite on July 23, 1967, with the options of U.S. statehood, independence, or commonwealth. Although the commonwealth option won with a comfortable margin (60.4 percent, statehood 39.0 percent, independence 4.3 percent),[6] it was evident that becoming a commonwealth had not solved the problem of the island's political status. In 1952, although a segment of the population abstained from voting, the referendum on Law 600 that paved the way for the establishment of the commonwealth won with 76 percent of the electorate. By 1967 many Puerto Ricans were aware of the shortcomings of the PPD and commonwealth status and expressed their displeasure at the ballot box.

The main problem with commonwealth status, according to the Estadista movement, was Puerto Rico's lack of full parity with the benefits—political and economic—of U.S. citizenship vis-à-vis citizens in any other U.S. state. Another clear limit was the lack of sovereignty over international diplomacy, as seen with the problems of the Cuban visas in the X CACG. Interestingly the next time a plebi-

scite on Puerto Rico's political status was held, in 1993, again organized by the PNP, the *estadistas* had just won the general elections,
which coincided with Puerto Rico's second CACG, this time in the
city of Ponce.

No matter their political or sport status, Puerto Ricans are, according to Muñoz Marín, a people on the march and on their way to better things. Like a tireless statesman, Muñoz Marín did not surrender
to criticism and upheld the PPD's strength and mission. He skillfully
used the Olympic motto "Higher, Farther, Stronger" to claim that
the PPD's program still had a purpose. And, like his predecessors in
the 1930s, he was aware that international participation was a good
way to make Puerto Rico visible in other places, to increase tourism, and to continue attracting foreign investment. The Puerto Rican
autonomist movement appeared to have finally carved a significant
niche and consolidated itself within the island's political, social, and
cultural imaginaries.

Behind Muñoz Marín's call for better local facilities was the desire
for the socioeconomic and political benefits of sport for the country.
Regardless of the fact that the PPD and the commonwealth had been
criticized for their political status, their local sport and recreational
programs had definitely left a positive mark on the people. Building better facilities for the masses was a successful social justice and
populist agenda that helped the PPD keep its hegemonic control for
more than a quarter century. New and better sporting facilities also
showed Puerto Rican athletic maturity and recreational culture to
tourists arriving for the X CACG, and a good athletic showing sent
a positive message of U.S.-sponsored athletic modernization. As a
showcase of democracy and capitalism, Puerto Rico contributed
to the U.S. side in the cold war. More broadly, just as Puerto Rican
industrialization by invitation was a model for the developing world,
sport modernization, though modest, was a contribution to other
parts of the world.

To some extent Puerto Rican sport leaders influenced world

Olympism. In addition to all of his local recognitions and awards, Monagas was awarded the Olympic Order (silver), the highest award conferred by the IOC, on April 5, 1984. Ironically, early in his career Monagas did not see international competition as a priority in Puerto Rican sport development. However, his view changed, and he embraced Puerto Rican Olympic participation and became a leader in hemispheric Olympism. In doing so he contributed significantly to Pan-American Olympism and to Puerto Rican national identity.

The Olympic participation of Puerto Rico as an unincorporated territory of the United States should not be considered a contradiction within Olympism or U.S. politics. Puerto Ricans utilized colonial loopholes to gain access to international competition. An invitation from a U.S. ambassador to participate at the 1930 CACG in Havana was accepted and applauded by locals and became the springboard for continuing participation. The rise of nationalism and debates of national identity fueled the idea of a Puerto Rican—not a U.S.—delegation at these regional games. Equally important, the IOC's need to legitimate its movement and to increase the participation of other countries, territories, and colonies provided the opportunity and platform for performing the nation. The populist politics of the 1930s, the disapproval of imperialism after World War II, and a vested interest in winning the cold war were reasons enough for the United States to allow Puerto Ricans their own national delegation and engage in athletic diplomacy. Monagas negotiated all of these political pressures in Puerto Rico, at the U.S. and Latin American levels and with the IOC. He solidified the commonwealth and its ties with the United States while insisting that Puerto Rico become an international presence. He showcased and strengthened Puerto Rico's national identity while en route to political autonomy and cultural sovereignty.

Monagas certainly left a distinctive mark on Anglo and Latin American Olympism. The April 1984 Olympic Order medal ceremony was held in a joint session of the legislature in the Puerto

Rican Capitol, with a speech by IOC president Juan Antonio Sama-ranch.[7] Monagas was only the second person in the Americas to receive the award, the first being Peter Ueberroth (gold) from the United States. To the sorrow of many, the Father of Puerto Rican Olympism died only three months later, on July 14.

Four other Puerto Ricans have received the honor of the Olym-pic Order medal from the IOC. In 1989 Rafael Hernández Colón, a prominent member of the PPD and governor of Puerto Rico in 1972–76 and 1984–92, received the Olympic Order medal. Germán Rieck-ehoff Sampayo, a nationalist turned *popular* who was vital in the resolution of the Cuban visa problem in the 1966 CACG, received the Olympic Order medal in 1990 and the Olympic Centenary award in 1994. Also in 1994 Eugenio Guerra, another close collaborator with the PPD, received the IOC honor, as did Genaro "Tuto" Marchand, another prominent figure in the defense of Puerto Rican Olympic sovereignty, in 2007. Among other local and international positions of leadership, Marchand was president of the Federación Interna-cional de Baloncesto and a member of the Executive Committee of COPR. Rieckehoff Sampayo, probably the second most influen-tial sport leader in Puerto Rican history, never truly abandoned his nationalist leanings. He continued his involvement with sport, serving as president of COPR from 1977 to 1990 and presiding over CACSO from 1978 to 1985. He was made an IOC member in 1977 and became a lifetime IOC member in 1990.

Eugenio "Trinitario" Guerra is distinct among Puerto Rican IOC Olympic Order recipients, as he was the only athlete and physical educator. Guerra was an eight-time Olympian, and as such became a national hero. After his athletic years he helped organize local sport activities well into his eighties. He was an enduring star in both local and Olympic sport, connecting the importance of physical education and the modernization of sport. As a teacher he educated a new gen-eration of athletes and physically minded citizens. As a promoter of sports he constantly advocated for more and better athletic facilities, not just for Olympic athletes but for all citizens. In 1994, Guerra fell gravely ill, and the Olympic Order award ceremony was held in the Auxilio Mutuo Hospital of San Juan, with Olympic leaders, family, and friends in attendance.[8]

Guerra died five days later, a sport hero with a new nickname, "El Eterno Guerrero" (the Eternal Warrior). Before he died he asked to have his ashes scattered on the "battlegrounds" that had made him a hero decades earlier: the tracks of the College of Agriculture and Mechanic Arts in Mayagüez, the Paquito Montaner Stadium in Ponce, the Sixto Escobar Stadium in San Juan, and the University of Puerto Rico in Río Piedras.

Guerra's ashes were received with the pomp of a national hero.[9] On its way to the university's Main Tower, Guerra's caravan entered through the front gate, which was lined with athletes. The university's interim president, the chancellor, deans, and children from local schools received his remains. After a presidential honorary salute to Guerra's son, Gino Guerra, the cortège proceeded to the tracks, where an honor guard of fellow athletes awaited. The president gave a speech, and the ashes were scattered. A starting pistol signaled children to scatter flower petals along the track. The ceremony ended with another athlete-led procession, followed by family and friends, distinguished guests, colleagues, and the public to the exit gate.

Olympic Whistles and Boos: The Inheritance of 1966 and the Consolidation of Colonial Olympism

This book ends with the events and problems of the X CACG for a reason. The award ceremony for Monagas on April 29, 1967, marks the consolidation of the sport modernization process. By 1966 the Puerto Rican institutions of sport had endured a series of changes and challenges, conflicts and reorganizations, which managed to solidify a culture of sport as well as a culture of Olympism. From this moment on, Puerto Rican sport followed parameters established in the early twentieth century. The formation of Puerto Rican sport institutions, the politics of their leaders, and the popularity of sport are by no means unique and actually resemble similar processes in other countries. But Puerto Rico stands out in one particular characteristic: the politics of enduring colonialism.

After beginning with an ill-equipped, nineteenth-century Spanish sport culture, Puerto Rican leadership and institutions of sport would become increasingly organized thanks to the work of the U.S. Army and Navy YMCA (1899), the development of sports at the University of Puerto Rico (1903), the creation of the Commission of Sport (1927), and the introduction of physical education in schools. As a result, and parallel to these processes, sport became increasingly popular. By 1966 sport institutions were an integral part of the executive branch of government. After 1966 the Public Parks and Recreation Administration (today's Departamento de Recreación y Deportes) had the task of setting the parameters, purpose, and meaning of sport and recreation as a constitutional right to safeguard a healthy citizenry. The Parks Commission, formed in 1917 to maintain the Luis Muñoz Rivera Park in San Juan, in 1961 became the Compañía de Fomento Recreativo de Puerto Rico (today the Compañía de Parques Nacionales de Puerto Rico), in charge of maintaining parks and athletic fields and building and expanding sport and recreational infrastructure. These reorganizations were done in response to Monagas's pressure and his vision of a Puerto Rican athletic and recreational culture.

These institutions fed Puerto Rico's Olympic movement. From initial attempts in 1933 to establish a Comité Olímpico de Puerto Rico, Olympism in Puerto Rico was stabilized by 1966. There was no longer doubt over the existence of a Puerto Rican national Olympic delegation, despite continuing problems over colonialism. Regardless of his early doubts about international competition, Monagas was paramount in the island's Olympic presence by managing to secure participation at the 1948 Olympics in London and continually sending delegations to all the Olympic Games in the 1950s and 1960s. From 1966 on, Puerto Rico was a legitimate member of the international Olympic community, on and off the field.

Similar to other countries, Puerto Ricans fully and effectively engaged in Olympic international diplomacy such as the Good Neighbor policy, the international decolonization movement, and the cold war. Puerto Rico's role as a piece of U.S. diplomacy in the Americas was envisioned by the PPD and proponents of autonomy under the commonwealth and also by the Estadista leadership in their ideal of an "annexed independent" state of the Union.[10] Seeing Puerto Rico as a culturally independent U.S. state allows many *estadistas* to reconcile Puerto Rican Olympism and U.S. statehood.

Monagas's success in leading Puerto Rican Olympic delegations to international participation resulted in the consolidation of national identity. After 1966 there was no question of Puerto Rico's nationhood, if only in matters of sport. If Puerto Rico's participation at the CACG in the 1930s was the dubious performance of a U.S. territory or colony, then its participation in the Olympic Games since 1948 and Pan-American Games after 1955 was the exhibition of a nation. Monagas was fully aware of Olympic nationalistic and political implications, but he gradually pursued more Olympic participation because it became a vital part of the commonwealth's legitimacy. Hosting the 1966 CACG in San Juan was the best way to exhibit the uniqueness, traditions, and culture of the Puerto Rican nation.

Consolidation of sport and recreational culture did not come free of problems and setbacks. Even though there were more athletic fields, stadiums, courts, playgrounds, and recreational areas in the 1940s and 1950s, there were not enough to host the CACG in 1966. The limitations were visible when compared to other places with better facilities. Only the comparison to the low-key 1962 games in Jamaica helped persuade Monagas to host the 1966 games in San Juan. For all the achievements in athletic infrastructure and all the accomplishments of the governing PPD, there was awareness that modernization was full of shortcomings.

By hosting the 1966 games, Puerto Ricans showcased the vitality of their nation, but what was this nation that sport was helping to create? Puerto Ricans demonstrated that they could host mega-sporting events but, in light of the problems with the Cuban visas, also demonstrated that Olympic sovereignty does not equal political sovereignty. Although willing to fight, Puerto Ricans were ultimately at the mercy of the U.S. State Department and IOC. It did not matter that the Puerto Rican government was opposed to granting visas to the Cuban athletes because the final decision was made in Washington DC and Lausanne, well beyond Puerto Rico's national borders. This lack of state political agency in international sporting affairs is precisely one of the consequences of sport development in this Caribbean island, and it is what makes Puerto Rico unique in the Latin American experience. This is because the Olympic movement in Puerto Rico revolved around the particular context of a colonial society. Colonial Olympism had been present since Puerto Rico's first appearance at the Central American and Caribbean Games in 1930 and still lingers today. Despite the political leadership that claims to have decolonized the island in 1952, colonial Olympism is still apparent and alive.

Nonetheless problems of colonialism should not cloud Puerto Rican agency in matters of sport and Olympism. Puerto Ricans actively challenge colonialism and uphold their national identity by attending Olympic tournaments and displaying their national flag. Though Monagas and Fred Guillermety were fierce rivals during the mid-1950s, they had one goal in common: to make Puerto Rico a visible and legitimate member of the Olympics, which granted a degree of sovereignty and legitimized an autonomy-driven political movement. Different shades and intensities of national pride helped create, maintain, and consolidate Puerto Rican Olympism. After all the problems of colonialism, Puerto Ricans found and fought for a stage on which to display the nation. Every time Puerto Ricans participate in an international sporting event that allows them to wave their flag and play their national anthem, they are challenging colonialism. It just so happens that each time they partake in these sporting events as both a nation and a colony, they uphold the same structures that allow colonialism and nationalism to happen in the first place.

Puerto Ricans were not alone in challenging the colonialism that denied an Olympic national persona. First, Avery Brundage and the IOC, regardless of their post–World War II Olympic-political interests, became the premier sponsors of a Puerto Rican Olympic nationality. Brundage continually helped Puerto Ricans participate at regional and worldwide Olympic events as their own nation, often going against the mandates of his own country. No less important was the support from the Latin American community. As early as 1935 in El Salvador, Salvadorians joined Puerto Ricans in hoisting the Puerto Rican flag, and in the absence of a Puerto Rican national anthem they played their own. One Salvadorian journalist proclaimed, to the disgust of the U.S. Consulate in San Salvador, that they had witnessed the "birth of the Puerto Rican nation" at those games. Fifteen years later, in Guatemala at the 1950 CACG, the local band played "La Borinqueña" during the opening ceremonies instead of the programmed "Star-Spangled Banner" and protested the U.S. flag carried by the Puerto Rican delegation. A few months later a group of nationalists rebelled against the colonial government and declared the island the Republic of Puerto Rico. Sixteen years after that, sovereignty was supported by the Cuban delegation in the CACG of 1966 by demanding unrestricted and direct athletic diplomacy between Havana and San Juan. But regardless of these challenges to colonialism and regardless of the support for Puerto Rican sovereignty, power over the island's affairs remained outside territorial limits, either in the United States or the IOC.

Problems of colonial Olympism lingered after 1966, particularly during the second time Puerto Ricans, now under Rieckehoff Sampayo's leadership, hosted the 1979 Pan-American Games in San Juan. The same problems of the 1966 CACG were replayed, mainly battles over official state symbols: Puerto Rican versus U.S. flags and anthems. The press called the conflict the "war of the anthems and flags."[11]

During the 1979 Pan-American Games local administration was in the hands of the *estadista* PNP, so any statement of sport autonomy projecting Puerto Rican national sovereignty was frowned upon. Carlos Romero Barceló, mayor of San Juan between 1969 and 1976, helped to bring the Pan-American Games to San Juan. However, once he became governor in 1976, he changed Olympic protocol to fit Puerto Rico's political situation. After taking office in 1977, Romero Barceló ruled that the Puerto Rican flag could not be hoisted alone at the games but would be displayed alongside the U.S. flag, as stipulated in the Puerto Rican Constitution of 1952. He argued that both the Puerto Rican and U.S. flags and anthems be used in every ceremony, including every time a Puerto Rican won a medal.[12]

According to Romero Barceló, flying the Puerto Rican flag by itself constituted an illegal display of Puerto Rican symbols. However, Rieckehoff Sampayo, other Olympic officials, and the local sport community argued that, within the Olympic movement, Puerto Rico was a separate nation from the United States. Hoisting both flags together at the Pan-American Games was against Olympic rules. In Olympism, and especially at the Pan-American and Olympic Games, Puerto Rico and the United States are two separate nations. Reaction to Romero Barceló's claims led to discussions among athletes, sporting leaders, and civil society; the majority among these groups wanted the Puerto Rican flag flown alone at the games. Consequently a group of athletes, trainers, and other citizens created the Asociación de Atletas y Deportistas de Puerto Rico to confront Romero Barceló's mandate in island-wide talks, educational seminars, and even striking in front of the governor's mansion, La Fortaleza (see fig. 16).

Fig. 16. Miche Medina, cartoon of the war of the flags in Puerto Rican Olympism. Source: Carlos Uriarte González, *Puerto Rico en el Continente, 1951–2011: 60 años de los Juegos Panamericanos* (N.p.: Nomos Impresores, 2011), 121. Courtesy of Carlos Uriarte González.

Regardless of the popular unity and support for national Olympic sovereignty, Romero Barceló was adamant in using both Puerto Rican and U.S. symbols. He had arranged for the band to play both the Puerto Rican and the U.S. national anthems during the games' opening state ceremony. In a historic moment of popular preference for Puerto Rican sporting autonomy, the public loudly booed and whistled during the U.S. anthem and Romero Barceló's opening remarks. This event became known as "la Pitada Olímpica" (the Olympic Whistle).[13]

La Pitada Olímpica of 1979 evidenced, once again, that Puerto Ricans still live under the problems of a colonial relationship. It also demonstrated the *estadistas*' recognition that the Olympic tradition in Puerto Rico was powerful enough to constitute a major roadblock for eventual U.S. statehood. To this day debates over the possibility of U.S. statehood for Puerto Rico revolve around the COPR. On

November 6, 2012, Puerto Ricans voted on a local and controversial plebiscite on Puerto Rico's status, one that is still not recognized by the U.S. Congress. The plebiscite had two questions: "Do you agree to keep the current political territorial condition?" and "Which status option would you prefer, Statehood, Enhanced Commonwealth, or Independence?" To the first question, a slight majority of voters voted no (970,910; yes, 828,077; blank, 67,267; contested, 12,948); on the second question the status with most votes was statehood, with 61 percent. *Estadistas* celebrated Puerto Ricans' desire for U.S. statehood. However, Governor-elect Alejandro García Padilla, who had denounced the plebiscite for not following proper democratic procedure, had asked his constituents to vote yes to the first question and to leave blank the second.[14] Following this line of reasoning, adding the 498,604 blank ballots to the 454,768 votes for enhanced commonwealth would yield 953,372 votes. When compared to the 834,191 votes for statehood, *populares* claimed, Puerto Ricans had once again rejected U.S. statehood. (Independence received 74,895 votes, 5.49 percent.)[15] Once taking his seat as governor, García Padilla appointed David Bernier as his secretary of state. Bernier had served as COPR's president since 2008 and as secretary of the Department of Recreation and Sports since 2005. A Central American and Caribbean and Pan-American athlete, Bernier was part of the fencing team that won bronze at the 2003 Pan-American Games in Santo Domingo, Dominican Republic. In 2004 he was selected to be the flag bearer at the 2004 Olympic Games in Athens.

Among the different elements in the discussion over Puerto Rico's status are the Olympic Committee and beauty pageants. Although some *estadistas* affirm the possibility of keeping the Puerto Rican National Olympic Committee under U.S. statehood, the U.S. Congress passed the Ted Stevens Olympic and Amateur Sports Act (36 USC Sec. 220501) in 1998, which states that there can be only one NOC that represents the United States.[16] Genaro Marchand and Richard Carrión, both IOC members, have said that Puerto Rico would not keep its NOC under U.S. statehood.[17] Taking all arguments together, and due to the U.S. federal law that recognizes only one USOC, it seems highly unlikely that the United States would allow Puerto Ricans to keep their NOC in the case of statehood. The power and popularity of COPR for Puerto Ricans is noted by the *estadistas*, and rejecting the COPR under U.S. statehood does not seem to be a favorable political position.

The political battles of Puerto Rico's colonial Olympism continued into the 1980 Olympic Games, when COPR and Rieckehoff Sampayo made a historic stand-off against both the United States and Romero Barceló's administration. Those Games were held in Moscow and became an example of worldwide cold war politics when the United States led an international boycott in response to the Soviet Union's invasion of Afghanistan. This boycott should not be taken lightly, since it marked a test of East versus West alliances that threatened not only the legitimacy of the Olympic Games but also international relations. Romero Barceló's government also supported the Olympic boycott, but Rieckehoff Sampayo, citing COPR's Olympic sovereignty, declared that Puerto Rico would participate.

In response to Rieckehoff Sampayo's decision, Romero Barceló withdrew all government support from COPR. However, after an ardent defense of sport sovereignty before both the U.S. and Puerto Rican governments, Rieckehoff Sampayo's COPR managed to send a small delegation of three athletes and two delegates to Moscow. As part of the intense negotiations, Rieckehoff Sampayo managed to get official, full, and undisputed recognition of COPR's sovereignty from the U.S. State Department.[18] At the opening ceremony in Moscow, leaders of COPR debated whether or not to parade with the Puerto Rican flag and assert their sport sovereignty and national identity; they chose instead to parade with the Olympic flag.[19] Puerto Ricans were not alone in the decision to hide their national flag. Other nations did the same, and some nations did not even participate in the opening procession.[20] Nevertheless, by attending the Moscow

Games, Rieckehoff Sampayo's COPR had reasserted Puerto Ricans' sport autonomy and their right to belong to the international Olympic movement. This political and nationalistic message was forceful and visible and helped bring attention to Puerto Rico's colonial situation. Once again sport sovereignty did not equate to political sovereignty.

Puerto Rico has hosted two major Olympic tournaments since then. The cities of Ponce and Mayagüez hosted the CACG of 1993 and 2010, respectively. On both occasions the government was Estadista after a long PPD rule, and on both occasions there were political problems characteristic of all Olympic tournaments of the late twentieth and early twenty-first centuries.[21] However, just as Puerto Rico is a unique place in Latin America, these games had conflicts specific to the island. The 1993 games in Ponce coincided with celebrations of the five-hundred-year anniversary of Christopher Columbus's landing in Puerto Rico, giving it an expanded air of Hispanic and Spanish American cultural identity. Still, with another Estadista governor in power, Pedro Roselló, the games became a political battle for local authority and the definition of sovereignty. Political battles ensued after a push to relocate some events to San Juan, a cut in central government funding, and, a few days prior to the opening ceremony, the staging of another plebiscite to yet again determine the island's political status.[22]

The results of these political clashes were a victory for the PPD's Rafael Cordero, mayor of Ponce (1988–2004), who managed to keep all events close to the Ponce region; a plebiscite victory for the commonwealth (albeit by a narrower margin than in 1967);[23] and another popular expression of disapproval when Governor Roselló was booed during the opening ceremony. Unlike in 1966, the Cuban delegation attended the games without visa restrictions in a direct flight from Havana to San Juan.[24] The Cubans attended with a record number of 786 in their delegation, of whom 565 were athletes. Puerto Rico had its largest delegation ever, with 741 persons, of whom 544 were athletes.

After the 1993 games were over and the Estadistas' loss in the status plebiscite, Roselló did not quell his U.S. statehood desires. In November 1995 he made an infamous public statement affirming that Puerto Rico "is not and has never been a nation." A large segment of the civil society and political parties—including the Congreso Nacional Hostosiano, Nuevo Movimiento Independentista, the autonomist wing of the PPD, and even some *estadistas*—were outraged. In response a multiparty, multisector coalition organized a public demonstration, called La Nación en Marcha, to refute Roselló's statement and declare that Puerto Rico *is* a nation. The march was held on July 14, 1996, in Fajardo. According to some estimates, it drew more than two hundred thousand people.[25]

The 2010 CACG in Mayagüez were also organized and executed under much political controversy. In preparation, the city undertook a series of infrastructural projects, not without doubts of their success. Old structures were demolished, and new parks and buildings were created to show the wonders and progress of the west coast. Once again the PNP was in power, after an eight-year PPD government. José Guillermo Rodríguez, in his fifth term as Mayagüez's mayor, was a major figure within the PPD. Governor Luis Fortuño, from the PNP and a member of the U.S. Republican Party, began his tenure in 2009 after winning the 2008 elections by the largest margin of votes in Puerto Rican history. The political controversies revolved around Fortuño's neoliberal reforms that included government layoffs of thirty thousand workers, plus visa restrictions to the Cuban delegation due to the 1996 Helms-Burton U.S. law. In reaction to the latter, the Cuban delegation decided not to attend the games, claiming that Cuba's participation was a "right," and they must not receive "special treatment."[26] As in 1966, they recognized Puerto Rico's sovereignty and wished to have politico-cultural relations directly between Havana and San Juan.

Much anticipation surrounded the opening ceremonies in Mayagüez. The city, and all of Puerto Rico, hoped to stage a show worthy of admiration by their Latin American brothers and sisters. The stakes were high, as these games were proof of Puerto Rico's twenty-first century progress and the nation's vitality. Fortuño, aware of the booing episodes for the two previous Estadista governors, had nonetheless planned a full speech to open the games. The president of CACSO at the time, the Puerto Rican Héctor Cardona, delivered his long speech as expected. When he finished, in what appeared to be a sudden change in plans, Fortuño stood up from his chair and, without delivering his speech, declared the twenty-first CACG open.

Fortuño thus did not give the spectators time to boo. However, among the cheers (and vuvuzelas) were also a few "hundred spectators booing the mandatary."[27] A group of Puerto Rican athletes demonstrated their political agency and discontent with Fortuño when they walked to the field and displayed a large banner that read "Red Card for the Puerto Rican Government." Though the athletes later declared that their act was "alluding to non-sport issues," they did use the Olympic stage to present their political sentiments.[28]

The athletes' protest speaks of two central issues in Olympism: the politics at Olympic events and national identity. Hoisting a Puerto Rican flag to protest Puerto Rico's government at an international event taking place in Puerto Rico sent several messages. It protested neoliberal policies and asserted nationhood against a colonial government that sees Puerto Ricans as "U.S. citizens residing in Puerto Rico." It protested Fortuño's government and asserted that Puerto Rico is a Latin American and Caribbean nation. The name *Puerto Rico* on the athletes' banner was the color of the blue sky, the same color as the triangle in the flag used presently by *independentistas*, who claim it was the original design of the Puerto Rican anti-Spanish and republican flag of 1895.

The events at the Olympic, Pan-American, and Central American and Caribbean Games after 1966 are exactly what sport and Olympism has meant for Puerto Ricans throughout the twentieth century and into the twenty-first. Sport has been a site of contested politics, popular agency, political autonomy, colonialism, progress, national identity, and international belonging. The leaders of institutions of sport and recreation since their initial stages in the 1920s saw their purpose as delineating the parameters of a developed and healthy society. Particular to Puerto Ricans was that this desire and the guidelines for progress were, and still are, carried out under U.S. colonialism with a certain degree of autonomy. As the athletes' banner at the 2010 games (or 1979 or 1993) illustrates, colonialism was not always directed unilaterally from the United States, for Puerto Ricans themselves have had a direct role in it.

This political relation has not worked against Puerto Rican claim to a sense of nationhood, at least culturally. From the early decades of the twentieth century Puerto Ricans have understood that sport is a cultural activity, that it contains values of progress and modernity, and that certain games are sponsored by the IOC. The IOC's definition of Olympism upholds the value and desirability of nationhood. That is, to be modern is to have a healthy and vibrant sport culture, but also to participate in and belong to the Olympic cycle as a nation. Puerto Ricans took this call seriously as part of their own search for nationhood. Along the way they achieved membership in the international Olympic movement and also became involved in and at times led international diplomacy during conflicts.

Ultimately the politics and culture of sport in Puerto Rico help us to understand the significance of the 2004 basketball game between Puerto Rico and the United States in Athens as described in the introduction. As this book conveys, Puerto Ricans have a particular reason to exist as a nation at the Olympic Games, and playing against the United States at the Olympics has a special meaning. Their basketball victory in 2004, which, more than anything else, illustrates a long list of small but transcendental twentieth-century Olympic achievements, sent a message few outside Puerto Rico have comprehended, except those who have experienced and endured the variants of political subjugation and cultural survival: a twenty-first-century colonial nation can dramatically beat its colonial masters at their own game.

The Puerto Rican national basketball team did not win a medal at the Olympic Games in Athens; they finished in sixth place overall. Nonetheless this small and peripheral colonial nation won something else, a different battle, which for many is the most important of all: world exposure and a national existence.

Notes

Introduction

1. USA Men's National Team, USA Basketball, http://archive.usab.com/mens/national/history.html (accessed November 21, 2014); Associated Press, "U.S.: 3-for-24 from 3-Point Range," ESPN Olympic sports, August 17, 2004, http://sports.espn.go.com/oly/summer04/basketball/news/story?id=1859825 (accessed August 18, 2014).
2. For an analysis of the U.S.-Soviet basketball rivalry during these decades, see Witherspoon, "'Fuzz Kinds' and 'Musclemen.'"
3. Associated Press, "U.S.: 3-for-24 from 3-Point Range."
4. Wojnarowski, "No Longer America's Sport"; Caple, "Those Absent Share the Blame."
5. Ramsay, "The World Is in the Zone."
6. Ramsay, "The World Is in the Zone"; Wojnarowski, "No Longer America's Sport."
7. MacAloon, *This Great Symbol*, 138–44.
8. Moraña et al., *Coloniality at Large*.
9. Here I make direct reference to Anderson's classic work, *Imagined Communities*. However, Lomnitz argues in "Nationalism as a Practical System" that Spanish American national identity has been a process in the making for over five hundred years and that this identity comes from heterogeneous populations creating meaning through "bonds of dependence." I agree with a group of scholars who have criticized Anderson for not providing enough concrete historical proof for his claims of the construction and spread of the idea of the nation. With a profound and documented study of the institutions and individuals who actively aided in the construction of the idea of a Puerto Rican nation we can arrive at the conclusion of an imagined, better yet, performed Puerto Rican nation. See Castro-Klarén and Chasteen, *Beyond Imagined Communities*.
10. See Gellner, *Nations and Nationalism*; Hobsbawm and Ranger, *The Invention of Tradition*; Hobsbawm, *Nations and Nationalism since 1780*.
11. Arbena, "Sport and the Promotion of Nationalism in Latin America";

Lever, *Soccer Madness*; Kittleson, *The Country of Football*; Ruiz Patiño, *La política del sport*.

12. Villena Fieno, "Fútbol, *mass media* y nación en la era global."
13. Hobsbawm, *Nations and Nationalism since 1780*, 143.
14. Galeano, *Soccer in Sun and Shadow*, 45.
15. Chatterjee, *The Nation and Its Fragments*, 5–6.
16. Hutchinson, "Cultural Nationalism and Moral Regeneration."
17. Duany, *The Puerto Rican Nation on the Move*; Carrión, *Voluntad de nación*; Sotomayor, "Patron Saint Festivities, Politics, and Culture."
18. López Rojas, *El debate por la nación*, 14, 81.
19. Guerra, *Popular Expression and National Identity in Puerto Rico*; Scarano, "The *Jíbaro* Masquerade and the Subaltern Politics of Creole Identity Formation in Puerto Rico"; Torres, "La gran familia puertorriqueña 'Ej prieta de beldá.'"
20. Benítez Rojo, *La isla que se repite*.
21. Huertas González, *Deporte e identidad*.
22. Carpentier and Lefèvre, "The Modern Olympic Movement, Women's Sport and the Social Order during the Inter-war Period."
23. Dyreson, "Prolegomena to Jesse Owens."
24. United Nations, Department of Public Information, News and Media Division, "Special Committee on Decolonization Approves Text Calling upon United States to Initiate Self-Determination Process for Puerto Rico."
25. For a detailed study of Puerto Rican autonomists, see Negrón-Portillo, *El autonomismo puertorriqueño, su transformación ideológica (1895–1914)*.
26. Cabán, *Constructing a Colonial People*, 51–65.
27. ¿Desaparece la camiseta boricua de las Olimpiadas bajo la estadidad?," *Primera Hora*, August 8, 2012, http://www.primerahora.com/noticias/gobierno-politica/nota/desaparecelacamisetaboricuadelasolimpiadas bajolaestadidad-680594/ (accessed October 29, 2013); "Richard Carrión aclara sus expresiones sobre el Copur y la estadidad," *Primera Hora*, November 29, 2011, http://www.primerahora.com/noticias/gobierno-politica/nota/richardcarrionaclarasusexpresionessobreelcopurylaestadidad-585044/ (accessed October 29, 2013).
28. Albizu Campos, *República de Puerto Rico*; Torres, *Pedro Albizu Campos*, vols. 1–3.
29. Silén, *Pedro Albizu Campos*; Prieto, *Albizu Campos y el independentismo puertorriqueño*; Carrión et al., *La nación puertorriqueña*; Power, "Nationalism in a Colonized Nation: The Nationalist Party and Puerto Rico."
30. José Santori Coll, personal interview, September 22, 2014.

31. Torres, *Pedro Albizu Campos*, 3:15.

32. Power, "The Puerto Rican Nationalist Party, Transnational Latin American Solidarity, and the United States during the Cold War," 25–26.

33. Coubertin, "Athletic Colonization" and "Athletic Unification" in *Olympism*, 703, 697.

34. Elias, *The Empire Strikes Out*, 42, 109–10.

35. Gems, *The Athletic Crusade*, 1–16.

36. Torres, "Peronism, International Sport, and Diplomacy," 175.

37. For the legal basis and analysis of the legal and constitutional parameters of the colonial relationship between Puerto Rico and the United States, see Thomas, "A Constitution Led by the Flag"; Rivera Ramos, "Deconstructing Colonialism"; Trías Monge, "Injustice According to Law"; Johnson, "Anti-Imperialism and the Good Neighbor Policy"; Bolívar Fresnada, *Guerra, [Banca] y Desarrollo*; Unger, "Industrialization vs. Agrarian Reform"; Ince, "Nationalism and Cold War Politics at the Pan American Games"; Sheinin, "The Caribbean and the Cold War."

38. For an analysis of Puerto Rico's position as an example to the developing world during the 1940s and 1950s, see Rivera Batiz and Santiago, *Island Paradox*.

39. See Wells, *The Modernization of Puerto Rico*, 200–202.

40. Pantojas-García calls Operation Bootstrap a "capital-importation/export-processing" strategy (*Development Strategies as Ideology*, 61). For a brief account of Benítez's role in PPD politics and his vision of a Puerto Rican "universal culture" rather than a "national culture," see Ayala and Bernabe, *Puerto Rico in the American Century*, 203. On Ricardo Alegría, see Duany, *The Puerto Rican Nation on the Move*; Dávila, *Sponsored Identities*. On Roberto Sánchez Vilella, see Wells, *The Modernization of Puerto Rico*, 380. On Antonio Fernós Isern, see Trías Monge, *Puerto Rico*.

41. Villaronga, "Constructing Muñocismo."

42. Dietz, *Puerto Rico*.

43. Beezley and Curcio-Nagy, *Latin American Popular Culture*, 1–6.

44. Chakravarty, "The Muddle of Modernity."

45. For an explanation of Puerto Rico's place in Latin American nationalism, see Maldonado Denis, "Prospects for Latin American Nationalism."

46. Benítez Rojo, *The Repeating Island*, particularly the introduction and part 1, "Society."

47. Knight, *The Caribbean*.

48. Morse, "The Caribbean."

49. Palmié and Scarano, introduction.

50. For example, politically both the U.S. and the British Virgin Islands have colonial relations with their respective metropoles, but this has not denied them their own constructions of national identity. See Cohen, "'This Is de Test,'" 200.

51. Bass, "State of the Field," 150.

52. Johns, "Introduction," 3.

53. Here I refer to the performative characteristic of sport represented in the human body. See Blake, *The Body Language*. For Eduardo Galeano, play in Latin America "has become spectacle, with few protagonists and many spectators" (*Soccer in Sun and Shadow*, 2).

54. For a general survey of sport as culture and as a product of the modern world, see Mandell, *Sport*. For a collection of essays dealing with the politics and culture of sport in Latin America, see Arbena and LaFrance, *Sport in Latin America and the Caribbean*; Mangan and DaCosta, *Sport in Latin American Society*.

55. Puig Barata, "Emociones en el deporte y Sociología."

56. Guttmann, *From Ritual to Record*; Hargreaves, *Sport, Power, and Culture*; MacAloon, *This Great Symbol*; Mangan, *The Games Ethic and Imperialism*.

57. See Guttmann, *From Ritual to Record*.

58. Coubertin, *Olympism*.

59. Hargreaves, *Sport, Power, and Culture*.

60. Guttmann, "Capitalism, Protestantism, and the Rise of Modern Sport"; Pope, "An Army of Athletes."

61. Mrozek, *Sport and the American Mentality*.

62. Blake, *The Body Language*, 20, 49.

63. See Keys, *Globalizing Sport*; Tomlinson and Young, *National Identity and Global Sports*, 1.

64. Dichter and Johns, *Diplomatic Games*.

65. Wagg and Andrews, *East Plays West*, 2.

66. Krüger, "The Unfinished Symphony," 13.

67. See Dubois, *Soccer Empire*, chapter 2, "Caribbean France," 47–72.

68. Hargreaves, *Freedom for Catalonia?*

69. Krüger, "The Unfinished Symphony," 9, 19.

70. James, *Beyond a Boundary*. For more recent scholarship on sport in Latin America, see, for example, Arbena, *Latin American Sport*; Arbena, and LaFrance, *Sport in Latin America and the Caribbean*; Mangan and DaCosta, *Sport in Latin American Society*; Alabarces, *Peligro de Gol*; Alabarces, *Futbologías*; Lever, *Soccer Madness*. For more recent work on soccer, see Elsey, *Citizens and Sportsmen*; Dubois, *Soccer Empire*; Ribeiro,

"Futebol, sentimento e política" (an entire journal issue on soccer in Brazil); Wood, "Sport and Latin American Studies."

71. Arbena, *Sport and Society in Latin America*; Guttmann, *From Ritual to Record*; Guttmann, "Our Former Colonial Masters."

72. Guttmann, *Games and Empires*, 2–3. Here Guttmann applies his seven-point outline of sport in their relation to imperial interests of Europe and the United States toward other parts of the world. The original work that addresses his seven-point outline of modern sport can be found in Guttmann, *From Ritual to Record*.

73. Mangan, "Prologue," 1.

74. Arbena, "Sport and the Promotion of Nationalism in Latin America," 3–4.

75. See Pérez, "Between Baseball and Bullfighting."

76. Pérez, *On Becoming Cuban*, 256.

77. Huyke, *Los deportes en Puerto Rico*; Varas, *La verdadera historia de los deportes puertorriqueños*; De la Roda, *Puerto Rico en los Juegos Centroamericanos*; Torres, *Historia de las Justas*; Colón Delgado et al., *50 años de historia deportiva puertorriqueña*; Fonseca Barahona, *Puerto Rico*; Stewart, *El baloncesto en San Germán*; Álvarez and Lorenti, *Fútbol puertorriqueño*; Uriarte González, *80 años de acción y pasión*; Uriarte González, *Puerto Rico en el Continente*; Uriarte González, *De Londres a Londres*.

78. For example, Van Hyning, *Puerto Rico's Winter League*; Van Hyning, *The Santurce Crabbers*; Colón Delgado, *Santurce Cangrejeros*; Maraniss, *Clemente*; Iber et al., *Latinos in U.S. Sports*; Regalado, *Viva Baseball*.

79. See Pike, *Hispanismo*; Ferrao, "Nacionalismo, hispanismo y élite intelectual en el Puerto Rico de los años treinta"; Pérez Montfort, *Hispanismo y Falange*.

80. Pedreira, *Insularismo*, 104, 192.

81. Negrón-Muntaner, "Showing Face," 98.

82. Here I am following the example of *Before the Eyes of the World*, Kevin Witherspoon's study of the 1968 Olympic Games in Mexico City and the real political significance for Mexico not only domestically but, most important, at the international level.

83. MacAloon, "La pitada Olímpica," 315.

1. Sport in Imperial Exchanges

1. Quoted in López Cantos, *Fiestas y juegos en Puerto Rico*, 280.

2. For an analysis of blasphemous speech in colonial Mexico, see Villa-Flores, *Dangerous Speech*.

3. Guttmann, *Games and Empires*, 2–3. Here Guttmann applies his seven-

point outline of sport in relation to imperial interests of Europe and the United States toward other parts of the world. The original work that addresses his seven-point outline of modern sport is *From Ritual to Record*. See also this definition and its application to this book in the introduction.

4. For a comprehensive documented history of baseball in Puerto Rico, see Varas, *La verdadera historia del deporte puertorriqueño* (1984); Huyke, *Los Deportes en Puerto Rico*. For more academic or analytic works on baseball in Puerto Rico, see Van Hyning, *Puerto Rico's Winter League*; Rodríguez Juliá, *Peloteros*; Van Hyning, *The Santurce Crabbers*; Regalado, "Roberto Clemente."

5. The Reconquista (Reconquest) refers to the period, roughly from 722 to 1492, when the Christian inhabitants of the Iberian Peninsula fought to expel the invading Muslim forces from their territory. For an explanation of how the Reconquista affected the exploration, conquest, and colonization of the New World, see Chasteen, *Born in Blood and Fire*; Bakewell, *A History of Latin America*.

6. Quoted in López Cantos, *Fiestas y juegos en Puerto Rico*, 132.

7. "Subieron a caballo con diferentes trajes a holgarse y jugaron a cañas y toros y siempre de noche y de día" (quoted in López Cantos, *Fiestas y juegos en Puerto Rico*, 166). This medieval performance mainly occurred during monarchical achievements, births, or marriages probably on an island-wide spectrum, yet we do not have additional mentions of it after 1722. Similar knightly games were played in other parts of Spanish America, such as Villaclara, Cuba, in 1737 for the proclamation of the future King Charles III; in Cali, Colombia, in honor of Ferdinand VII; in Jalapa, Mexico, for Charles III; and in Nirgua, Venezuela, for Our Lady of Victory (168).

8. *El Ponceño*, August 7, 1852, 1, Personal Archive of Benjamín Lúgaro Torres, Ponce, Puerto Rico.

9. See Pedreira, *Un hombre del pueblo, José Celso Barbosa*, 100–106; Huyke, *Los deportes en Puerto Rico*, 194–98.

10. Mejía Garcés, *Estampas de San Germán y algo más*.

11. See Guttmann, *From Ritual to Record*, 57–89; Mangan, *The Games Ethic and Imperialism*, 44–69; Davies, *Sports in American Life*, 60–78.

12. See Sánchez Agustí, *La educación española a finales del XIX*, chapters 4 and 5.

13. López Fernández, "The Social, Political, and Economic Contexts to the Evolution of Spanish Physical Educationalists," 1639.

14. Beeman, "The Anthropology of Theater and Spectacle."

15. Osuna, *A History of Education in Puerto Rico*, 86.

16. Huyke, *Los deportes en Puerto Rico*, 79.

17. Huyke, *Los deportes en Puerto Rico*, 217; "Químicos y Gimnásticos," *El Fénix*, June 7, 1856, 2.

18. Although the Spanish-American War in Puerto Rico lasted around a month, the aftermath of the invasion included local bands of rebellious peasants revolting against all sorts of authority, be they Spanish or Puerto Rican landowners or U.S. armed forces. See Picó, *1898*.

19. Cuba had been fighting and winning a liberation war against Spain since 1895. The entry of the United States in the Cuban fight for independence was a move to protect U.S. interests when the Cubans finally achieved their freedom. See Pérez, *Cuba*. Puerto Rico was attacked and occupied in order to ensure that there would not be any Spanish influence in the Caribbean. See Trías Monge, *Puerto Rico*, 23–26.

20. See Cabán, *Constructing a Colonial People*, 118.

21. For a more developed analysis of this idea and its relationship with the Insular Cases, which "clarified" the colonial status of Puerto Rico under the infamous legal category "unincorporated territory," see Trías Monge, "Injustice According to Law"; Thomas, "A Constitution Led by the Flag."

22. See Trías Monge, *Puerto Rico*, 41–44.

23. Trías Monge, *Puerto Rico*, chapter 6, 67–76.

24. By making Puerto Ricans U.S. citizens the U.S. Congress made sure that they were inside the system, making them subject to U.S. rule yet not granting full protection due to Puerto Rico's being an unincorporated territory. The United States was seen as benevolent for recognizing Puerto Ricans as citizens, yet in practice this recognition was limited, making Puerto Ricans a sort of second-class citizen. See Rivera Ramos, *The Legal Construction of Identity*.

25. Quoted in Rivera Ramos, *The Legal Construction of Identity*, 52.

26. For a brief account of the general outlines of initial political parties and their ideologies, see Trías Monge, *Puerto Rico*, chapter 5.

27. See Dietz, *Economic History of Puerto Rico*, 82–84.

28. As the nineteenth century was coming to a close, Puerto Rican leaders had an admiration, almost a persistent determination for a modern way of life, with the United States being one of the role models. See Álvarez Curbelo and Castro, *Un país del porvenir*.

29. Wells, *The Modernization of Puerto Rico*, 88–89.

30. Negrón de Montilla, *Americanization in Puerto Rico and the Public-School System*; Barreto, *The Politics of Language in Puerto Rico*.

31. Osuna, *A History of Education in Puerto Rico*, 209.

32. Del Moral, "Colonial Citizens of a Modern Empire."

33. See, for example, Ruiz Patiño, *La política del sport*, 45; Neto-Wacker and Wacker, *Brazil Goes Olympic*, 68–70.

34. Álvarez and Lorenti, *Fútbol puertorriqueño*, 45–57, 90. In the public school system during the first two decades of U.S. rule, sports included baseball, basketball, and track and field. Soccer did not feature in the school's athletic teams. Osuna, *A History of Education in Puerto Rico*, 239–41.

35. Arbena and LaFrance, *Sport in Latin America and the Caribbean*.

36. Gems, *The Athletic Crusade*.

37. Varas, *La verdadera historia de los deportes puertorriqueños* (1985); Huyke, *Los deportes en Puerto Rico*; Álvarez and Lorenti, *Fútbol puertorriqueño*.

38. Wangerin, *Distant Corners*, 139–41.

39. Álvarez and Lorenti, *Fútbol puertorriqueño*, 89–90.

40. Álvarez and Lorenti, *Fútbol puertorriqueño*, 92.

41. Ramos Méndez, *Posesión del ayer*, 23–24; Meléndez, *Movimiento anexionista en Puerto Rico*, 18–20.

42. See Práxedes M. Sagasta, "Presidencia del Consejo de Ministros," *Gaceta de Madrid*, May 12, 1901. Thanks to Eduardo Colón for clarifying this point and sending the Spanish source.

43. The Young Women's Christian Association (YWCA) was founded in 1866, but the YMCA has expanded more widely.

44. Even though the YMCA was a Christian missionary organization it may have been responsible for the secularization of U.S. colleges. According to Setran in *The College "Y,"* this is because, being the center of religious life on campuses, its focus became too general for a unilateral Christian belief. That is, in order for the YMCA to fit into different Christian denominations, it had to loosen its "belief" core and focus on a Christian "way of life."

45. Hopkins, *History of the YMCA in North America*, chapter 8, particularly 347–50; Latourette, *World Service*, chapter 11, 201–44.

46. It should be noted that the YMCA had been establishing alliances with the U.S. Army and Navy since the Civil War in order to provide spiritual and physical recreation to the Northern troops. See Lancaster, *Serving the U.S. Armed Forces*.

47. Soldiers detached from their families and stationed in army camps or near battlefields were prone to the moral decadence that war produced. "Remove the safeguards, and add the idle hours of a waiting campaign, the discomforts of enforced camp life in a crowd, the disappointments of

inactive service, together with trying climatic and sanitary conditions, and large bodies of men are predisposed toward evil. Then it is that profanity, gambling, intemperance and impurity flourish. One great curse of some of the camps last summer was the regimental beer canteen. In these army grog shops many a young man learned to take his first glass of liquor, for the temptation to drink was exceedingly strong" (Setran, *The College "Y,"* ii).

48. Silva Gotay, *Protestantismo y política en Puerto Rico.*

49. Dómenech Sepúlveda, *Historia y pensamiento de la educación física y el deporte,* 270.

50. Picó, *1898.* Picó argues that the "war after the war" lasted until the establishment of the civil government in 1900. Popular insurgencies, known as the *tiznados,* were common in former Spanish or elite haciendas, retaliating for years of social and economic abuse. Resistance to incoming U.S. military authority occurred within the popular classes but did not grow into a mass movement.

51. "In Porto Rico, owing to the somewhat different conditions, the Committee has inaugurated another plan of service. In San Juan a building centrally located has been secured and fitted up with a restaurant, reading, correspondence and recreation rooms for the use of the soldiers and sailors. Everything has started most auspiciously. All from the commanding general down, welcome the undertaking" (my emphasis). YMCA, *Yearbook of the Young Men's Christian Association* (1899), xvi.

52. San Juan and Manila were the only two "permanent" libraries in the Army and Navy Department of the YMCA. Other Army and Navy YMCAs had traveling libraries. See YMCA, *Yearbook of the Young Men's Christian Association* (1900), 16.

53. Zerah C. Collins, "With the Army YMCA in the Spanish-American War and in the Philippine Islands," unpublished manuscript, 1922, 15, Box 239, Armed Services YMCA, Kautz Family YMCA Archives, University of Minnesota, Twin Cities.

54. YMCA, *Yearbook of the Young Men's Christian Association* (1902), 21.

55. Varas, *La verdadera historia de los deportes puertorriqueños* (1984), 556–57.

56. Martínez-Fernández, *Protestantism and Political Conflict in the Nineteenth-Century Spanish Caribbean;* Silva Gotay, *Protestantismo y política en Puerto Rico.*

57. Arbena, "Sport and the Promotion of Nationalism in Latin America," 3–4.

58. Ruiz Patiño, *La política del sport,* 58–73.

59. Urbina Gaitán, "Origen del deporte en El Salvador," 20–21.

60. Del Moral, "Colonial Citizens of a Modern Empire."

61. The U.S. occupations of the Dominican Republic and Haiti in the 1910s were characterized by what some call "benevolent imperialism" in which the United States established schools in addition to improving the infrastructure and providing security and political stability. Yet these occupations pursued more than a "benevolent" occupation to bring freedom and democracy; they were actually strategic moves in order to secure these lands and mitigate revolts so that U.S. economic interests could prosper. See Renda, *Taking Haiti*; Pérez, *Cuba*; Calder, *The Impact of Intervention*. Nonetheless, and central to this study, regardless of the power of U.S. interests in these territories, local leaders accepted and sponsored these actions, taking a leading role in the establishment of the U.S. presence in their lands. See Gobat, *Confronting the American Dream*.

62. Georges Rioux, "Pierre de Coubertin's Revelations," in Coubertin, *Olympism*, 23–31.

63. Norbert Muller, "Coubertin's Olympism," in Coubertin, *Olympism*, 33–48.

64. See Negrón de Montilla, *Americanization in Puerto Rico and the Public-School System*; del Moral, *Negotiating Empire*, 24–57.

65. Navarro Rivera, *Universidad de Puerto Rico*.

66. Barreto, *The Politics of Language in Puerto Rico*.

67. Del Moral, *Negotiating Empire*, 6–17.

68. Elsey, *Citizens and Sportsmen*, 35, 36.

69. Departamento de Educación Física, Exposición narrativa de trabajo en re-examen del Depto. de Educación Física-Recinto de Río Piedras-Universidad de Puerto Rico, 1975, 1, Organizaciones y sus funciones, FDO E5, Historia Departamento Educación Física, 1975, Circular Número 75-12, Archivo Central de la UPR, Fondo.

70. Osuna, *A History of Education in Puerto Rico*, 160.

71. Report of Committee of Nominations and Appointments of the Board of Trustees of the UPR, 1904, Informes Anuales, folio 74, Archivo Junta de Síndicos de la UPR.

72. Commissioner of Education of Puerto Rico Samuel McCune Lindsay, reporting at a teachers' meeting (quoted in Osuna, *A History of Education in Puerto Rico*, 165).

73. Varas, *La verdadera historia de los deportes puertorriqueños* (1984), 23.

74. University of Puerto Rico Board of Trustees, "Minutes of a regular meeting of the Board of Trustees of the University of Puerto Rico held in the Executive House, in San Juan, on Tuesday, January 2, 1906," 15, Book 2, Actas de la Junta de Síndicos de la Universidad de Puerto Rico, Archivo de la Junta

de Síndicos. Another report from October that same year increased the funding for the athletic field. University of Puerto Rico Board of Trustees, "Minutes of a regular meeting of the Board of Trustees of the University of Puerto Rico held in the Executive House, in San Juan, on Tuesday, October 1, 1906," 43, Book 2, Actas de la Junta de Síndicos de la Universidad de Puerto Rico, Archivo de la Junta de Síndicos.

75. Varas, *La verdadera historia de los deportes puertorriqueños* (1984), 28.

76. "Un espectáculo muy agradable é interesante," *Puerto Rican Eagle*, May 13, 1905, Personal Archive of Benjamín Lúgaro Torres, Ponce, Puerto Rico.

77. Osuna, *A History of Education in Puerto Rico*, 628.

78. Del Moral, "Colonial Citizens of a Modern Empire," 48–49.

79. Del Moral, *Negotiating Empire*, 104–6.

80. Schoenrich, "An Interscholastic Basketball League for Porto Rico," 38–40. There were other U.S. teachers who did not behave in a paternalistic Americanizing attitude in Puerto Rico. The premier example is George Keelan, from Dedham, Massachusetts, who fell in love with Puerto Rican culture, became fluent in Spanish, married into a Puerto Rican family, and even later in life declared that he felt like a Puerto Rican. Keelan became the principal of the University High School in 1926, also serving as the athletics director, and often wrote in the sports section of the *Porto Rican School Review*. In 1930 he became the first head of the Puerto Rican Olympic delegation at the Central American Games in Havana. See Tomasini, *Honor a los maestros de educación física y propulsores del deporte puertorriqueño*, 145–46.

81. Pike, *Hispanismo*, 1971.

82. Gil, "Educación Física," 13.

83. Gil, "Educación Física," 12–13.

84. Del Moral, *Negotiating Empire*, 19.

85. Mechikoff and Estes, *A History of Philosophy of Sport and Physical Education*; see also Hartwell, "Peter Henry Ling, the Swedish Gymnasiarch."

86. Mechikoff and Estes, *A History of Philosophy of Sport and Physical Education*.

87. Krüger, "The Unfinished Symphony," 9–10.

88. "Champion puertorriqueño," *La Democracia*, December 6, 1912.

2. Rise of a Colonial Olympic Movement

1. Dietz, *Economic History of Puerto Rico*, 139.

2. See Van Dalen, "Physical Education and Sports in Latin America." For communist countries, see Riordan, "The Impact of Communism on Sport."

3. Cosme Beitía, *Annual Report of the Athletic Director of the University of Porto Rico, 1931–32,* 1932, Archivo Central, Universidad de Puerto Rico.

4. Devés Valdés in his book *El pensamiento latinoamericano en el siglo XX* argues that Latin American thought throughout the nineteenth and twentieth centuries can be seen in waves of dissimilar yet complementary ways of thinking between modernization and identity. According to Devés Valdés, during the 1930s Latin America was going through a period of transition between the identity phase of nationalism and a growing concern to modernize that later would be epitomized by the Comisión Económica para la América Latina. By the 1930s the identity movement that began with Rodó's "Ariel" and contained a strong cultural discourse had been transformed into one that blended different versions of economic and political nationalism and a persistent search for self-definition. He argues that authors such as José Vasconcelos, Gilberto Freyre, and Manuel Gamio made vital contributions to the understanding of national compositions. In Puerto Rico this task was carried out by authors such as Antonio Pedreira (*Insularismo*) and Tomás Blanco (*El prejuicio racial en Puerto Rico*). Nevertheless, with the worldwide crisis after the economic collapse in 1929, there was a growing concern regarding economic dependence on the United States by Latin American economies. As a consequence there was growing pressure and impetus to carry out the complete modernization of these Latin American societies. The emphasis was to industrialize economies that for centuries were relegated to being providers of raw material for export to the modern centers of production.

5. Torres, "'Corrió por el prestigio de su país,'" 3.

6. Jarvie and Walker, *Scottish Sport in the Making of the Nation*; Hargreaves, *Freedom for Catalonia?*; James, *Beyond a Boundary*.

7. Act No. 15, *Acts and Resolutions of the Second Regular Session and Second Special Session of the Eleventh Legislature of Porto Rico,* 1927, 439–49, Biblioteca Legislativa de Puerto Rico Tomás Bonilla Feliciano (hereafter BLPRTBF).

8. See Act No. 73, *Acts and Resolutions of the Third Regular Session of the Eleventh Legislature of Porto Rico,* 1928, 518–24, BLPRTBF.

9. See Act No. 9, *Acts and Resolutions of the Second Special Session and the Fourth Regular Session of the Twelfth Legislature of Porto Rico,* 1932, 182–90, BLPRTBF.

10. See Act No. 5, *Acts and Resolutions of the Fourth and Fifth Special Session of the Twelfth Legislature of Porto Rico and of the First Regular Session of the Thirteenth Legislature of Puerto Rico,* 1933, 188–94, 672–74, BLPRTBF.

11. Athletic Commission of Puerto Rico, *Sixth Annual Report, Fiscal Year 1932–33*, 1933, 2, 3, Exhibit D, Archivo General de Puerto Rico (hereafter AGPR).

12. See Martínez-Rousset, *50 años de Olimpismo*, 66–78.

13. Letter dated May 12, 1933, addressed to Teófilo Maldonado, Fondo Oficina del Gobernador, Tarea 96-20, Caja 245, AGPR.

14. R.C. No. 8, "Resolución conjunta para crear el Comité Olípico de Puerto Rico," in Martínez-Rousset, *50 años de Olimpismo*, 73. "Por Cuanto: la juventud de Puerto Rico ha demostrado siempre su amor e interés a su desarrollo físico, participando en competencias insulares deportivas y varias veces en torneos internacionales; Por Cuanto: en el año 1930, Puerto Rico participó en las Olimpiadas Centroamericanas efectuadas en la ciudad de la Habana, Capital de Cuba, terminando en cuarto puesto con solo cuatro atletas nativos representando a nuestra Isla; Por Cuanto: un año más tarde una selección nativa de basket-ball visitó la República de Venezuela, resultando invicta en todos los partidos de este deporte en dicho país efectuados; Por Cuanto: Puerto Rico carece al presente de asociaciones solventes que puedan acarrear los gastos originados por el envío de nuestras mejores selecciones atléticas a las competencias Antillanas, Centroamericanas e internacionales. Por Cuanto: el desarrollo cultural de la juventud puertorriqueña depende en gran parte del desarrollo físico de la misma."

15. Martínez-Rousset, *50 años de Olimpismo*, 74.

16. Sesión del Comité Olímpico de Puerto Rico, Mayo 1933, Fondo Oficina del Gobernador, Tarea 96-20, Caja 245, AGPR.

17. "Vamos encaminados a salvar el amateurismo y habremos de conseguirlo. El espíritu del deporte se levanta airoso en todo Puerto Rico y el sentimiento atlético de todas nuestras clases se va uniendo para formar un bloque formidable y vigoroso. Presentimos que se está acercando ya una nueva era, una nueva época; como un despertar más claro y más diáfano para los deportes atléticos en Puerto Rico y para la juventud que hasta hace poco estuvo huérfana de mentores, de organizadores y de orientadores desinteresados" (in Martínez-Rousset, *50 años de Olimpismo*, 78).

18. Martínez-Rousset, *50 años de Olimpismo*, 68.

19. "Memorial que eleva al Hon. Robert Hayes Gore, Gobernador de Puerto Rico, La Federación Deportiva de Puerto Rico," Fondo Oficina del Gobernador, Tarea 96-20, Caja 1799, 190, AGPR.

20. See Keys, *Globalizing Sport*; Mason, "England 1966." The involvement of the state in the development of sport, particularly to prove the strength

of the nation, was particularly present in communist states. See Riordan, "The Impact of Communism in Sport."

21. "Felicidad de nuestro pueblo." In this case the word *pueblo* could mean people or country.

22. "Libre acción natural del individuo de la juventud de Puerto Rico, demostrada en su afición hacia la práctica deportiva como un medio eficaz de obtener su mejor desarrollo cultural y físico" ("A los miembros del Senado y Cámara de Representates de Puerto Rico," Fondo Oficina del Gobernador, Tarea 96-20, Caja 1799, 190, AGPR).

23. Diez de Andino does not actually name these individuals, but it is likely they are the ones he is referring to.

24. Act No. 11, *Acts and Resolutions of the Second Regular Session of the Thirteenth Legislature of Puerto Rico*, 1934, 218, BLPRTBF.

25. Johnson, "Anti-Imperialism and the Good Neighbor Policy," 93.

26. Act No. 11, *Acts and Resolutions of the Second Regular Session of the Thirteenth Legislature of Puerto Rico*, 1934, 234, BLPRTBF.

27. See Dietz, *Economic History of Puerto Rico*, 146–58.

28. Radiogram received May 21, 1938, No. 229, May 20, Box 963, RG 126, Office of Territories Classified Files, 1907–51, File 9887, Recreation and Sports, General, National Archives and Records Administration (hereafter NARA).

29. See Johnson, "Anti-Imperialism and the Good Neighbor Policy." For example, he helped write the Tydings Bill to decolonize Puerto Rico, and he agreed with a local sugar baron's complaints and dismissed the Puerto Rican Liberal Party's Chardón Plan, which sought government-run industries in order to implement agricultural cooperatives that mirrored Mexican president Plutarco Elías Calles's economic reforms. These policies were aimed at making the United States look good to Latin American governments for the anti-imperialist policies and the empowerment of peasants. However, the Tydings Bill ended up as a punitive measure, to which he had not originally agreed, and the rejection of the Chardón Plan came as a blow to Puerto Rican leadership, which regarded the plan highly.

30. For an explanation of the New Deal in Puerto Rico, see Dietz, *Economic History of Puerto Rico*, 143–46.

31. Letter sent to Ernest Gruening, Director, Division of Territories and Insular Possessions, October 3, 1938, Box 963, RG 126, Office of Territories Classified Files, 1907–51, File 9887, Recreation and Sports, General, NARA.

32. Letter dated February 3, 1939, to Ernest Gruening, Division of Insular Possessions and Territories, Box 963, RG 126, Office of Territories Classified Files, 1907–51, File 9887, Recreation and Sports, General, NARA.

33. Letter dated February 15, 1939, to Teofilo Maldonado, Amusement and Sports Commissioner, Box 963, RG 126, Office of Territories Classified Files, 1907–51, File 9887, Recreation and Sports, General, NARA.

34. Letter to Hon. Blanton Winship, Governor of Puerto Rico, February 15, 1939, Box 963, RG 126, Office of Territories Classified Files, 1907–51, File 9887, Recreation and Sports, General, NARA.

35. See Tomlinson and Young, *National Identity and Global Sports*.

36. Ruiz Patiño, *La política del sport*; Carter, *The Quality of Home Runs*.

37. Huertas González, *Deporte e identidad*, 11–17, 13–14.

38. For example, in "The Invention of Tradition" Trevor-Roper demonstrates the way Highland tradition, so important for Scottish national identity, was actually invented or developed by Englishmen in the eighteenth century. Thanks to Benjamin Geer at "H-Nationalism" for suggesting this reading. In "Football and the Idea of Scotland," Bairner demonstrates that the apparent cohesiveness of the Scottish nation is highly artificial due to the conflictive, regional, and divisive loyalties of different socioeconomic and ethnic groups. Cases of the "invention" of the "nation" in Latin America are abundant and well researched; see Annino and Guerra, *Inventando la nación*.

39. Torres, "'Spreading the Olympic Idea' to Latin America."

40. Huertas González, *Deporte e identidad*, 38.

41. Huertas González, *Deporte e identidad*, 42.

42. Although Torres's analysis in "The Limits of Pan-Americanism" of the "failed 1942 Pan-American Games" in Argentina provides crucial insights into Pan-American Olympism and U.S.–Latin American diplomatic relations through sport, he does not mention that the Central American and Caribbean Games had dealt with these issues since the 1930s with the participation of Puerto Rico. See also Sotomayor, "Colonial Olympism."

43. See, for example, Bucheli, *Bananas and Business*; Gobat, *Confronting the American Dream*; Renda, *Taking Haiti*; Pérez, *Cuba*, 1995.

44. See Duany, *The Puerto Rican Nation on the Move*, 59–62, 89–90.

45. See Duffy Burnett and Marshall, "Between the Foreign and the Domestic," in *Foreign in a Domestic Sense*, 7–13.

46. Huertas González, *Deporte e identidad*, 43–44. Mayo Santana, *El juguete sagrado*.

47. This is according to the research of Félix Ortiz, director of the Museo Olímpico de Puerto Rico in Salinas, and his interviews with a former Puerto Rican Olympic athlete of the 1930s (author interview with Félix Ortiz).

48. Silén, *Pedro Albizu Campos*, 47.

49. Memorandum dated January 22, 1954, from SA Charles B. Peck to SAC, San Juan (100–3), 5, 1133760-000-100-SJ-4014-Section 21, 4 August 1953–January 25 1954, Partido Independentista Puertorriqueño Collection, FBI Library, Archives Unbound, online (accessed September 29, 2014).

50. Tomasini, *Honor a los maestros de educación física y propulsores del deporte puertorriqueño*, 114–18.

51. Huertas González, *Deporte e identidad*, 41.

52. Letter dated December 14, 1932, addressed to His Excellency Theodore Roosevelt, Governor of Puerto Rico, Fondo Oficina del Gobernador, Tarea 96-20, Caja 1799, 190, AGPR.

53. Letter dated December 31, 1931, addressed to George W. Graves, Treasurer, American Olympic Committee, Fondo Oficina del Gobernador, Tarea 96-20, Caja 1799, 190, AGPR.

54. Letter dated July 20, 1933, addressed to Governor, Fondo Oficina del Gobernador, Tarea 96-20, Caja 1799, 190, AGPR.

55. See Wilson, "Recent Works on Tourism in Latin America"; Zauhar, "Historical Perspectives of Sports Tourism."

56. Merrill, *Negotiating Paradise*.

57. Quoted in Johnson, "Anti-Imperialism and the Good Neighbor Policy," 94. Roosevelt's statement came in an article published in 1934: "Puerto Rico: Our Link with Latin America," *Foreign Affairs*, July 1934, 271–80.

58. "Podría muy bien solicitarse del Gobierno de los Estados Unidos la aportación de su cooperación y buenos deseos para que nuestros emisarios a El Salvador el año próximo, que son ciudadanos americanos y que además de representar a Puerto Rico llevan la representación de la gran república Americana, cediera pasajes gratis, de San Juan a Panama [sic] en uno de los transportes de la nación, a las selecciones portorriqueñas. Ello equivaldría, además de estrechar lazos de confraternidad entre Puerto Rico, Centroamérica y Estados Unidos, a mermar los gastos de viaje de nuestros compatriotas" (Memorandum to Hon. Robert Hayes Gore, Presidente del "Comité Olímpico de Puerto Rico" en relación con la organización en nuestra isla de las primeras coompetencias atleticas insulares y el envoi de nuestras mejores selecciones a los Juegos Deportivos Centroamericanos de "El Salvador," Fondo Oficina del Gobernador, Tarea 96-20, Caja 1799, 190, AGPR).

59. Radiogram sent to Director of the Division of Territories and Island Possessions, dated October 25, 1934, Fondo Oficina del Gobernador, Tarea 96-20, Caja 1799, 190, AGPR.

60. Letter dated February 12, 1934, to Señor don José Prados Herrero, Secretario General de la Federación Deportiva de Puerto Rico, Fondo Oficina del Gobernador, Tarea 96-20, Caja 1799, 190, AGPR.

61. Letter dated May 17, 1934, addressed to The Honorable The Governor of Puerto Rico, Fondo Oficina del Gobernador, Tarea 96-20, Caja 1799, 190, AGPR.

62. Letter dated October 30, 1934, addressed to The Honorable Marvin H. McIntire, The White House, Box 963, RG 126, Office of Territories Classified Files, 1907–51, File 9887, Recreation and Sports, Central American and Caribbean Games, NARA.

63. Uriarte González, *80 años de acción y pasión*, 18.

64. Power, "The Puerto Rican Nationalist Party, Transnational Latin American Solidarity, and the United States during the Cold War," 25–26.

65. Huyke, *Los deportes en Puerto Rico*, 270.

66. Uriarte González, *80 años de acción y pasión*, 19.

67. Urbina Gaitán, "Origen del deporte en El Salvador," 55–56, 73–74.

68. Letter dated March 21, 1935, addressed to The Honorable Secretary of State, Box 963, RG 126, Office of Territories Classified Files, 1907–51, File 9887, Recreation and Sports, Central American and Caribbean Games, NARA.

69. Acosta, *La mordaza*.

70. Letter dated October 11, 1934, addressed to The Honorable The Secretary of State, Box 963, RG 126, Office of Territories Classified Files, 1907–51, File 9887, Recreation and Sports, Central American and Caribbean Games, NARA.

71. Letter dated October 23, 1934, Box 963, RG 126, Office of Territories Classified Files, 1907–51, File 9887, Recreation and Sports, Central American and Caribbean Games, NARA.

72. Letter dated February 28, 1935, to Exmo. Señor Dr. Don Frank P. Corrigan, Ministro de los E.U. de América, Fondo Oficina del Gobernador, Tarea 96-20, Caja 1799, 190, AGPR. Also in letter dated March 1, 1935, No. 85, to Gruening, Division of Territories and Island Possessions, Fondo Oficina del Gobernador, Tarea 96-20, Caja 1799, 190, AGPR.

73. "Local Editorial Regarding Puerto Rico," letter dated April 5, 1935, No. 200, Box 963, RG 126, Office of Territories Classified Files, 1907–51, File 9887, Recreation and Sports, Central American and Caribbean Games, NARA.

74. Uriarte González, *80 años de acción y pasión*, 24.

75. Huertas González, *Deporte e identidad*, 51–52; Rodríguez Tapia, *Rafael Hernández Marín*.

76. Huertas González, *Deporte e identidad*, 50.

77. "¡Ese es Puerto Rico! ¡Ese es Puerto Rico encarnado en Figueroa, tirándose contra el suelo al romper la marca olímpica por 1 centímetro, y en Luyanda, haciendo un esfuerzo sobre-humano para derrotar a Bello, de Cuba, en el triple salto, por escasamente otro centímetro! Ese es Puerto Rico ausente, desbordándose en el corazón de sus hijos, que contra inconvenientes y vicisitudes han logrado hoy que el nombre de nuestra pequeña isla sea repetido con admiración y respeto por todas las naciones que, formando un enorme corazón en el mapa, son el núcleo de repúblicas hispanas, espinazo y médula de nuestra raza?" (in Huertas González, "Deporte e identidad en Puerto Rico").

78. See Uriarte González, *De Londres a Londres*, 53–55.

79. Fernando Rodil, "¿Irá Malavé a Princeton?," *El Mundo*, June 12, 1936, Digital Library of the Caribbean, http://www.dloc.com/CA03599022/01205/7x (accessed November 24, 2014).

80. Fernando Rodil, "Gestiona que algunos atletas portorriqueños sean incluidos en el equipo olímpico de Estados Unidos," *El Mundo*, May 23, 1936, Digital Library of the Caribbean, http://www.dloc.com/CA03599022 /01186/6x?vo=3 (accessed November 24, 2014).

81. Nieves Falcón, *Un siglo de represión política en Puerto Rico*, 100–111.

82. Letter dated January 15, 1935, addressed to J. R. Cabrera, Amusements and Sports Commission, Fondo Oficina del Gobernador, Tarea 96-20, Caja 1799, 190, AGPR.

83. "Extienda en mi nombre felicitaciones efusivas nuestros atletas. Puerto Rico orgulloso de su triunfo. Adelante" (cablegram to Frank Campos, March 23, 1935, Fondo Oficina del Gobernadorr, Tarea 96-20, Caja 1799, 190, AGPR).

84. Administrative Bulletin No. 520, Puerto Rican Olympic Games, Box 963, RG 126, Office of Territories Classified Files, 1907–51, File 9887, Recreation and Sports, General, NARA.

85. Radio address by Governor Winship over station WKAQ, December 16, 1937, Fondo Oficina del Gobernador, Tarea 96-20, Caja 1799, 190, AGPR.

86. See Trías Monge, *Puerto Rico*.

87. Letter dated December 26, 1934, to the Honorable Blanton Winship Governor of Puerto Rico, Fondo Oficina del Gobernador, Tarea 96-20, Caja 1799, 190, AGPR; letter dated May 29, 1937, addressed to Hon. Blannton Winship Governor of Puerto Rico, Fondo Oficina del Gobernador, Tarea 96-20, Caja 1799, 190, AGPR.

88. 4th Endorsement, Office of the Auditor of Puerto Rico, San Juan, October 29, 1937, Fondo Oficina del Gobernador, Tarea 96-20, Caja 1799, 190, AGPR.

89. Letter dated November 29, 1937, addressed to Gilberto González Juliá, Fondo Oficina del Gobernador, Tarea 96-20, Caja 1799, 190, AGPR.

90. Letter dated May 24, 1937, addressed to Hon. Blanton Winship, Fondo Oficina del Gobernador, Tarea 96-20, Caja 1799, 190, AGPR.

91. USA Baseball Congress, letter dated June 28, 1937, addressed to Hon. Señor Blanton Winship, Fondo Oficina del Gobernado, Tarea 96-20, Caja 1799, 190, AGPR.

92. Letter dated August 3, 1937, addressed to Leslie Mann, Fondo Oficina del Gobernador, Tarea 96-20, Caja 1799, 190, AGPR.

93. Letter dated August 9, 1937, addressed to Justo Rivera Cabrera, Amusement and Sports Commissioner, Fondo Oficina del Gobernador, Tarea 96-20, Caja 1799, 190, AGPR.

94. Second Session, Monday, February 14, Actas de las sesiones de la Junta Ceneral de Delegados, in *La Junta Nacional Panameña*, 295.

95. Huertas González, *Deporte e identidad*, 57.

96. Uriarte González, *80 años de acción y pasión*, 42.

3. Legitimizing Colonial Olympism

1. Dubois, *Soccer Empire*, 50.

2. See, for example, Rein, "'El Primer Deportista.'"

3. Ayala, "From Sugar Plantations to Military Bases."

4. Bolívar Fresnada, *Guerra, [Banca] y Desarrollo*, 7.

5. García Reyes, "Olimpiadas y Copa Mundial de Fútbol."

6. Tomasini, *Honor a los maestros de educación física y propulsores del deporte puertorriqueño*, 162.

7. Tomasini, *Honor a los maestros de educación física y propulsores del deporte puertorriqueño*, 162.

8. Letter dated October 10, 1941, to Sr. Luis Muñoz Marín, Sección IV, Luis Muñoz Marín, Presidente del Senado, Serie 3, Archivo Fundación Luis Muñoz Marín, San Juan, Puerto Rico (hereafter AFLMM).

9. For a full analysis of Monagas's alliance with the PPD and his leadership in the development of Puerto Rico's sport infrastructure in the 1940s, see Sotomayor, "Un parque para cada pueblo."

10. See Dubois, *Soccer Empire*, chapter 2, 47–71.

11. "Nueve Millones pide Monagas para proyectos de recreación," *El Mundo*, May 29, 1945. "Tengo el firme convencimiento de que Puerto Rico debe encauzar sus planes de competencia internacional hacia los Estados Unidos ya que es a este país a quien más ligados nos encontramos en el presente y de quien recibimos más publicidad en cualquier actividad, aparte

de la similitud en las prácticas deportivas que venimos observando en la isla últimamente."

12. "El deporte popular: Tres aspectos del deporte en Puerto Rico," *Puerto Rico Ilustrado*, November 29, 1947, 70–71.

13. Wilbur et al., *White House Conference on Child Health and Protection*.

14. Colón Ocasio, *Antonio Fernós Isern soberanista, Luis Muños Marín autonomista*, 145–56; Bolívar Fresnada, *Guerra, [Banca] y Desarrollo*, 46–47.

15. Bushnell, *Report of the United States Olympic Committee*, 16.

16. Bushnell, *Report of the United States Olympic Committee*, 17.

17. López Rojas, *El debate por la nación*, 60–61.

18. Ayala and Bernabe, *Puerto Rico in the American Century*, 150.

19. Bolívar Fresnada, *Guerra, [Banca] y Desarrollo*, 29–30.

20. Letter dated October 4, 1950, sent to Sr. Julio Enrique Monagas, Administrador de Parques y Recreo, Fondo Oficina del Gobernador, Tarea 96-20, Caja 1881, 273, Recreational Facilities and Equipment, AGPR.

21. "El Caucus reafirma su confianza al Comisionado de Deportes," *El Mundo*, April 8, 1948.

22. José Seda, "Seda afirma que la Isla no ha progresado en varios deportes," *El Mundo*, September (?), 1945.

23. Tomasini, *Honor a los maestros de educación física y propulsores del deporte puertorriqueño*, 234–37.

24. "Puerto Rico tiene aún problemas que precisa resolver rápidamente," *El Mundo*, October 17, 1946.

25. See Uriarte González, *80 años de acción y pasión*.

26. "Se adoptan las reglas de aficionismo de Puerto Rico," *El Mundo*, March 22, 1944.

27. Gelpí, *Literatura y paternalismo en Puerto Rico*; Roy-Féquière, *Women, Creole Identity, and Intellectual Life in Early Twentieth-Century Puerto Rico*.

28. MacAloon, "La pitada Olímpica."

29. Roberto Sánchez Vilella, secretary; Alberto Guerrero, treasurer of Puerto Rico; and Jorge Jiménez, commissioner of the interior. Transcription of the original letter, in Comité Olímpico de Puerto Rico, *Puerto Rico y la Educación Olímpica*, 28. See also another transcription in Martínez-Rousset, *50 años de Olimpismo*, 31.

30. Martínez-Rousset, *50 años de Olimpismo*, 36.

31. Comité Olímpico de Puerto Rico, *Puerto Rico y la Educación Olímpica*, 29.

32. "Nouveaux CNO: . . . Les demandes de Syrie et de Porto Rico seront proposées avec préavis favorable" (in Martínez-Rousset, *50 años de Olimpismo*, 39, 43).

33. "No se podrá hacer una excepción con Puerto Rico," "no se le ha otorgado reconocimento oficial alguno" (quoted in Martínez-Rousset, *50 años de Olimpismo*, 51).

34. Transcription of the original letter, in Comité Olímpico de Puerto Rico, *Puerto Rico y la Educación Olímpica*, 29.

35. Invitation sent to National Olympic Association, Puerto Rico, Box 963, RG 126, Office of Territories Classified Files, 1907–51, File 9887, Recreation and Sports, General, NARA.

36. Personal interview with Martínez-Rousset, 2009.

37. "Juan Juarbe tuvo incidente en acto Bogotá," *El Mundo*, April 1948.

38. Juarbe again represented the PN at the ninth Pan-American Conference, also in Bogotá, in April 1948, presenting seventeen points why the United States should give independence to Puerto Rico. "Tratarán caso de Puerto Rico en Colombia," *El Mundo*, April 9, 1948.

39. Note dated April 15, 1948, Box 963, RG 126, Office of Territories Classified Files, 1907–51, File 9887, Recreation and Sports, General, NARA.

40. Jamaica's NOC was recognized by the IOC in 1936. Jamaicans first participated in the Olympics in 1948.

41. Fondo Oficina del Gobernador, Tarea 96-20, Caja 443, 21-2, Athletic Delegations, Comisión Parques y Recreo, AGPR.

42. Letter dated May 18, 1948, to Sr. Roberto Colón, Fondo Oficina del Gobernador, Tarea 96-20, Caja 443, 21-2, Athletic Delegations, Comisión Parques y Recreo, AGPR; Uriarte González, *De Londres a Londres*, 64.

43. Jaime Partsch McMillan, oral history interview with José Vicente Chandler, May 2, 2007, Río Piedras, Puerto Rico, Jesús T. Piñero Oral History Collection, Universidad del Este, Carolina, Puerto Rico.

44. Jaime Partsch McMillan, oral history interview with José C. Barbosa, May 23, 2007, Río Piedras, Puerto Rico, Jesús T. Piñero Oral History Collection, Universidad del Este, Carolina, Puerto Rico. "El Comité Olímpico Americano podía vetar eso. Ellos podrían decir: 'Ellos son ciudadanos americanos. Si van a competir, tienen que competir con nosotros.'"

45. Huyke, *Los deportes en Puerto Rico*, 279.

46. "JP: Entiendo que usted fue el abanderado, ¿verdad? JV: Sí. JP: Hábleme de eso. JV: (Se ríe.) El que iba a ser el abanderado de Puerto Rico era Barasorda. Pues, entonces, hubo un conflicto con la bandera. Muñoz no quería que usaran la bandera de Puerto Rico porque en aquel tiempo era un símbolo nacionalista. JP: ¿Eso fue Muñoz? JV: Muñoz. Le había dicho a Monagas que no podía usar la bandera de Puerto Rico porque tenía unas connotaciones con el nacionalismo que nos perjudicaba. Entonces lleva-

mos el escudo de Puerto Rico. Hubo una discusión en la cual yo no participé. Yo sólo sé es [sic] que Mongas me dijo 'Fofó, como tú habías sido soldado, sabes marchar, tú eres el que va a llevar la bandera. Punto.' Así que me tocó por carambola. (Se ríe.) JP: ¿Y qué pasó con Barasorda? No se la dieron, ¿por qué? JV: No se. [sic] Me dijeron que él quería llevar la bandera de Puerto Rico y no lo dejaron." Jaime Partsch McMillan, oral history interview with José Vicente Chandler, May 2, 2007, Río Piedras, Puerto Rico, Jesús T. Piñero Oral History Collection, Universidad del Este, Carolina, Puerto Rico.

47. Acosta, *La Mordaza*; Nieves Falcón, *Un siglo de repression política en Puerto Rico*, 115.

48. Jaime Partsch McMillan, oral history interview with José Vicente Chandler, May 2, 2007, Río Piedras, Puerto Rico, Jesús T. Piñero Oral History Collection, Universidad del Este, Carolina, Puerto Rico.

49. Fonseca Barahona, *Puerto Rico*, 13.

50. Negrón-Muntaner, "Showing Face."

51. Uriarte González, *80 años de acción y pasión*, 33, 49.

52. "Piñero aprobó participación de la Isla en justas mundiales," *El Mundo*, September 18, 1948. "Es motivo de satisfacción para nuestra Isla que Puerto Rico haya sido reconocido por las más importantes federaciones deportivas internacionales y que se le haya concedido el derecho de participación en propiedad en competencias internacionales. . . . Es de justicia hacer claro que todas estas gestiones y esos logros se han alcanzado desde julio 1ero de 1947 hasta la fecha y que corresponde a la Comisión de Parques y Recreos del Gobierno de Puerto Rico el crédito por el éxito obtenido."

53. "Rosario señala auge deportivo en Puerto Rico: Hablando en Venezuela, declaró hay entusiasmo inusitado para X Serie," *El Mundo*, September 20, 1948. "Por primera vez en la historia contamos con un Gobierno que cree en la práctica deportiva. . . . En pocas palabras, podría decir que nos hemos puesto los pantalones largos en deportes. Enviamos un equipo de nueve hombres a las Olimpiadas, y logramos cuatro puntos. Tenemos peloteros profesionales en las Ligas menores y de Color y nuestros Guantes Dorados han ganado el campeonato nacional de boxeo amateur de Estados Unidos. Con una población de dos millones y medio de habitantes, Puerto Rico indudablemente está dando una lección en deportes a muchos países de mayor número de habitantes."

54. Bosque Pérez and Colón Morera, *Las carpetas*; Bosque Pérez and Colón Morera, *Puerto Rico under Colonial Rule*.

55. See Ayala and Bernabe, *Puerto Rico in the American Century*.

4. Colonial Sovereignty through Olympism

1. Colón Ocasio, *Antonio Fernós Isern soberanista, Luis Muños Marín autonomista*, 201.
2. As Colón Ocasio argues in his book, Fernós, the mastermind behind the political and legal dimensions of the commonwealth, thought that the political formula of 1952 still had much room for development in regard to more local sovereignty and outside the sphere of U.S. sovereignty (*Antonio Fernós Isern soberanista, Luis Muños Marín autonomista*, 216–17).
3. Malavet, *America's Colony*, 42–48. For a study of the contentious creation of the commonwealth, see Colón Ocasio, *Antonio Fernós Isern soberanista, Luis Muños Marín autonomista*.
4. Betts, *Decolonization*.
5. Beck, "The British Government and the Olympic Movement."
6. Ramón Villares argues that Galician intellectual leaders during the Spanish Civil War sought to cultivate a sense of cultural distinctiveness instead of a political separation from Spain. This sense of cultural separation was promoted through popular culture, particularly language and literature (*Historia de Galicia*, 366). See Abell, "'They Seem to Think "We're Better Than You"'"; Curran, "Sport and Cultural Nationalism."
7. See Duany, *The Puerto Rican Nation on the Move*, 17–18; Sotomayor, "Patron Saint Festivities, Politics, and Culture," 111–19.
8. Dietz, *Economic History of Puerto Rico*, 244.
9. Russell, "Operation Bootstrap and NAFTA."
10. Dietz, *Economic History of Puerto Rico*, 244; Ayala and Bernabe, *Puerto Rico in the American Century*, 205–8.
11. Dietz, *Economic History of Puerto Rico*, 261.
12. Fiftieth Annual Report of the Governor of Puerto Rico, 1, Fondo Oficina del Gobernador, Tarea 96-20, Caja 840, AGPR.
13. Reorganization Plan No. 2 of 1950, Public Parks and Recreation Administration, Acts of the Second Special Session, Second Regular Session and Fourth Special Session of the Seventeenth Legislature of Puerto Rico, 1950, 18–20, BLPRTBF.
14. Emilio E. Huyke, "Los Deportes en el Mundo: Señor Gobernador," *El Mundo*, November 7, 1956.
15. Sotomayor, "Operation Sport."
16. Fiftieth Annual Report of the Governor of Puerto Rico, Honorable Luis Muñoz Marín, for the Fiscal Year 1949–50, 13, Fondo Oficina del Gobernador, Tarea 96-20, Caja 840, Informes Gobernador, AGPR.

17. Luis Muñoz Marín, "Puerto Rico since Columbus," Commonwealth of Puerto Rico, Department of Labor, Migration Division/Columbia Broadcasting System, November 19, 1953, 1, Box 4465, RG 59, 1950–54, NARA.

18. For a complete and well-documented account of the rebellion, later called "Grito de Jayuya," see Seijo Bruno, *La insurrección nacionalista en Puerto Rico.*

19. "Despiden a 'Lolita,'" *El Nuevo Día,* August 2, 2010.

20. Ramos Méndez, *Posesión del ayer,* 98–100.

21. Handy, "The Guatemalan Revolution and Civil Rights."

22. "Por el bien del deporte, fraternidad de los pueblos y grandeza de América" (quoted in Uriarte González, *80 años de acción y pasión,* 58).

23. "Guatemala no reconoce colonia, estamos en contra del coloniaje en América" (quoted in Uriarte González, *80 años de acción y pasión,* 58).

24. Memorandum dated January 22, 1954, from SA Charles B. Peck to SAC, San Juan (100-3), 5, 1133760-000-100-SJ-4014-Section 21, August 4, 1953–January 25, 1954, Partido Independentista Puertorriqueño Collection, FBI Library, Archives Unbound, online (accessed September 29, 2014).

25. See Barbosa Muñiz, *La era de oro del atletismo puertorriqueño,* 80.

26. "Fue apoteósico, cientos y cientos de automóviles, miles y miles de entusiastas, a pie, por las aceras, por los balcones de las casas aplaudían y vitoreaban a nuestros campeones . . . la procesión triunfal fue por la avenida Fernández Juncos y luego por la Ponce de León, no parecía tener fin, allí llegó la banda del Colegio y tocó 'La Borinqueña' y también el Star Bangled Banner, para evitar problemas" (quoted in Uriarte González, *80 años de acción y pasión,* 64).

27. Memorandum of Conversation dated December 12, 1950, Box 4465, RG 59, Department of State, 1950–1954, File 811, NARA.

28. Letter dated November 20, 1950, to Senor Julio Monagas, Box 143, Comite Olimpico de Puerto Rico, 1935, 1947–62, Avery Brundage Collection, University Archives, University of Illinois at Urbana-Champaign (hereafter ABCUIUC).

29. Letter dated November 25, 1950, to Forney Roskin, Box 143, Comite Olimpico de Puerto Rico, 1935, 1947–62, ABCUIUC.

30. Letter dated December 14, 1950, Box 143, Comite Olimpico de Puerto Rico, 1935, 1947–62, ABCUIUC.

31. Letter dated December 23, 1950, to Daniel J. Farris, Box 143, Comite Olimpico de Puerto Rico, 1935, 1947–62, ABCUIUC.

32. Letter dated February 1, 1951, to Senor Julio E, Monagas, Parks and Public Recreation, Box 143, Comite Olimpico de Puerto Rico, 1935, 1947–62, ABCUIUC.

33. Quoted in the letter dated September 19, 1951, to Hon. Luis Muñoz Marín, Fondo Oficina del Gobernador, Tarea 96-20, Caja 1882, 273.3, Olympic Games, AGPR. The trail of paperwork pertaining to the negotiations to allow Puerto Ricans to participate at the Helsinki Olympics has not been found yet; this points to the need for further research at the archives of the IOC in Lausanne.

34. See Wagg and Andrews, *East Plays West*.

35. Flores Collazo, *25/4 julio*.

36. Granted, it is also flown by itself during beauty pageants, yet these events are of a different, though not less important, nature.

37. "La delegación boricua en correcta formación y llevando al pecho la mano derecha, debió haber oído La Borinqueña en la lejanía, ante un sol brillante, más brillante que nunca en el cielo de Finlandia, al ver izarse lentamente y por primera vez la bandera de la estrella solitaria en el asta de la Villa Olímpica. . . . Eran las once de la mañama y, de donde escribo, veo y no me canso de mirar nuestra bandera, flotando orgullosa y majestuosa junto a las demás banderas del mundo . . . el inicio para nuestro pueblo de mayor dignidad dentro de la familia mundial de los deportes" (quoted in an exhibit at the Museo Olímpico de Puerto Rico, Salinas).

38. See López Rojas, *El debate por la nación*.

39. Olimpiadas Melbourne Repiten Ceremonias de Reconocimiento Nacional a Puerto Rico, 1, Fondo Oficina del Gobernador, Tarea 96-20, Caja 1882, 273, Equipo y Facilidades para Recreación, AGPR.

40. For an extensive explanation of Operation Serenity and Muñoz Marín's usage of the concept of "personality," see Duany, *The Puerto Rican Nation on the Move*, chapter 5, "A Postcolonial Colony? The Rise of Cultural Nationalism in Puerto Rico during the 1950s," 122–36. His mention of the concept of "personality" may be found on 126–27.

41. "Es ahora en Melbourne, Australia, que vuelve Puerto Rico al escenario de la mayor representación internacional de los deportes, para confirmar una vez más el reconocimiento de su personalidad nacional ante la representación de la juventud selecta del mundo y de los dignatarios de mayor rango para el deporte en el campo internacional. . . . Cuando fuimos a Londres, todavía Puerto Rico no se había emancipado de los rasgos coloniales que aún prevalecían en sus relaciones políticas y de gobierno. . . . Pero esta gloria fué [*sic*] más elocuente y fundamental cuando frente a nuestra bandera y bajo los aires de nuestro himno desfiló la delegación completa de los Estados Unidos, presidida por su Embajador y su bandera para rendir entonces y en aquel momento el saludo y reconocimiento

y cordial afecto de aquella distinguida representación norteamericana a la representación nacional de nuestro pueblo" (Olimpiadas Melbourne Repiten Ceremonias de Reconocimiento Nacional a Puerto Rico, 1–3, Fondo Oficina del Gobernador, Tarea 96-20, Caja 1882, 273, Equipo y Facilidades para Recreación, AGPR).

42. "Simpático reconocimiento a la personalidad puertorriqueña en medio de la admiración y aplausos de más de 110,000 espetadores extranjeros." "If we have contributed to it all along it has been always with the best of motivations to honor our country and to comply with loyalty and devotion to the best inspirations of our people and the Government to which we serve." "Si a ello hemos contribuído fué siempre con las mejores motivaciones para honrar a nuestro país y por cumplir con lealtad y devoción a las mejores inspiraciones de nuestro pueblo y del Gobierno a quien servimos" (Olimpiadas Melbourne Repiten Ceremonias de Reconocimiento Nacional a Puerto Rico, 4. Fondo Oficina del Gobernador, Tarea 96-20, Caja 1882, 273, Equipo y Facilidades para Recreación, AGPR).

43. "Se ha establecido la personalidad propia de Puerto Rico y su derecho a participar separadamente de las delegaciones de Estados Unidos." R. Santiago Rosa, "Reconocido Derecho PR Competir Solo," *El Nuevo Día*, December 11, 1957.

44. Teófilo Maldonado, "Monagas Preside Comité Estatutos," *El Nuevo Día*, March 8, 1955.

45. José Prados Herrero, "Escogen a Puerto Rico Pais Coordinador Juegos de 1959," *El Mundo*, January 25, 1956.

46. Robert Creamer, "Of Greeks—and Russians," *Sports Illustrated*, February 6, 1956.

47. "Olympic Rule Nr. 25," National Olympic Committees (adopted at the Session of the IOC in Athens, May 1954), Comité Internationale Olympique, Lausanne, 1954, 1, http://www.olympic.org/Documents/Olympic%20Charter/Olympic_Charter_through_time/1954-Olympic_Charter-Olympic_Rule_Nr25.pdf (accessed August 21, 2014).

48. Letter dated July 27, 1954, to Avery Brundage, Series 26/20/37, Box 63, IOC Members, Moenck, Dr. Miguel A., 1954–56, ABCUIUC.

49. Exhibit B, "Excluyen Argentina Juegos Olímpicos porque gobierno designa delegados," in a letter dated September 22, 1956, to the IOC, Series 26/20/37, Box 146, ABCUIUC.

50. Letter dated February 9, 1955, to Avery Brundage, Series 26/20/37, Box 63, IOC Members, Moenck, Dr. Miguel A., 1954–56, ABCUIUC. For Guillermety's chronology of events of this controversy, see letter dated September 22, 1956, to the IOC, Series 26/20/37, Box 146, ABUIUC.

51. Letter sent August 23, 1956, to Julio E. Monagas, President National Olympic Committee of Puerto Rico, Series 26/20/37, Box 146, ABCUIUC.

52. Exhibit D, Article "Bullseye" by Fred Guillermety, August 28, 1956, *El Mundo*, letter dated September 22, 1956, to the IOC, Series 26/20/37, Box 146, ABCUIUC.

53. Exhibit I, cablegram dated September 15, 1956, to the IOC, the International Shooting Union, and Avery Brundage, Series 26/20/37, Box 146, ABCUIUC.

54. Letter dated September 4, 1956, to Avery Brundage, Series 26/20/37, Box 143, ABCUIUC.

55. Letter dated October 10, 1956, to H. J. Holt, Comité d'Organisation de la VXIe Olympiade from Otto Mayer, Series 26/20/37, Box 146, ABCUIUC.

56. "Crean mañana nueva asociacion deportiva," *El Mundo*, July 13, 1957; Emilio E. Huyke, "Los Deportes en el Mundo," *El Mundo*, July 23, 1957.

57. Letter dated July 15, 1957, to Dr. Miguel A. Moenck, Miembro Comité Olímpico Internacional, Series 26/20/37, Box 146, ABCUIUC.

58. Letter dated July 18, 1957, to Otto Mayer, Chancellor, IOC, Series 26/20/37, Box 146, ABCUIUC.

59. Letter dated July 22, 1957, to Julio E. Monagas, Series 26/20/37, Box 146, ABCUIUC.

60. Letter dated August 5, 1957, to The Marquess of Exeter, Series 26/20/37, Box 146, ABCUIUC.

61. Letter sent August 13, 1957, to Avery Brundage, Series 26/20/37, Box 146, ABCUIUC.

62. Letter dated May 13, 1957, to Otto Mayer, Series 26/20/37, Box 146, ABCUIUC. See also letter dated December 11, 1957, from Otto Mayer to Fred Guillermety, Asociación Olímpica de Puerto Rico, Series 26/20/37, Box 146, ABCUIUC. For Dr. Manuel Alsina Capó's claims, see Miguel Rivera, "Federación Atletismo Protesta Contra la Actitud de Monagas," *El Mundo*, March 26, 1958. For Monagas's reaction, see "Habla Monagas," *El Mundo*, March 28, 1958.

63. See cable dated May 23, 1958, from Julio Monagas to Avery Brundage, Series 26/20/37, Box 146, ABCUIUC.

64. Letter dated May 13, 1957, to Otto Mayer, Series 26/20/37, Box 146, ABCUIUC.

65. Letter dated May 29, 1958, to Avery Brundage, Series 26/20/37, Box 146, ABCUIUC.

66. Letter dated May 24, 1958, to Dr. Miguel A. Moenck, Series 26/20/37, Box 146, ABCUIUC.

67. The AOPR and the COPR were supposed to hold a meeting at San Juan

International Airport on May 23, 1958, but Monagas and his group did not attend. See letter dated May 29, 1958, from Fred Guillermety to Otto Mayer, Series 26/20/37, Box 146, ABCUIUC.

68. See letter dated August 18, 1958, to Avery Brundage from Lt. Col. H. R. Brewerton, Series 26/20/37, Box 146, ABCUIUC.

69. "De aquí salió Rolando Cruz con una pértiga de palo a disputarle el campeonato panamericano a Don Bragg, que ya tenía, desde hace años, una pértiga de fibra de cristal que le concede varias pulgadas adicionales en su salto." "Esa es la realidad y no es duro decirlo, porque precisamente esa realidad agiganta aún más nuestros logros del pasado. En materia de facilidades deportivas, y de programación, estamos en una tierna infancia y vivimos en una infantil inocencia, y no hemos logrado la madurez que nos creemos tener." "Lo esencial es competir y eso es lo que hacemos. Cumplimos con el mandato, la ley y el espíritu olímpico." Emilio E. Huyke, "El Balance de Puerto Rico en Chicago," *El Mundo*, September 8, 1959.

70. Santiago Sosa, "Equipo de Puerto Rico Clasificado Subcampeón Baloncesto," *El Mundo*, September 8, 1959.

71. Pepo Talavera, "Estatura fue Factor Decisivo Juego Perdió PR Frente a E.U.," *El Mundo*, September 3, 1959.

72. For a version of Puerto Rican success at international tournaments, see Gems, *The Athletic Crusade*, 99–114. Although Gems's analysis of Puerto Rican sport as a symbol of national pride makes a good contribution to the field, his short chapter has various mistakes as far as Puerto Rican history goes. For example, he says that in 1897 Puerto Rico was an independent country, which is false. The Autonomous Charter of 1897 from Spain did not grant Puerto Rico its independence but made it an autonomous province of Spain. Otherwise his analysis of sport as inherently political and a source of identity is well taken. See also Dómenech Sepúlveda, *Historia y pensamiento de la educación física y el deporte*, 284.

73. Letter sent July 28, 1959, to Julio E. Monagas, PR Lawn Tennis Federation, Series 26/20/37, Box 146, ABCUIUC.

74. Letter sent on August 6, 1959, to Asa S. Bushnell, Series 26/20/37, Box 146, ABCUIUC.

75. The United Nations, at the request of the United States, actually took Puerto Rico off the list of colonial territories on November 27, 1953, under Resolution 748 (VIII). For a complete analysis of this process, see Trías Monge, *Puerto Rico*, chapter 11, "The Big Sleep," 119–35.

76. Letter sent September 23, 1959, to Averill [sic] Brundage, Series 26/20/37, Box 146, ABCUIUC.

77. Letter sent November 30, 1959, to Dr. Pedro Ramos Casellas, Series 26/20/37, Box 146, ABCUIUC.
78. Rafael Santiago Sosa, "Monagas consultará con gobernador sobre gira atletas boricuas sur," *El Mundo*, September 7, 1959.

5. A Cold War Playing Field

1. Hutchinson, "Cultural Nationalism and Moral Regeneration"; Chatterjee, *The Nation and Its Fragments*. For an explanation on the concept of a cultural nation or cultural nationalism, see the introduction.
2. Atiles Osoria, "Pro-State Violence in Puerto Rico."
3. Atiles Osoria, "Pro-State Violence in Puerto Rico,"131; Nieves Falcón, *Un siglo de represión política and Puerto Rico*, 149–63.
4. Jaime Plenn, "Surge movimiento para eliminar a Cuba," *El Mundo*, May 10, 1962; Jess Losada, "Caso de Cuba ante los Juegos Centroamericanos y del Caribe," *Boletín Deportivo*, Unión Deportiva Cuba Libre, Año II, no. 3 (April 1965), 1, 6, Sección VI, Senador por Acumulación, Serie 17, Archivo Misceláneo, Cartapacio 273.3, Décimos Juegos Centro Americanos y del Caribe (hereafter JCAC), Administración Parques y Recreo, AFLMM.
5. Krüger, "The Unfinished Symphony," 11, 18.
6. "Brundage hace elogios a labor de J. E. Monagas," *El Mundo*, September 24, 1962. Indonesia denied visas to Israel and the Republic of China (Taiwan) to attend the fourth Asian Games in Jakarta. This occurred due to political and religious pressure from Arab countries and from the People's Republic of China. As a result the IOC terminated Indonesia's IOC membership, preventing it from participating in future IOC-sponsored Olympic Games.
7. I. Aleksandrov, "Washington's 'Iron Curtain,'" *Pravda*, June 28, 1966, in Joint Committee on Slavic Studies, *Current Digest of the Soviet Press* 18, no. 22 (1966): 18.
8. Letter dated February 10, 1960, to Avery Brundage, Series 26/20/37, Box 199, ABCUIUC.
9. "Personalmente estoy en contra de esta decisión porque considero que vamos a hacer un gran ridículo." Letter dated December 3, 1962, to Roberto Sánchez Vilella, Sección VI, Senador por acumulación, Serie 17, Archivo Misceláneo, Cartapacio 273.3, Décimos JCAC, Compañía de Fomento Recreativo 1964–62, AFLMM.
10. "Memoria X Juegos Centroamericanos y del Caribe," June 25, 1966, no page number, Sección VI, Senador por Acumulación, Serie 17, Archivo Misceláneo, Cartapacio 273.3, Décimos JCAC, Administración Parques y Recreo, AFLMM.

11. "Memoria X Juegos Centroamericanos y del Caribe."

12. Emilio E. Huyke, "Los Juegos Centroamericanos," *El Mundo*, November 13, 1961.

13. "Comité Olímpico gestiona sede para juegos de 1966," *El Mundo*, July 31, 1962.

14. Pepe Seda, "X Juegos de San Juan—1966," *El Mundo*, September 8, 1962.

15. "Entiende el Comité Olímpico de Puerto Rico que no corresponde a la historia deportiva de nuestra isla, ni a la etapa de progreso gigante que vive Puerto Rico, continuar aceptando invitaciones sin que ahora invitemos nosotros a los demás pueblos del circuito a visitarnos." "Comité Olímpico PR pide entrevista al gobernador," *El Mundo*, March 2, 1962.

16. Antonio Cañas S., "Juegos Deportivos Centroamericanos y del Caribe," Sección VI, Senador por Acumulación, Serie 17, Archivo Misceláneo, Cartapacio 273.3, Décimos JCAC, Administración Parques y Recreo, AFLMM.

17. "Memoria X Juegos Centroamericanos y del Caribe."

18. "Demostrar que es verdad que nuestro adelanto deportivo es tal, que hay que mirar a nuestra isla y a nuestros hombres para orientación y guía." Pepe Seda, "Misión-Juegos de S.J. 1966," *El Mundo*, July 4, 1963.

19. Letter addressed to "Honorable Legislador" sent May 16, 1966, Sección VII, Senador por Acumulación, Serie 17, Archivo Misceláneo, Cartapacio 273.3, Memoria de los Décimos Juegos Deportivos Centroamericanos y del Caribe, 1966, AFLMM.

20. Letter to Julio E. Monagas dated August 13, 1962, Sección VI, Senador por Acumulación, Serie 17, Archivo Misceláneo, Cartapacio 273.3, Décimos JCAC, Administración Parques y Recreo, AFLMM.

21. "Posibles mejoras dentro de la realidad económica de Puerto Rico." Cable from Emilio Huyke to Julio E. Monagas, 1962, Sección VI, Senador por Acumulación, Serie 17, Archivo Misceláneo, Cartapacio 273.3, Décimos JCAC, Administración Parques y Recreo, AFLMM.

22. "Comité Olímpico de PR trabaja ya en planes organización de décimos juegos," *El Mundo*, August 31, 1962.

23. "Memoria X Juegos Centroamericanos y del Caribe."

24. "Este Gobierno se opone decididamente a que venga un equipo cubano a Puerto Rico a participar en dichos juegos mientras el presente régimen cubano gobierne en aquella isla. No creemos que su presencia pueda servir propósito alguno sino que, por el contrario, tendría a crear una situación difícil e intolerable en el país." Draft of "Letter to the Governor" by Roberto Sánchez Vilella to Julio E. Monagas, Delegación cubana a Juegos Centroamericanos 1966, dated April 17, 1964, Sección VI, Senador por

Acumulación, Serie 17, Archivo Misceláneo, Cartapacio 273.3, Décimos jcac, Administración Parques y Recreo, AFLMM.

25. "La actitud de agresividad que han demostrado . . . tanto en Jamaica como en Brasil y otros lugares en el hemisferio donde se han celebrado competencias atléticas." "Puerto Rico será libre por la lucha de su pueblo y la solidaridad de todos los pueblos de este continente y del mundo. . . . Puerto Rico será libre como lo será Vietman del Sur, que está luchando contra el imperialismo norteamericano, y como lo serán Angola y Venezuela" (Sánchez Vilella, draft of "Letter to the Governor").

26. "Ni aún en el campo de los deportes." "Combatiremos activamente cualquier gestión ante el Gobierno de los Estados Unidos tendiente a permitir la entrada de la delegación de Cuba a . . . Puerto Rico" (Sánchez Vilella, draft of "Letter to the Governor").

27. For a discussion of Olympic Rule No. 25 regarding political interference or discrimination, see my discussion of the reorganization of COPR in chapter 4.

28. Joaquín Martínez-Rousset, "No tenemos aún Villa Olímpica para X Juegos, dice Monagas," *El Mundo*, February, 16, 1965.

29. "¿Qué sucederá si Cuba envía unos doscientos atletas a los X Juegos y aquí se encuentran con unos 20,000 compatriotas exiliados dispuestos y listos a enviarlos al paredón? . . . problema de gobierno a gobierno . . . pintado de rojo. . . . Es posiblemente la situación más explosiva con que se ha tropezado el COI en toda su historia." Joaquín Martínez Rousset, "Visas para los cubanos," *El Mundo*, February 22, 1965.

30. See Guttmann, *The Games Must Go On*.

31. "Puede ser causa de una tragedia en una actividad que está supuesta a incrementar la confraternidad entre los distintos países del mundo" (quoted in Juan Cepero, "El problema de PR es muy complicado: Brundage," *El Mundo*, February 24, 1965).

32. R. Santiago Sosa, "Secretario de Estado de PR Dr. Lastra reafirma decisión de no pedir visas para cubanos," *El Mundo*, February 25, 1965.

33. Leogrande and Kornblue, *Back Channel to Cuba*.

34. Sosa, "Secretario de Estado de PR."

35. "Puerto Rico ni tiene ni ha solicitado sede para los Juegos Olímpicos Mundiales." Juan Cepero, "Sec General de FAIA promete ayudar a resolver caso de PR y los X Juegos," *El Mundo*, February 25, 1965.

36. Juan Cepero, "Declara don Julio Enrique Monagas 'Puerto Rico no le ha ofrecido a nadie la sede de los X Juegos,'" *El Mundo*, February 22, 1965.

37. Joaquín Martínez-Rousset, "Este cohete no llegó a la luna," *El Mundo*, February 24, 1965.

38. "Brundage Is Critical of Excluding Cuba Athletes," *Santa Barbara News-Press*, February 24, 1965.

39. Juan Cepero, "Sec General de FAIA promete ayudar a resolver caso de PR y los X Juegos," *El Mundo*, February 25, 1965.

40. "Caracas Resolution," Caracas, March 16, 1965, Series 26/20/37, Box 199, ABCUIUC.

41. Letter dated March 30, 1965, to Avery Brundage, Series 26/20/37, Box 199, ABCUIUC.

42. "Resolution No 1. Whereas: 1) The Organizing Committee of the X Central American and Caribbean Games, which are to be held in San Juan, Puerto Rico in 1966, has informed the Executive Committee that the Government of that country does not consider it advisable at this time nor in the immediate future, for security reasons, to grant visas to the Cuban Delegation. 2) The organizing Committee of the X Central American and Caribbean Games, consequently feels that in view of the high importance of these Games, Cuba should not be invited to participate in them and that any request from Cuba to be represented in them should be denied, solely for security reasons. 3) The Constitution of Central American and Caribbean Sports Organization, states in article 2, paragraph 1, that one of its objectives is to 'assure the periodic holding of the Central American and Caribbean Games,' and in its article 23, section b), charges the Executive Committee with the direction and organization of all matters of the CACSO to be 'discharged in the most efficient manner and in accordance with the general interest of all concerned.' 4) In article 23, section f, second paragraph, the Executive Committee is empowered 'to adopt any measures it may consider necessary to safeguard the high interests of amateur sport and those of the Central American and Caribbean Sport Organization.' Be it Resolved: 1. to authorize, the Organizing Committee of the X Central American and Caribbean Games to continue its work and to hold the Games in 1966, without the participation of Cuba; 2. to empower the Organizing Committee, whenever the problem of security dessappear [*sic*], to invite and to accept the participation of Cuba in the X Central American and Caribbean Games; 3. to send the present resolution to the International Olympic Committee and the National Olympic Committees members of the CACSO for whatever action may be deemed necessary. Caracas, March 16, 1965." Caracas Resolution, Series 26/20/37, Box 199, ABCUIUC.

43. Probably the withdrawal of IOC recognition to the X CACG or Puerto Rico's ban from hosting an Olympic Games.

44. Letter to Avery Brundage, marked CONFIDENTIAL, no date, Series 26/20/37, Box 199, ABCUIUC.

45. Letter addressed to ODECABE, COPUR, and Comité Organizador de los X Juegos Centroamericanos y del Caribe, no date, Series 26/20/37, Box 199, ABCUIUC.

46. Letter to A. Illueca dated April 15, 1965, Series 26/20/37, Box 199, ABCUIUC.

47. Jamaica Cabinet Submission (JCS), "Entry of Cubans into Jamaica," January 10, 1962, cited in Lipman, "Between Guantánamo and Montego Bay," 37, 32–33.

48. For a complete biography of Rieckehoff Sampayo, see Mayo Santana, *El juguete sagrado*.

49. Letter to Avery Brundage dated September 5, 1965, Series 26/20/37, Box 199, ABCUIUC.

50. At this time CACSO was led by Monagas, COPR was under the brief presidency of Francisco Bueso, the Organizing Committee was led by Emilio Huyke, and the PRPA was now under the presidency of Octavio Wys. Letter to Ing. José de J. Clark Flores dated November 17, 1965, Series 26/20/37, Box 199, ABCUIUC. See also Informe semanal 41, October 5–13, 1965, Administración de Parques y Recreos Públicos, Fondo Oficina del Gobernador, Serie Informes Semanales de los Jefes de Agencias de Gobierno al Gobernador de Puerto Rico, 1965–68, AGPR. It seems probable that Rieckehoff Sampayo had a role in making Puerto Rican Olympic and sport institutions change their policy regarding the Cuban visas. See Mayo Santana, *El juguete sagrado*.

51. Juan Manuel Ocasio, "Lastra: Hands Off Policy for Cubans," *San Juan Star*, November 11, 1965.

52. Memorandum to Avery Brundage dated November 26, 1965, Series 26/20/37, Box 199, ABCUIUC.

53. Letter to Avery Brundage dated December 7, 1965, Series 26/20/37, Box 199, ABCUIUC.

54. Cable to Torregrosa dated December 5, 1965, Series 26/20/37, Box 199, ABCUIUC.

55. As presented in memorandum dated December 11, 1965, Series 26/20/37, Box 199, ABCUIUC.

56. I. Aleksandrov, "Washington's 'Iron Curtain,'" *Pravda*, June 28, 1966, in Joint Committee on Slavic Studies, *Current Digest of the Soviet Press* 18, no. 22 (1966): 18.

57. Letter to Felicio Torregrosa dated December 13, 1965, Series 26/20/37, Box 199, ABCUIUC.

58. Cable to Felicio Torregrosa dated December 15, 1965, Series 26/20/37, Box 199, ABCUIUC; letter dated January 5, 1966, Series 26/20/37, Box 199, ABCUIUC.

59. See letter to Avery Brundage dated December 15, 1965, Series 26/20/37, Box 199, ABCUIUC.

60. Letter from Avery Brundage to K. Andrianov, Comite Olympique d'URSS, Skatertnyj 4, Moscow, Series 26/20/37, Box 199, ABCUIUC.

61. Memorandum for agenda items at the sixty-fourth meeting of the IOC in 1966 by K. Andrianov, Chancellery of the International Olympic Committee, I. Political interference into sports, Series 26/20/37, Box 199, ABCUIUC.

62. Cablegram sent June 4, 1966, to Avery Brundage, Series 26/20/37, Box 199, ABCUIUC.

63. See Ayala and Bernabe, *Puerto Rico in the American Century*, 226–29.

64. "Los atletas cubanos no estarán solos. Allí estarán los deportistas e independentistas puertorriqueños para ponerle coto a los planes de provocación contra Cuba que pretende llevar a cabo el imperialismo yanqui y para contestar, junto a los atletas cubanos si es que éstos se ven obligados a hacerlo también, dichas provocaciones en las formas que sean necesarias. El pueblo de Puerto Rico, ciertamente no permitirá que gusanos y lacayos usurpen su representación y mucho menos que mancillen nuestro prestigio y dignidad nacional." "Los atletas cubanos no estarán solos: Denuncia el MPI las maniobras del imperialismo contra Cuba en los Juegos Centroamericanos," *Granma*, March 24, 1966, Series 26/20/37, Box 85, ABCUIUC. This letter was actually written by Narciso Gabell Martínez, mission chief of the MPI in Cuba, for *Granma*.

65. Letter sent to Avery Brundage dated February 22, 1966, Series 26/20/37, Box 199, ABCUIUC.

66. Letter to Monagas dated March 21, 1966, Series 26/20/37, Box 199, ABCUIUC.

67. See Mayo Santana, *El juguete sagrado*, 180–81.

68. Morris W. Rosenberg, "'Threats' at the Games Here," *San Juan Star*, July 1, 1966.

69. "Lo asociado le impide ser libre," "Temas del día," Cuban newspaper clipping, Series 26/20/37, Box 85, ABCUIUC.

70. Personal report by Avery Brundage dated June 30, 1966, Series 26/20/37, Box 199, ABCUIUC.

71. The alleged political interference was a "so-called 'Olympic Oath' and the anthem of the 1st National Sport Games" and other politically oriented statements made by some sports leaders, as published in *Granma* on Octo-

ber 21, 1965. Letter to Comité Olímpico Cubano dated February 16, 1966, Series 26/20/37, Box 85, ABCUIUC.

72. Letter to Avery Brundage sent March 30, 1966, Series 26/20/37, Box 199, ABCUIUC.

73. Meeting of the Executive Board of the IOC, April 21–24, 1966, 7, Series 26/20/37, Box 84, ABCUIUC.

74. Marrero, *Nos vimos en Puerto Rico*, 9–15.

75. "Y JURO, en nombre de los mártires de 'Cerro Pelado' y en el de todos los que han hecho posible nuestra dedicación al deporte, defenderlo con la vida si fuera necesario" (Marrero, *Nos vimos en Puerto Rico*, 17).

76. Cable to Avery Brundage from Moscow URSSGOVT, Series 26/20/37, Box 199, ABCUIUC.

77. Cablegram from Andrianov, Moscow URSSGOVT, to Avery Brundage, June 10, 1966, Series 26/20/37, Box 199, ABCUIUC.

78. "TASS Statement," *Pravda*, May 30, 1966; "Cuba Has Loyal Friends," *Izvestia*, May 31, 1966, both in Joint Committee on Slavic Studies, *Current Digest of the Soviet Press* 18, no. 22 (1966): 27.

79. "13th Congress of the Communist Party of Czechoslovakia: Speech by Comrade L. I. Brezhnev, General Secretary of the Central Committee of the CPSU," *Pravda*, June 1, 1966, in Joint Committee on Slavic Studies, *Current Digest of the Soviet Press* 18, no. 22 (1966): 24.

80. Ramón Rodríquez, "Revelan Yate MPI salió tras cubanos," *El Mundo*, June 10, 1966, Series 26/20/37, Box 199, ABCUIUC.

81. Rafael López Sosa, "Acusa a E.U. de interferir con cubanos," *El Mundo*, June 13, 1966.

82. See transcription of interview with Rieckehoff Sampayo in Mayo Santana, *El juguete sagrado*, 176–80.

83. "Este barco es propiedad del gobierno de Cuba, el cual se ha incautado de la propiedad de muchos de los cubanos que viven en Puerto Rico, sin el debido procedimiento de ley. Si este barco entra a las aguas de Puerto Rico y, bajo la ley de almirantazgo, un cubano inicia una acción contra el gobierno de Cuba, este barco queda arrestado en aseguramiento de sentencia y van a pasar muchos años en que el mismo va a estar en Puerto Rico bajo arresto" (quoted in Mayo Santana, *El juguete Sagrado*, 179).

84. Cable sent to Avery Brundage from Moscow, Series 26/20/37, Box 199, ABCUIUC.

85. "Estamos listos para bajar y dejamos el barco aquí" (quoted by Rieckehoff in Mayo Santana, *El juguete Sagrado*, 179).

86. Cable to Avery Brundage, June 10, 1966, Series 26/20/37, Box 199, ABCUIUC.

87. "Interferir, entorpecer y retrasar." Rafael López Rosas, "Acusa a E.U. de interferir con cubanos," *El Mundo*, June 13, 1966.

88. "Patria O Muerte Venceremos," "Saludamos Atletas Cubanos."

89. The only political incident at the opening ceremonies consisted of the Dominican Republic flag being hoisted halfway by their NOC president to protest the presence of the international peacekeeping forces in his country.

90. For a complete overview of the X CACG, including scores, teams, sports, and other statistical information, see Uriarte González, *80 años de acción y pasión*, 111–37.

91. See "Memoria X Juegos Centroamericanos y del Caribe."

92. Rafael Collazo, "Atleta cubano pide asilo politica PR," *El Día*, June 14, 1966, Series 26/20/37, Box 199, ABCUIUC; "Alega régimen Castro puso ELA en ridículo," *El Mundo*, June 22, 1966, Series 26/20/37, Box 199, ABCUIUC.

93. Guillermo Hernández, "Creen que está incomunicada atleta cubana quiere quedarse en PR," *El Imparcial*, June 22, 1966, Series 26/20/37, Box 199, ABCUIUC.

94. Salvador Guzmán, "Llanuza dice frustra 2 atentados a su vida," *El Imparcial*, June 24, 1966, Series 26/20/37, Box 199, ABCUIUC.

95. Letter from Dr. Carlos Lastra to Salvador Rodríguez Aponte, Police Superintendent, dated June 3, 1966, Fondo Oficina del Gobernador, Informes Semanales de los Jefes de Agencias de Gobierno al Gobernador de Puerto Rico, AGPR.

96. This is according to the COC's president, Manuel González Guerra, which José de J. Clark certified as true and accurate. See letter from Manuel González Guerra to Emilio Huyke dated June 14, 1966, Series 26/20/37, Box 199, ABCUIUC.

97. "Hijos de tal cosa." Letter from González Guerra to Huyke.

98. This is according to Juan Pablo Vega in an interview after his defection. See Ismael Fernández, "Revelan hay agentes secretos delegación cubana," *El Día*, June 14, 1966, Series 26/20/37, Box 199, ABCUIUC.

99. "Iniciar su fuga hacia la libertad." "¿No se queda nadie aquí?" Letter from González Guerra to Huyke.

100. Letter from González Guerra to Huyke.

101. Antonio Miranda, "Alega el MPI tergiversó incidente," *El Mundo*, June 21, 1966, Series 26/20/37, Box 199, ABCUIUC.

102. Letter from González Guerra to Huyke.

103. "Dirigidos exclusivamente por la Agencia Central de Inteligencia de Estados Unidos." "No son directamente responsables de los mismos." "Guerra sicológica." Salvador Guzmán, "Llanuza dice frustra 2 atentados a su vida," *El Imparcial*, June 24, 1966, Series 26/20/37, Box 199, ABCUIUC.

104. "Fidel Castro ha puesto en ridículo al Gobierno del Estado Libre Asociado." "El ridículo del pueblo de Puerto Rico consiste en que haciendo alardes de soberanía, invita con gran fanfarria a los atletas cubanos, y cuando llegan a escasamente 3 millas de nuestras playas, una simple orden de un empleado subalterno de la Guardia Costanera, detiene fuera de nuestras playas a la embarcación cubana. Esto es evidente de que no existe la soberanía de Puerto Rico." "Senador Ortiz Toro alega régimen Castro puso ELA en ridículo," *El Mundo*, June 22, 1966, Series 26/20/37, Box 199, ABCUIUC.

105. See Mayo Santana, *El juguete sagrado*, 234–35.

106. The average attendance per day for all sports combined was 18,017. The sports with most attendance were swimming with 56,971; track and field with 51,586; baseball with 29,459; basketball with 29,127; and volleyball with 25,854. Comité Organizador Décimos Juegos, "Memorias de los décimos juegos Centroamericanos y del Caribe celebrados en San Juan de Puerto Rico del 11 al 25 del mes de junio de 1966," Fundación Luis Muñoz Marín, Sección VII, Senador por acumulación, Serie 17, Archivo Misceláneo, Cartapacio 273.3, Memoria de los Décimos JCAC, 1966, n.p.

107. "Comenzó la penosa tarea de 'desvestir' la Villa Deportiva Central. . . . Ya todo había concluido. Se recogió el mobiliario y se hizo la limpieza general. La Villa Deportiva Central regresó al papel que el progreso le ha encomendado en la vida de Puerto Rico: Urbanización Pública Las Virtudes. . . . En el silencio de un atardecer de Puerto Rico los hombres que terminaron la labor de quitarle a aquellas estructuras el ropaje deportivo con que se habían engalanado, lloraron como niños. Como niños a quienes se les había quitado un juguete. El mejor juguete que el deporte podía ofrecerle a hombres como ellos. . . . Los Décimos Juegos Deportivos Centroamericanos y del Caribe." Organizador Décimos Juegos, "Memorias de los décimos juegos Centroamericanos y del Caribe celebrados en San Juan de Puerto Rico del 11 al 25 del mes de junio de 1966," Fundación Luis Muñoz Marín, Sección VII, Senador por acumulación, Serie 17, Archivo Misceláneo, Cartapacio 273.3, Memoria de los Décimos JCAC, 1966, n.p.

6. The Eternal Overtime?

1. "Un pueblo necesita determinación para luchar dedicadamente e incansablemente por el mejoramiento de toda la comunidad. Paciencia porque los problemas a que nos enfrentamos no se resuelven con meramente aprobar una ley, sino que requieren el esfuerzo colectivo, a largo plazo, de todos los ciudadanos. Honradez-honor-porque hay que entender que no hay empresa más noble que el servicio, sin esperar recibir recompensa, a todos nuestros compatriotas. Nuestro pueblo ha cumplido responsablemente y cabalmente con ambos campos en los útlimos años." "Muñoz destaca logros de Julio E. Mongas," *El Mundo*, May 1, 1967.

2. "Sumergido en la desesperanza." "Aportación al deporte y a la vida de nuestro pueblo es grande." "Al rendirle tributo a Julio Enrique Monagas le rendimos tributo a nuestro pueblo. Un pueblo que se empeña, como nosotros nos hemos empeñado, en trabajar duro y bien, en ampliar y profundizar nuestros valores, nuestro sistema democrático de vida, en las oportunidades de mejoramiento para todos nuestros compatriotas es un pueblo que vale. Es un pueblo que merece progresar y merece que no se le pongan obstáculos en su camino, pero si se le pusieran sabría salvarlos con la misma limpieza como los que ya dejamos atrás." "Muñoz destaca logros de Julio E. Mongas," *El Mundo*, May 1, 1967.

3. "Nos podemos sentir orgullosos de haber sido los anfitriones. A pesar de los problemas con que nos enfrentamos, auspiciamos unos juegos, que si no superan, ciertamente comparan favorablemente con los mejores presentados hasta ahora en su categoría. Independientemente del buen papel que en las competencias hicimos, demostramos antes que nada, que somos un pueblo hospitalario, consciente de su tradición, serio y dedicado. Pero lo más importante fue demostrar que somos un pueblo en marcha, un pueblo que vive a tono con la noble exigencia del lema olímpico: 'Más alto, más lejos, más fuerte.' Sigamos honrando y haciendo realidad ese lema. Elevemos nuestra vista más alto y más lejos en nuestro horizonte deportivo. Ampliemos nuestra participación internacional y recibamos con los brazos abiertos a los que de otros países vengan aquí a compartir. Fortalezcamos nuestra juventud, estimulándolos a participar, no a ser espectadores en el deporte y en la solución de problemas que aún tenemos que resolver. Vamos a proveerle más facilidades para que se puedan desarrollar físicamente y que puedan recoger en su entendimiento lo que el deporte y su pueblo son y significan. Más aún, que toda esa energía, física y mental, se canalice en pro del bienestar de todo nuestro pueblo. Vamos a alzar los

niveles de vida en todos los órdenes de Puerto Rico. Miremos decididos la meta difícil, pero ciertamente no imposible de una gran civilización para nuestro país. Fortalezcamos nuestras instituciones principales para poder enfrentarnos mejor al futuro y para poder hacer contribución, aunque sea modesta, a la felicidad y bienestar de otros. Si logramos esto habremos alcanzado nuestro propósito." "Muñoz destaca logros de Julio E. Mongas," *El Mundo*, May 1, 1967.

4. Meléndez, *Movimiento anexionista en Puerto Rico*.

5. Nieves Falcón, *Un siglo de represión política en Puerto Rico*.

6. Ayala and Bernabe, *Puerto Rico in the American Century*, 224–26.

7. See Tomasini, *Honor a los maestros de educación física y propulsores del deporte puertorriqueño*, 164.

8. Olympic leaders included Germán Rieckehoff Sampayo, Puerto Rican IOC member Richard Carrión, President Héctor Cardona of COPR, the chancellor of the UPR, the president of Sacred Heart University, and the president of American University. "Parte de Prensa: Comité Olímpico de Puerto Rico," Fondo Organizaciones y sus Funciones, Guerra, Caja H5, Archivo Central, Universidad de Puerto Rico (hereafter ACUPR).

9. "Homenaje a Don Geño Guerra, Programa Tentativo," Fondo Organizaciones y sus Funciones, Guerra, Caja H5, ACUPR.

10. Ramos Méndez, *Posesión del ayer*, 98–100.

11. "Guerra de los himnos y las banderas." Mayo Santana, *El juguete sagrado*, 247.

12. For a brief documentary account of this issue, see Uriarte González, *Puerto Rico en el Continente*, 120–22; Mayo Santana, *El juguete sagrado*, 247–94.

13. MacAloon, "La Pitada Olímpica."

14. "García Padilla exhorta a dejar la segunda pregunta en blanco," *El Nuevo Día*, February 11, 2012.

15. "Resultados Plebiscito 2012: Consulta sobre el estatus Político de Puerto Rico 6 de noviembre de 2012," Comisión Estatal de Elecciones Estado Libre Asociado de Puerto Rico, http://64.185.222.182/REYDI_Escrutinio12 /index.html#es/default/OPCIONES_NO_TERRITORIALES_ISLA.xml (accessed May 18, 2015).

16. Héctor Ríos Amaury, "Estadidad y Olimpismo," *El Vocero*, August 2, 2012, www.estado51prusa.com/?p=19535 (accessed October 29, 2013). Act 220501, chapter 2205, U.S. Olympic Committee, www.soccerpark.com /TedStevens.pdf (accessed October 29, 2013).

17. "¿Desaparece la camiseta boricua de las Olimpiadas bajo la estadidad?,"

Primera Hora, August 8, 2012, http://www.primerahora.com/noticias /gobierno-politica/nota/desaparecelacamisetaboricuadelasolimpiadas bajolaestadidad-680594/ (accessed October 29, 2013); "Richard Carrión aclara sus expresiones sobre el Copur y la estadidad," *Primera Hora*, November 29, 2011, http://www.primerahora.com/noticias/gobierno-politica/nota /richardcarrionaclarasusexpresionessobreelcopurylaestadidad-585044/ (accessed October 29, 2013).

18. Mayo Santana, *El juguete sagrado*, 298, 309. For an overview of the events around the Olympic boycotts in Puerto Rico, see chapter 14, "Los boicoteos olímpicos."

19. José Santori Coll, personal interview, September 13, 2011. It is important to know that both "Fufi" Santori Coll and Germán Rieckehoff Sampayo later regretted their decision on parading with the Olympic flag.

20. Riordan and Krüger, *The International Politics of Sport in the 20th Century*, 22.

21. A recent case was the 2010 Commonwealth Games in India, which was full of controversy over how prepared India was to be the host. India's capacity to organize and host these games was seen as a test of its modernization and as a marker of the vitality of the nation. The organizational problems that arose made India's modernization questionable. See Pankaj Mishra, "Games India Isn't Ready to Play," *New York Times*, October 2, 2010, accessed online October 3, 2010; Jim Yardley, "As Games Begin, India Hopes to Save Its Pride," *New York Times*, October 2, 2010, accessed online October 3, 2010.

22. See Uriarte González, *80 años de acción y pasión*, 289–90.

23. Commonwealth 48.6 percent, statehood 46.3 percent, independence 4.4 percent (Ayala and Bernabe, *Puerto Rico in the American Century*, 293–94).

24. "Cuba: Asistir a los Juegos Centroamericanos 2012 es un derecho," *Al Momento*, January 10, 2010, www.almomento.net (accessed July 21, 2010).

25. Amanda Ulman and Ruth Machado, "Marchers in Puerto Rico Say: We Are a Nation," *Militant*, August 5, 1996.

26. "Cuba: Asistir a los Juegos Centroamericanos 2012 es un derecho," *Al Momento*, January 10, 2010, www.almomento.net (accessed July 21, 2010).

27. Luis Santiago Arce, "Fortuño evade abucheo Centroamericano," *El Nuevo Día*, July 18, 2010.

28. "Tarjeta Roja para el Gobierno de Puerto Rico." "Amonestan atletas boricuas," *El Nuevo Día*, July 19, 2010. A red card is a card used in various sports, most notably soccer, to indicate a serious offense, which results in an automatic ejection of the player for the rest of the game.

Bibliography

Archival Sources

Archive of the Board of Trustees of the Universidad de Puerto Rico, San Juan
Archivo Central of the Universidad de Puerto Rico en Río Piedras
Archivo Fundación Luis Muñoz Marín, San Juan
Archivo General de Puerto Rico, San Juan
Ateneo Puertorriqueño, San Juan, Puerto Rico
Avery Brundage Collection, University of Illinois at Urbana-Champaign
Biblioteca Legislativa de Puerto Rico Tomás Bonilla Feliciano, San Juan
Colección Jesús T. Piñero, Universidad del Este
Colección Puertorriqueña, Universidad de Puerto Rico en Río Piedras
Kautz Family YMCA Archives, University of Minnesota, Twin Cities
Museo Olímpico de Puerto Rico at the Villa Olímpica Germán Rieckehoff
   Sampayo, Salinas
National Archives and Records Administration, Washington DC
Personal Archive of Benjamín Lúgaro Torres, Ponce, Puerto Rico
Seymour Library, Knox College, Galesburg, Illinois
University Library, University of Illinois at Urbana-Champaign

Published Sources

Abell, Jackie. "'They Seem to Think "We're Better Than You"': Framing Football Support as a Matter of 'National Identity' in Scotland and England." *British Journal of Social Psychology* 50, no. 2 (2011): 246–64.
Academia Olímpica de Puerto Rico. *Puerto Rico y el Movimiento Olímpico.* San Juan: Comité Olímpico de Puerto Rico, 1995.
Acevedo, Héctor L., ed. *Don Jaime Benítez: Entre la universidad y la política.* San Juan: Universidad Interamericana de Puerto Rico, 2008.
Aching, Gerard. *Masking and Power: Carnival and Popular Culture in the Caribbean.* Minneapolis: University of Minnesota Press, 2002.
Acosta, Ivonne. *La mordaza.* Río Piedras, Puerto Rico: Edil, 1987.
Acosta, Úrsula. "La inmigración germánica a Puerto Rico a principios del siglo XIX." *Revista de Historia* 1, no. 1 (1985): 139–44.

Acosta-Belen, Edna, ed. *The Puerto Rican Woman: Perspectives on Culture, History, and Society.* New York: Praeger, 1986.

Agosto Cintrón, Nélida. *Religión y cambio social en Puerto Rico (1898–1940).* Río Piedras, Puerto Rico: Ediciones Huracán, 1996.

Aguiló, Sylvia. *Idea y concepto de la cultura puertorriqueña en la década del 50.* San Juan: Centro de Estudios Avanzados de Puerto Rico y el Caribe, 1987.

Alabarces, Pablo, ed. *Futbologías: Fútbol, identidad y violencia en América Latina.* Buenos Aires, Argentina: Consejo Latinoamericano de Ciencias Sociales, 2003.

————. *Peligro de Gol: Estudios sobre deporte y sociedad en América Latina.* Buenos Aires, Argentina: CLACSO, 2000.

Albizu Campos, Pedro. *Cuatro discursos, dos extractos, una entrevista.* San Juan, Puerto Rico: Editorial Patria Nuestra, 1969.

————. *República de Puerto Rico: Libro de Bolsillo.* Montevideo, Uruguay: El Siglo Ilustrado, 1972.

Albizu-Campos Meneses, Laura, and Mario A. Rodríguez León, eds. *Albizu Campos escritos.* Hato Rey, Puerto Rico: Publicaciones Puertorriqueñas, 2007.

Alegría, Ricardo E. *Ball Courts and Ceremonial Plazas in the West Indies.* New Haven CT: Yale University Press, 1983.

————. *El Instituto de Cultura Puertorriqueña: Los primeros cinco años, 1955–1960.* San Juan: Instituto de Cultura Puertorriqueña, 1960.

————. *El Instituto de Cultura Puertorriqueña, 1955–1973: Dieciocho años contribuyendo a fortalecer nuestra conciencia nacional.* San Juan: Instituto de Cultura Puertorriqueña, 1978.

————. *Descubrimiento, conquista y colonización de Puerto Rico, 1493–1599.* San Juan, Puerto Rico: Editorial Edil, 1969.

————. "The Fiesta of Santiago Apóstol (St. James the Apostle) in Loíza, Puerto Rico." *Journal of American Folklore* 69, no. 272 (1956): 123–34.

Álvarez, Luis Reinaldo, and Tony Lorenti. *Fútbol puertorriqueño: Crónica de alegrías, sueños y desencantos.* Vol. 1, *1911–1949.* Humacao: Museo Casa Roig, Universidad de Puerto Rico en Humacao, 2007.

Álvarez Curbelo, Sylvia, and María E. Rodríguez Castro. *Del nacionalismo al populismo: Cultura y política en Puerto Rico.* Río Piedras, Puerto Rico: Ediciones Huracán, 1993.

————. "Las fiestas públicas en Ponce: Políticas de la memoria y cultura cívica." In *Los arcos de la memoria: El '98 de los pueblos puertorriqueños,* edited by Silvia Álvarez Curbelo, Mary Frances Gallart, and Carmen I. Raffucci. San Juan: Oficina del Presidente de la Universidad de Puerto Rico, 1998.

————. *Un país del porvenir: El afán de modernidad en Puerto Rico (siglo XIX)*. San Juan, Puerto Rico: Ediciones Callejón, 2001.

Anderson, Benedict. *Imagined Communities: Reflections on the Origin and Spread of Nationalism*. London: Verso, 1991.

Anderson, Thomas P. *The War of the Dispossessed: Honduras and El Salvador, 1969*. Lincoln: University of Nebraska Press, 1981.

Andreu Iglesias, César. *Cosas de aquí: Una visión de la década del '60 en Puerto Rico*. San Juan, Puerto Rico: Publicaciones Atenea, 1975.

Annino, Antonio, and François-Xavier Guerra, eds. *Inventando la nación: Iberoamérica. Siglo XIX*. Mexico City: Fondo de Cultura Económica, 2003.

Arbena, Joseph L. *Latin American Sport: An Annotated Bibliography, 1988–1998*. New York: Greenwood Press, 1999.

————, ed. *Sport and Society in Latin America: Diffusion, Dependency, and the Rise of Mass Culture*. New York: Greenwood Press, 1988.

————. "Sport and the Promotion of Nationalism in Latin America: A Preliminary Interpretation." *Studies in Latin America Popular Culture* 11 (1992): 143–56.

Arbena, Joseph L., and David G. LaFrance, eds. *Sport in Latin America and the Caribbean*. Wilmington DE: Scholarly Resources, 2002.

Archetti, Eduardo P. "The Meaning of Sport in Anthropology: A View from Latin America." *European Review of Latin American and Caribbean Studies* 65 (December 1998): 91–103.

Arroyo Muñoz, José Carlos. *Rebeldes al poder: Los grupos y la lucha ideológica: 1959–2000*. San Juan, Puerto Rico: Isla Negra, 2002.

Atiles Osoria, José M. "Pro-State Violence in Puerto Rico: Cuban and Puerto Rican Right-Wing Terrorism from the 1960s to the 1990s." *Socialism and Democracy* 26, no. 1 (2012): 127–42.

Ayala, César. "From Sugar Plantations to Military Bases: The U.S. Navy Expropriations in Vieques, Puerto Rico, 1940–1945." *CENTRO Journal* 13, no. 1 (2001): 22–44.

Ayala, César J., and Rafael Bernabe. *Puerto Rico in the American Century: A History since 1898*. Chapel Hill: University of North Carolina Press, 2007.

Babín, María Teresa. *Panorama de la cultura puertorriqueña*. New York: Las Americas Publishing, 1958.

Bairner, Alan. "Football and the Idea of Scotland." In *Scottish Sport in the Making of the Nation: Ninety-Minute Patriots?*, edited by Grant Jarvie and Graham Walker, 9–26. London: Leicester University Press, 1994.

Bakewell, Peter John. *A History of Latin America: C. 1450 to the Present*. Malden MA: Blackwell, 2004.

Barbosa Muñiz, José C. *La era de oro del atletismo puertorriqueño 1930–1960*. San Juan: Academia Puertorriqueña de la Historia, 2007.

Barreto, Amílcar Antonio. *The Politics of Language in Puerto Rico*. Gainesville: University of Florida Press, 2001.

Bass, Amy. "State of the Field: Sports History and the 'Cultural Turn.'" *Journal of American History* 101, no. 1 (2014): 148–72.

Beck, Peter. "The British Government and the Olympic Movement: The 1948 London Olympics." *International Journal of the History of Sport* 25, no. 5 (2008): 615–48.

Beckles, Hilary McD. "The Caribbean, Cricket and C. L. R. James." In "Report on Sport and Society." Special issue, *North American Congress on Latin America* 37, no. 5 (2004): 19–22.

Beeman, William O. "The Anthropology of Theater and Spectacle." *Annual Review of Anthropology* 22 (1993): 369–93.

Beezley, William H. "Bicycles, Modernization, and Mexico." In *Sport and Society in Latin America: Diffusion, Dependency, and the Rise of Mass Culture*, edited by Joseph L. Arbena, 15–28. New York: Greenwood Press, 1988.

Beezley, William H., and Linda A. Curcio-Nagy, eds. *Latin American Popular Culture: An Introduction*. Wilmington DE: Scholarly Resources, 2000.

Beezley, William, Cheryl English Martin, and William French, eds. *Rituals of Rule, Rituals of Resistance: Public Celebrations and Popular Culture in Mexico*. Wilmington DE: SR Books, 1994.

Bell, David A. *The Cult of the Nation in France: Inventing Nationalism, 1680–1800*. Cambridge MA: Harvard University Press, 2001.

Benítez, José A. *Puerto Rico and the Political Destiny of America*. Houston TX: Southern University Press, 1958.

Benítez Rojo, Antonio. *La isla que se repite: El Caribe y la perspectiva posmoderna*. Hanover NH: Ediciones del Norte, 1989.

———. *The Repeating Island: The Caribbean and the Postmodern Perspective*. Durham NC: Duke University Press, 2006.

Berman Santana, Déborah. *Kicking Off the Bootstrap: Environment, Development and Community Power in Puerto Rico*. Tucson: University of Arizona Press, 1996.

Bernier, David. *¡En guardia! Combates, conquistas y legados de Mayagüez 2010*. Guaynabo, Puerto Rico: Publicaciones Urbanas, 2010.

Betts, Raymond. *Decolonization*. New York: Routledge, 2004.

Bhana, Surendra. *The United States and the Development of the Puerto Rican Status Question, 1936–1968*. Lawrence: University Press of Kansas, 1975.

Blake, Andrew. *The Body Language: The Meaning of Modern Sport*. London: Lawrence & Wishart, 1995.

Blanco, Tomás. *El prejuicio racial en Puerto Rico*. New York: Arno Press, 1975.

Bolívar Fresnada, José. *Guerra, [Banca] y Desarrollo: El Banco de Fomento y la industrialización de Puerto Rico*. San Juan, Puerto Rico: Fundación Luis Muñoz Marín, 2011.

Bosch, Juan. *De Cristóbal Colón a Fidel Castro: El Caribe, frontera imperial*. Santo Domingo, Dominican Republic: Editora Alfa y Omega, 1988.

Bosque Pérez, Ramón, and José Javier Colón Morera, eds. *Las carpetas: Persecución política y derechos civiles en Puerto Rico*. Río Piedras, Puerto Rico: Centro para la Investigación y Promoción de los Derechos Civiles, 1997.

――, eds. *Puerto Rico under Colonial Rule: Political Persecution and the Quest for Human Rights*. New York: State University of New York Press, 2005.

Braudel, Fernand. *The Mediterranean and the Mediterranean World in the Age of Philip II*. New York: Harper & Row, 1972.

Breckinridge, Henry. "Recreation and Physical Education." In *White House Conference on Child Health and Protection*, edited by Ray L. Wilbur, H. E. Barnard, Katherine Glover, and Winifred Moses, 215–30. New York: Century, 1931.

Briggs, Laura. *Reproducing Empire: Race, Sex, Science, and U.S. Imperialism in Puerto Rico*. Berkeley: University of California Press, 2002.

Bucheli, Marcelo. *Bananas and Business: The United Fruit Company in Colombia, 1899–2000*. New York: New York University Press, 2005.

Bureau of the Budget. *Manuel de organización del Gobierno del Estado Libre Asociado de Puerto Rico*. San Juan: Estado Libre Asociado de Puerto Rico, Negociado del Presupuesto, 1966.

Burgos, Adrian. *Playing America's Game: Baseball, Latinos, and the Color Line*. Berkeley: University of California Press, 2007.

Burke, Peter. "The Invention of Tradition." *English Historical Review* 101 (January 1986): 316–17.

Bushnell, Asa S., ed. *Report of the United States Olympic Committee: Games of the XIVth Olympiad London, England, July 29 to August 14, 1948, Vth Olympic Winter Games, St. Moritz, Switzerland, January 30 to February 8, 1948*. New York: U.S. Olympic Association, 1948.

Cabán, Pedro. *Constructing a Colonial People: Puerto Rico and the United States, 1898–1932*. Boulder CO: Westview Press, 1999.

Cabrera Collazo, Rafael. *Los dibujos del progreso: El mundo caricaturesco de*

Filardi y la crítica al desarrollismo muñocista, 1950–1960. San Juan: Publicaciones Puertorriqueñas Editores, 2006.

Calder, Bruce. *The Impact of Intervention: The Dominican Republic During the U.S. Occupation of 1916–1924.* Austin: University of Texas Press, 1984.

Canales, Nemesio R. *Paliques.* Ponce, Puerto Rico: Tipografía "La Defensa," 1913.

Cañete Quesada, Carmen. "Reseña. Mercedes López Baralt. Sobre ínsulas extrañas: El clásico de Pedreira anotado por Tomás Blanco. San Juan: Universidad de Puerto Rico: 2001. 447 páginas." *Revista de Crítica Literaria Latinoamericana* 59 (September 2004): 336–38.

Cannadine, David, and Simon Price. *Rituals of Royalty: Power and Ceremonial in Traditional Societies.* Cambridge, England: Cambridge University Press, 1987.

Caple, Jim. "Those Absent Share the Blame." ESPN.com, August 15, 2004. http://espn.go.com/espn/print?id=1860013&type=story (accessed May 15, 2015).

Caro de Delgado, A. R. *Villa de San Germán: Sus derechos y privilegios durante los siglos XVI, XVII y XVIII.* San Juan: Instituto de Cultura Puertorriqueña, 1962.

Carpentier, Florence, and Jean-Pierre Lefèvre. "The Modern Olympic Movement, Women's Sport and the Social Order during the Inter-war Period." *International Journal of the History of Sport* 23, no. 7 (2006): 1112–27.

Carrión, Juan Manuel. *Voluntad de nación: Ensayos sobre el nacionalismo en Puerto Rico.* San Juan, Puerto Rico: Ediciones Nueva Aurora, 1996.

Carrión, Juan Manuel, Teresa C. Gracia Ruiz, and Carlos Rodríguez Fraticelli, eds. *La nación puertorriqueña: Ensayos en torno a Pedro Albizu Campos.* San Juan: Editorial de la Universidad de Puerto Rico, 1993.

Carter, Thomas. *The Quality of Hume Runs: The Passion, Politics, and Language of Cuban Baseball.* Durham NC: Duke University Press, 2008.

Castro-Klarén, Sara, and John Charles Chasteen, eds. *Beyond Imagined Communities: Reading and Writing the Nation in Nineteenth-Century Latin America.* Washington DC: Woodrow Wilson Center Press, 2003.

Chakravarty, Dipesh. "The Muddle of Modernity." In "AHR Roundtable: Historians and the Question of 'Modernity.'" Special issue, *American Historical Review* 116, no. 3 (2011): 663–75.

———. *Provincializing Europe: Postcolonial Thought and Historical Difference.* Princeton NJ: Princeton University Press, 2000.

Chant, Sylvia, and Nikki Craske. "Gender and Sexuality." In *Gender in Latin America,* edited by Sylvia Chant and Nikki Craske, 128–60. London: Latin American Bureau, 2003.

Chappell, Robert. "The Soviet Protégé: Cuba, Modern Sport, and Communist Comrade." *European Sports History Review* 3 (2001): 181–204.

Chasteen, John C. *Born in Blood and Fire: A Concise History of Latin America.* New York: Norton, 2001.

Chatterjee, Partha. *The Nation and Its Fragments: Colonial and Postcolonial Histories.* Princeton NJ: Princeton University Press, 1993.

Cobas, José A., and Jorge Duany. *Cubans in Puerto Rico: Ethnic Economy and Cultural Identity.* Gainesville: University Press of Florida, 1997.

Cohen, Colleen B. "'This Is de Test': Festival and the Cultural Politics of Nation Building in the British Virgin Islands." *American Ethnologist* 25, no. 2 (1998): 189–214.

Colby, Merle. *Puerto Rico: A Profile in Pictures.* New York: Duell, Sloan and Pearce, 1940.

Colón Delgado, Jorge. *Santurce Cangrejeros 1954–55: La Maquinaria Perfecta.* Self-published, 2007.

Colón Delgado, Jorge, Ferdinand Mercado, and Jorge L. Rosario. *50 años de historia deportiva puertorriqueña, 1952–2002.* San Juan, Puerto Rico: Comisión Especial para la Celebración del Cincuentenario de la Constitución del Estado Libre Asociado de Puerto Rico, 2002.

Colón Ocasio, Roberto. *Antonio Fernós Isern soberanista, Luis Muñoz Marín Autonomista: Divergencias ideológicas y su efecto en el desarrollo del Estado Libre Asociado de Puerto Rico.* San Juan, Puerto Rico: Fundación Educativa Antonio Fernós Isern, 2009.

Comité Olímpico de Puerto Rico. *Puerto Rico y la Educación Olímpica.* San Juan: Comité Olímpico de Puerto Rico, n.d.

Comité Organizador Décimos Juegos. *Memorias de los décimos juegos Centroamericanos y del Caribe celebrados en San Juan de Puerto Rico del 11 al 25 del mes de junio de 1966.* San Juan, Puerto Rico: Talleres Gráficos Interamericanos, 1966.

Coubertin, Pierre. *Olympism: Selected Writings.* Ed. Norbert Muller. Lausanne, Switzerland: International Olympic Committee, 2000.

Curet, Eliezer. *El desarrollo económico de Puerto Rico, 1940 a 1972.* Hato Rey, Puerto Rico: Management Aid Center, 1976.

Curran, Connor. "Sport and Cultural Nationalism: The Conflict between Association and Gaelic Football in Donegal, 1905–34." *Éire-Ireland: A Journal of Irish Studies* 48, nos.1–2 (2013): 79–94.

Da Costa, Lamartine P. "Epilogue: Hegemony, Emancipation and Mythology." In *Sport in Latin American Society: Past and Present*, edited by J. A. Mangan and Lamartine P. Da Costa, 181–96. London: Frank Cass, 2002.

Da Matta, Roberto. *Carnavales, malandros y héroes: Hacia una sociología del dilema brasileño*. Mexico City: Fondo de Cultura Económica, 2002.

Davies, Richard O. *Sports in American Life: A History*. Malden MA: Wiley-Blackwell, 2012.

Dávila, Arlene M. *Sponsored Identities: Cultural Politics in Puerto Rico*. Philadelphia: Temple University Press, 1997.

Davis, Natalie-Zemon. *Society and Culture in Early Modern France: Eight Essays*. Stanford: Stanford University Press, 1975.

Delano, Jack. *Puerto Rico Mio: Four Decades of Change / Cuatro décadas de cambio*. Washington DC: Smithsonian Institution Press, 1990.

De la Rosa, Víctor. *Puerto Rico en los Juegos Centroamericanos*. Puerto Rico: n.p., 1995.

del Moral, Solsiree. "Colonial Citizens of a Modern Empire: War, Illiteracy, and Physical Education in Puerto Rico, 1917–1930." *New West Indian Guide* 87 (2013): 30–61.

——. *Negotiating Empire: The Cultural Politics of Schools in Puerto Rico, 1898–1952*. Madison: University of Wisconsin Press, 2013.

Dent, David. *The Legacy of the Monroe Doctrine: A Reference Guide to U.S. Involvement in Latin American and the Caribbean*. Westport CT: Greenwood Press, 1999.

Devés Valdés, Eduardo. *El pensamiento latinoamericano en el siglo XX: Entre la modernización y la identidad*. Buenos Aires, Argentina: Biblios, 2000.

Díaz Quiñónez, Arcadio. "The Hispanic-Caribbean National Discourse: Antonio S. Pedreira and Ramiro Guerra y Sánchez." In *Intellectuals in the Twentieth-Century Caribbean*, vol. 2, *Unity in Variety: The Hispanic and Francophone Caribbean*, edited by Alistair Hennessy, 98–121. London: Macmillan, 1992.

Dichter, Heather L., and Andrew L. Johns, eds. *Diplomatic Games: Sport, Statecraft, and International Relations since 1945*. Lexington: University Press of Kentucky, 2014.

Dietz, James. *Economic History of Puerto Rico: Institutional Change and Capitalist Development*. Princeton NJ: Princeton University Press, 1986.

——. *Puerto Rico: Negotiating Development and Change*. Boulder CO: Rienner, 2003.

Diffie, Justine W., and Bailey W. Diffie. *Porto Rico: A Broken Pledge*. New York: Vanguard Press, 1931.

Dinwiddie, William. "Cock-Fighting in Puerto Rico." In *The Cockfight: A Casebook*, edited by Alan Dundes, 26–29. Madison: University of Wisconsin Press, 1994.

Dirks, Robert. *The Black Saturnalia: Conflict and Its Ritual Expression on British West Indian Slave Plantations*. Gainesville: University of Florida Press, 1987.

Dómenech Sepúlveda, Luis. *Historia y pensamiento de la educación física y el deporte*. Río Piedras, Puerto Rico: Publicaciones Gaviota, 2003.

Duany, Jorge. *The Puerto Rican Nation on the Move: Identities on the Island and in the United States*. Chapel Hill: University of North Carolina Press, 2002.

Dubois, Laurent. *Soccer Empire: The World Cup and the Future of France*. Berkeley: University of California Press, 2010.

Duffy Burnett, Christina, and Burke Marshall, eds. *Foreign in a Domestic Sense: Puerto Rico, American Expansion, and the Constitution*. Durham NC: Duke University, 2001.

Dunn, Richard. *Sugar and Slaves: The Rise of the Planter Class in the English West Indies, 1624–1713*. Chapel Hill: University of North Carolina Press, 1972.

Dyreson, M. "Prolegomena to Jesse Owens: American Ideas about Race and Olympic Races from the 1890s to the 1920s." *International Journal of the History of Sport* 25, no. 2 (2008): 224–46.

Eckstein, Susan E. *Back from the Future: Cuba under Castro*. Princeton NJ: Princeton University Press, 1994.

Eddy, John, and Deryck Schreuder. *The Rise of Colonial Nationalism: Australia, New Zealand, Canada and South Africa First Assert Their Nationalities, 1880–1914*. Sydney: Allen & Unwin, 1988.

Eley, Geoff, and Ronald Grigor Suny, eds. *Becoming National: A Reader*. Oxford: Oxford University Press, 1996.

Elias, Robert. *The Empire Strikes Out: How Baseball Sold U.S. Foreign Policy and Promoted the American Way Abroad*. New York: New Press, 2010.

Elsey, Brenda. *Citizens and Sportsmen: Fútbol and Politics in Twentieth-Century Chile*. Austin: University of Texas Press, 2011.

Escobar, Arturo, and Sonia Álvarez, eds. *The Making of Social Movements in Latin America: Identity, Strategy, and Democracy*. Boulder CO: Westview Press, 1992.

Fernández Méndez, Eugenio. *Galería Puertorriqueña: Tipos y caracteres, costumbres y tradiciones*. San Juan Bautista: Instituto de Cultura Puertorriqueña, 1958.

———. *La identidad y la cultura: Críticas y valoraciones en torno a Puerto Rico*. San Juan, Puerto Rico: Ediciones "El Cemí," 1959.

Fernández Retamar, Roberto. *Calibán: Apuntes sobre la cultura de nuestra América*. Buenos Aires, Argentina: La Pleyade, 1973.

Ferrao, Luis Angel. "Nacionalismo, hispanismo y élite intelectual en el Puerto Rico de los años treinta." In *Del nacionalismo al populismo: Cultura y política en Puerto Rico*, edited by Silvia Alvarez Curbelo and María Elena Rodríguez Castro, 37–60. Río Piedras, Puerto Rico: Ediciones Huracán, 1993.

———. *Pedro Albizu Campos y el nacionalismo puertorriqueño 1930–1939.* Harrisonburg VA: Banta, 1990.

Ferrer, Ada. *Insurgent Cuba: Race, Nation, and Revolution, 1868–1898.* Chapel Hill: University of North Carolina Press, 1999.

Fleagle, Fred K. *Social Problems in Porto Rico.* Boston: D. C. Heath, 1917.

Flores, Juan. *From Bomba to Hip-Hop: Puerto Rican Culture and Latino Identity.* New York: Columbia University Press, 2000.

———. *Insularismo e ideología burguesa.* Río Piedras, Puerto Rico: Ediciones Huracán, 1979.

———. "The Puerto Rico That Jose Luis Gonzalez Built: Comments on Cultural History." In "Destabilization and Intervention in the Caribbean." Special issue, *Latin American Perspectives* 11, no. 3 (1984): 173–84.

Flores Collazo, María Margarita. *25/4 julio: Conmemorar, festejar y consumir en Puerto Rico.* San Juan: Academia Puertorriqueña de la Historia y Centro de Investigaciones Históricas, 2004.

Fonseca Barahona, Marvin. *Puerto Rico: Cuna de campeones. 56 años de pura adrenalina, 1934–1990.* San Juan, Puerto Rico: Departamento de Recreación y Deportes/Best PR Boxing Promotions, 2008.

Freeman, William H. *Physical Education and Sports in a Changing Society.* Boston: Allyn & Bacon, 1997.

Galeano, Eduardo. *Soccer in Sun and Shadow.* London: Verso, 1998.

García Reyes, Karina G. "Olimpiadas y Copa Mundial de Fútbol: ¿Competencias deportivas o instrumentos políticos?" CONfines de relaciones internacionales y ciencia política 3, no. 6 (2007): 83–94.

Garrard-Burnett, Virginia. *On Earth as It Is in Heaven: Religion in Modern Latin America.* Wilmington DE: Scholarly Resources, 2000.

Garrido, Pablo. *Esoteria y fervor popular de Puerto Rico.* Madrid: Ediciones Cultura Hispánica, 1952.

Geary, Patrick J. *The Myth of Nations: The Medieval Origins of Europe.* Princeton NJ: Princeton University Press, 2002.

Geertz, Clifford. *Negara: The Theatre State in Nineteenth-Century Bali.* Princeton NJ: Princeton University Press, 1980.

Gellner, Ernest. *Nations and Nationalism.* Ithaca NY: Cornell University Press, 1983.

Gelpí, Juan G. *Literatura y paternalismo en Puerto Rico*. San Juan: Editorial de la Universidad de Puerto Rico, 1994.

Gems, Gerald. *The Athletic Crusade: Sport and American Cultural Imperialism*. Lincoln: University of Nebraska Press, 2006.

Gil, Pedro. "Educación Física." *Porto Rico School Review* 4, no. 10 (1920): 12–18.

Girón, Socorro. *Ponce, el teatro La Perla y la campana de la Almudaina: Historia de Ponce desde sus comienzos hasta la segunda década del siglo XX*. Ponce, Puerto Rico: Gobierno Municipal de Ponce, 1992.

Gobat, Michel. *Confronting the American Dream: Nicaragua under U.S. Imperial Rule*. Durham NC: Duke University Press, 2005.

Gómez Calvo, José L. "Deporte y conciencia nacional en Puerto Rico." In *Puerto Rico ¿La más antigua colonia mundial? Una paradójica realidad*, edited by Ramón-Darío Molinary, 111–28. Madrid: Fundación Francisco Carvajal, Casa de Puerto Rico en España, 1998.

González, José Luis. *El país de los cuatro pesos y otros ensayos*. Río Piedras, Puerto Rico: Ediciones Huracán, 1989.

Gordon, Maxine. "Cultural Aspects of Puerto Rico's Race Problem." *American Sociological Review* 15 (June 1950): 383–89.

Greenfeld, Liah. *Nationalism: Five Roads to Modernity*. Cambridge MA: Harvard University Press, 1992.

Grosfoguel, Ramón. *Colonial Subjects: Puerto Ricans in a Global Perspective*. Berkeley: University of California Press, 2003.

Guerra, Lillian. *Popular Expression and National Identity in Puerto Rico: The Struggle for Self, Community, and Nation*. Gainesville: University Press of Florida, 1998.

Guss, David M. *The Festive State: Race, Ethnicity, and Nationalism as Cultural Performance*. Berkeley: University of California Press, 2000.

Guttmann, Allen. "Capitalism, Protestantism, and the Rise of Modern Sport." In *Major Problems in American Sport History*, edited by Steven Riess, 5–14. Boston: Houghton Mifflin, 1997.

——. *From Ritual to Record: The Nature of Modern Sports*. New York: Columbia University Press, 1978.

——. *Games and Empires: Modern Sport and Cultural Imperialism*. New York: Columbia University Press, 1994.

——. *The Games Must Go On: Avery Brundage and the Olympic Movement*. New York: Columbia University Press, 1984.

——. *The Olympic Games: A History of the Modern Games*. Urbana: University of Illinois Press, 1992.

———. "'Our Former Colonial Masters': The Diffusion of Sports and the Question of Cultural Imperialism." *Stadion* 14, no. 1 (1988): 49–63.

Halperín-Donghi, Tulio. *The Contemporary History of Latin America*. Durham NC: Duke University Press, 1993.

Handy, Jim. "The Guatemalan Revolution and Civil Rights: Presidential Elections and the Judicial Process under Juan José Arévalo and Jacobo Arbenz Guzmán." *Canadian Journal of Latin American and Caribbean Studies* 10, no. 19 (1985): 3–21.

Hanson, Earl P. *Puerto Rico: Ally for Progress*. Princeton NJ: D. Van Nostrand, 1962.

Hargreaves, John. *Freedom for Catalonia? Catalan Nationalism, Spanish Identity and the Barcelona Olympic Games*. Cambridge, England: Cambridge University Press, 2000.

———. *Sport, Power, and Culture: A Social and Historical Analysis of Popular Sports in Britain*. New York: St. Martin's Press, 1986.

Harris, Max. "Masking the Site: The Fiestas de Santiago Apostol in Loíza, Puerto Rico." *Journal of American Folklore* 114, no. 453 (2001): 358–69.

Hartwell, Edward M. "Peter Henry Ling, the Swedish Gymnasiarch." *American Physical Education Review* 1, no. 1 (1896): 1–13.

Haslip-Viera, Gabriel. *Taino Revival: Critical Perspectives on Puerto Rican Identity and Cultural Politics*. Princeton NJ: Markus Wiener, 2001.

Hill, Christopher R. *Olympic Politics*. Manchester, England: Manchester University Press, 1996.

"Historians and the Question of 'Modernity.'" Special issue, *American Historical Review* 116, no. 3 (2011): 631–751.

Hobsbawm, Eric. *Nations and Nationalism since 1780: Programme, Myth, and Reality*. Cambridge, England: Cambridge University Press, 1990.

Hobsbawm, Eric, and Terence Ranger. *The Invention of Tradition*. Cambridge, England: Cambridge University Press, 1983.

Hoover, Herbert. "Address of President Hoover." In *White House Conference on Child Health and Protection*, edited by Ray L. Wilbur, H. E. Barnard, Katherine Glover, and Winifred Moses, 5–15. New York: Century, 1931.

Hopkins, C. Howard. *History of the YMCA in North America*. New York: Association Press, 1951.

Huertas González, Félix R. "Deporte e identidad en Puerto Rico." *Enciclopedia de Puerto Rico*, September 28, 2010. http://www.enciclopediapr.org/esp/print_version.cfm?ref=09021302 (accessed October 16, 2013).

———. *Deporte e identidad: Puerto Rico y su presencia deportiva internacional (1930–1950)*. San Juan, Puerto Rico: Terranova Editores, 2006.

Hutchinson, John. "Cultural Nationalism and Moral Regeneration." In *Nationalism*, edited by John Hutchinson and Anthony Smith, 122–31. Oxford: Oxford University Press, 1994.

Huyke, Emilio. *Los deportes en Puerto Rico*. Sharon CT: Troutman Press, 1968.

Iber, Jorge, Samuel O. Regalado, José M. Alamillo, and Arnoldo De León, eds. *Latinos in U.S. Sports: A History of Isolation, Cultural Identity, and Acceptance*. Champaign IL: Human Kinetics, 2011.

Ince, Basil. "Nationalism and Cold War Politics at the Pan American Games: Cuba, the United State and Puerto Rico." *Caribbean Studies* 27, nos. 1–2 (1994): 65–85.

James, C. L. R. *Beyond a Boundary*. Durham NC: Duke University Press, 1993.

Jarvie, Grant, and Graham Walker, eds. *Scottish Sport in the Making of the Nation: Ninety-Minute Patriots?* London: Leicester University Press, 1994.

Johns, Andrew. "Introduction: Competing in the Global Arena. Sport and Foreign Relations since 1945." In *Diplomatic Games: Sport, Statecraft, and International Relations since 1945*, edited by Heather L. Dichter and Andrew L. Johns, 1–15. Lexington: University Press of Kentucky, 2014.

Johnson, Robert D. "Anti-Imperialism and the Good Neighbor Policy: Ernest Gruening and Puerto Rican Affairs, 1934–1939." *Journal of Latin American Studies* 29, no. 1 (1997): 89–110.

Joseph, Gilbert. "Forging the Regional Pastime: Baseball and Class in Yucatán." In *Sport and Society in Latin America: Diffusion, Dependency, and the Rise of Mass Culture*, edited by Joseph L. Arbena, 29–62. New York: Greenwood Press, 1988.

Kemper, Kurt Edward. *College Football and American Culture in the Cold War Era*. Urbana: University of Illinois Press, 2009.

Keys, Barbara J. *Globalizing Sport: National Rivalry and the International Community in the 1930s*. Cambridge MA: Harvard University Press, 2006.

Kittleson, Roger. *The Country of Football: Soccer and the Making of Modern Brazil*. Berkeley: University of California Press, 2014.

Knight, Allan, and Will Pansters, eds. *Caciquismo in Twentieth-Century Mexico*. London: Institute for the Study of the Americas, 2005.

Knight, Franklin. *The Caribbean: The Genesis of a Fragmented Nationalism*. New York: Oxford University Press, 1990.

Krüger, Arnd. "The Unfinished Symphony: A History of the Olympic Games from Coubertin to Samaranch." In *The International Politics of Sport in the 20th Century*, edited by Jim Riordan and Arnd Krüger, 3–27. London: E&FN Spon, 1999.

La Junta Nacional Panameña de los IV Juegos Deportivos Centro Americanos y del Caribe: Memoria oficial de los IV Juegos Deportivos Centro Americanos y del Caribe. Panamá: La Junta, 1938.

Lancaster, Richard. *Serving the U.S. Armed Forces, 1861–1986: The Story of the YMCA's Ministry to Military Personnel for 125 Years*. Schaumburg IL: Armed Services YMCA of the USA, 1987.

Latourette, Kenneth S. *World Service: A History of the Foreign Work and World Service of the Young Men's Christian Associations of the United States and Canada*. New York: Association Press, 1957.

Leogrande, William M., and Peter Kornblue. *Back Channel to Cuba: The Hidden History of Negotiations between Washington and Havana*. Chapel Hill: University of North Carolina Press, 2014.

Lever, Janet. *Soccer Madness*. Chicago: University of Chicago Press, 1995.

———. "Sport in a Fractured Society: Brazil under Military Rule." In *Sport and Society in Latin America: Diffusion, Dependency, and the Rise of Mass Culture*, edited by Joseph L. Arbena, 85–96. New York: Greenwood Press, 1988.

Levine, Daniel H. *Religion and Politics in Latin America: The Catholic Church in Venezuela and Colombia*. Princeton NJ: Princeton University Press, 1981.

Lewis, Gordon. *Notes on the Puerto Rican Revolution: An Essay on American Dominance and Caribbean Resistance*. New York: Monthly Review Press, 1974.

———. *Puerto Rico: Freedom and Power in the Caribbean*. New York: Monthly Review Press, 1963.

Lidin, Carmen, and Elliott Castro Tirado. *¡Listos! Puerto Rico en el deporte internacional (1930–2004)*. San Juan, Puerto Rico: BPPR, 1996.

Lipman, Jana K. "Between Guantánamo and Montego Bay: Cuba, Jamaica, Migration and the Cold War, 1959–62." *Immigrants and Minorities* 21, no. 3 (2002): 25–51.

Lomnitz, Claudio. "Nationalism as a Practical System: Benedict Anderson's Theory of Nationalism from the Vantage Point of Spanish America." In *The Other Mirror: Grand Theory through the Lens of Latin America*, edited by Miguel Angel Centeno and Fernando López-Alves, 329–59. Princeton NJ: Princeton University Press, 2001.

López Cantos, Ángel. *Fiestas y juegos en Puerto Rico (siglo XVIII)*. San Juan: Centro de Estudios Avanzados de Puerto Rico y el Caribe, 1990.

López Fernández, Iván. "The Social, Political, and Economic Contexts to the Evolution of Spanish Physical Educationalists (1874–1992)." *International Journal of the History of Sport* 26, no. 11 (2009): 1630–51.

López López, Gabriel. "Geurra fría, propaganda y prensa: Cuba y México ante el fantasma del comunismo internacional, 1960–1962." *Revista Mexicana de Política Internacional* 100, no. 1 (2014): 127–46.

López Rojas, Luis A. *El debate por la nación: Ascenso y consolidación del muñocismo. Del afán por el poder hasta la discusión por el status entre Gilberto Concepción de Gracia y Luis Muñoz Marín (1932–1945).* San Juan, Puerto Rico: Isla Negra Editores, 2011.

Lupkin, Paula. *Manhood Factories: YMCA Architecture and the Making of Modern Urban Culture.* Minneapolis: University of Minnesota Press, 2010.

MacAloon, John. "La pitada Olímpica." In *Text, Play, and Story: The Construction and Reconstruction of Self and Society,* edited by Edward M. Bruner. Washington DC: American Ethnological Society, 1984.

——, ed. *Muscular Christianity in Colonial and Post-Colonial Worlds.* London: Routledge, 2008.

——. *This Great Symbol: Pierre de Coubertin and the Origins of the Modern Olympic Games.* London: Routledge, 2008.

Malavet, Pedro. *America's Colony: The Political and Cultural Conflict between the United States and Puerto Rico.* New York: New York University Press, 2004.

Maldonado Denis, Manuel. *Eugenio María de Hostos y el pensamiento social iberoamericano.* Mexico City: Fondo de Cultura Económica, 1992.

——. "Prospects for Latin American Nationalism: The Case of Puerto Rico." *Latin American Perspectives* 3 (1976): 36–45.

Mandell, Richard D. *Sport: A Cultural History.* New York: Columbia University Press, 1984.

Mangan, J. A. *The Games Ethic and Imperialism: Aspects of the Diffusion of an Ideal.* London: Frank Cass, 1998.

——. "Prologue: Emulation, Adaptation and Serendipity." In *Sport in Latin American Society: Past and Present,* edited by J. A. Mangan and LaMartine P. DaCosta, 1–8. London: Frank Cass, 2002.

——, ed. *Reformers, Sport, Modernizers: Middle-Class Revolutionaries.* Vol. 4 of *The European Sports History Review.* London: Frank Cass, 2002.

Mangan, J. A., and Colm Hickey. "Missing Middle-Class Dimensions: Elementary Schools, Imperialism and Athleticism." In *Reformers, Sport, Modernizers: Middle-Class Revolutionaries,* edited by J. A. Mangan, 73–90. Vol. 4 of *The European Sports History Review.* London: Frank Cass, 2002.

Mangan J. A., and LaMartine P. DaCosta, eds. *Sport in Latin American Society: Past and Present.* London: Frank Cass, 2002.

Maraniss, David. *Clemente: The Passion and Grace of Baseball's Last Hero.* New York: Simon & Schuster, 2006.

Marqués, René. *El puertorriqueño dócil y otros ensayos, 1953–1971*. Barcelona: Editorial Antillana, 1977.

Marrero, Juan. *Nos vimos en Puerto Rico: Crónicas*. Havana: Ediciones Granma, 1966.

Martínez-Fernández, Luis. *Protestantism and Political Conflict in the Nineteenth-Century Spanish Caribbean*. New Brunswick NJ: Rutgers University Press, 2002.

Martínez-Rousset, Joaquín. *50 años de Olimpismo*. San Juan, Puerto Rico: Editorial Edil, 2003.

Marx, Anthony W. *Faith in Nation: Exclusionary Origins of Nationalism*. Oxford: Oxford University Press, 2003.

Mason, Tony. "England 1966: Traditional or Modern?" In *National Identity and Global Sports Events: Culture, Politics, and Spectacle in the Olympics and the Football World Cup*, edited by Alan Tomlinson and Christopher Young, 83–98. Albany: State University of New York Press, 2006.

Mayo Santana, Raúl. *El juguete sagrado: Germán Rieckehoff Sampayo. Vida y leyenda*. San Juan, Puerto Rico: Editorial Plaza Mayor, 2000.

McCaffrey, Katherine. *Military Power and Popular Protest: The U.S. Navy in Vieques, Puerto Rico*. New Brunswick NJ: Rutgers University Press, 2002.

McCree, Roy. "Modern Sport, Middle Classes and Globalization 1945–1952: Variations on a Theme." *International Journal of Sport* 25, no. 4 (2008): 472–92.

Mechikoff, Robert A., and Steven G. Estes. *A History of Philosophy of Sport and Physical Education: From Ancient Civilizations to the Modern World*. Boston: WCB/McGraw-Hill, 1998.

Mejía Garcés, Reinaldo. *Estampas de San Germán y algo más . . . Recodando el ayer*. Sábana Grande, Puerto Rico: Imprenta Santana, 1995.

Meléndez, Edwin. *Movimiento anexionista en Puerto Rico*. Río Piedras: Universidad de Puerto Rico, 1993.

Merrill, Dennis. *Negotiating Paradise: U.S. Tourism and Empire in Twentieth-Century Latin America*. Chapel Hill: University of North Carolina Press, 2009.

Mintz, Sidney. *Caribbean Transformations*. Chicago: Aldine, 1974.

——— . *Worker in the Cane: A Puerto Rican Life History*. New York: Norton, 1974.

Mintz, Sidney, and Sally Price, eds. *Caribbean Contours*. Baltimore: Johns Hopkins University Press, 1985.

Morales Carrión, Arturo. *Puerto Rico y la lucha por la hegemonía en el Caribe: Colonialismo y contrabando, siglos XVI–XVIII*. San Juan: Centro de Investigaciones Históricas, Editorial de la Universidad de Puerto Rico, 1995.

Moraña, Mabel, Enrique Dussel, and Carlos A. Jáuregui, eds. *Coloniality at Large: Latin America and the Postcolonial Debate*. Durham NC: Duke University Press, 2008.

Morris, Nancy. *Puerto Rico: Culture, Politics, and Identity*. Westport CT: Praeger, 1995.

Morse, Richard M. "The Caribbean: Geopolitics and Geohistory." In *Caribbean Integration: Papers on Social, Political, and Economic Integration. Third Caribbean Scholar's Conference, Georgetown, Guyana, April 4–9, 1966*, edited by Sybil Lewis and Thomas G. Mathews, 155–73. Río Piedras: Institute of Caribbean Studies, University of Puerto Rico, 1967.

Mrozek, Donald J. *Sport and American Mentality, 1880–1910*. Knoxville: University of Tennessee Press, 1983.

Muñiz Hernández, Ramón. *Londres 1948: La verdadera historia de los primeros juegos olímpicos puertorriqueños*. Río Piedras, Puerto Rico: RMH, 1998.

Munton, Don, and David A. Welch. *The Cuban Missile Crisis: A Concise History*. Oxford: Oxford University Press, 2011.

Navarro Rivera, Pablo. *Universidad de Puerto Rico: De Control Político a Crisis Permanente, 1903–1952*. Río Piedras, Puerto Rico: Ediciones Huracán, 2000.

Negrón de Montilla, Aida. *Americanization in Puerto Rico and the Public-School System, 1900–1930*. Barcelona: Editorial Universitaria, Universidad de Puerto Rico, 1975.

Negrón-Muntaner, Frances. "Showing Face: Boxing and Nation Building in Contemporary Puerto Rico." In *Contemporary Caribbean Cultures and Societies in a Global Context*, edited by Franklin W. Knight and Teresita Martínez-Vergne, 97–116. Chapel Hill: University of North Carolina Press, 2005.

Negrón-Portillo, Mariano. *El autonomismo puertorriqueño, su transformación ideológica (1895–1914)*. Río Piedras, Puerto Rico: Ediciones Huracán, 1981.

Neto-Wacker, Marica de Franceschi, and Christian Wacker. *Brazil Goes Olympic: Historical Fragments from Brazil and the Olympic Movement until 1936*. Kassel, Germany: Agon Sportverlag, 2010.

Nieves Falcón, Luis. *Un siglo de represión política en Puerto Rico: 1898–1998*. San Juan, Puerto Rico: Ediciones Puerto, 2009.

Nugent, David. *Modernity at the Edge of Empire: State, Individual and Nation in the Northern Peruvian Andes, 1885–1935*. Stanford: Stanford University Press, 1997.

Oleksak, Michael M., and Mary Adams Oleksak. *Béisbol: Latin Americans and the Grand Old Game*. Grand Rapids MI: Masters Press, 1991.

Ollero Tassara, Andrés. *Universidad y política: Tradición y secularización en el siglo XIX*. Madrid: Instituto de Estudios Políticos, 1972.

Osuna, Juan J. *A History of Education in Puerto Rico*. Rio Piedras: Editorial de la Universidad de Puerto Rico, 1949.

Page, Joseph. "Soccer Madness: *Futebol* in Brazil." In *Sport in Latin America and the Caribbean*, edited by Joseph L. Arbena and David G. LaFrance, 33–50. Wilmington DE: Scholarly Resources, 2002.

Palmié, Stephan. *Wizards and Scientists: Explorations in Afro-Cuban Modernity and Tradition*. Durham NC: Duke University Press, 2002.

Palmié, Stephan, and Francisco A. Scarano, eds. *The Caribbean: A History of the Region and Its People*. Chicago: University of Chicago Press, 2011.

——— . Introduction to *The Caribbean: A History of the Region and Its People*, edited by Stephan Palmié and Francisco A. Scarano, 1–21. Chicago: University of Chicago Press, 2011.

Pantojas-García, Emilio. *Development Strategies as Ideology: Puerto Rico's Export-Led Industrialization Experience*. Boulder CO: Lynne Rienner, 1990.

——— . "End-of-the-Century Studies of Puerto Rico's Economy, Politics, and Culture." *Latin American Research Review* 35, no. 3 (2000): 227–40.

——— . "The Puerto Rican Paradox: Colonialism Revisited." *Latin American Research Review* 40, no. 3 (2005): 163–76.

Park, Roberta J. "'Forget about That Pile of Papers': Second World War Sport, Recreation and the Military on the Island of Puerto Rico." *International Journal of the History of Sport* 20, no. 1 (2003): 50–64.

——— . "From *la bomba* to *béisbol*: Sport and the Americanisation of Puerto Rico, 1898–1950." *International Journal of the History of Sport* 28, no. 17 (2011): 2575–93.

Pedreira, Antonio. *Insularismo: Ensayos de interpretación puertorriqueña*. San Juan: Biblioteca de Autores Puertorriqueños, 1957.

——— . *Un hombre del pueblo, José Celso Barbosa*. San Juan: Instituto de Cultura Puertorriqueña, 1965.

Pérez, Louis, Jr. "Between Baseball and Bullfighting: The Quest for Nationality in Cuba, 1868–1898." *Journal of American History* 81, no. 2 (1994): 493–517.

——— . *Cuba: Between Reform and Revolution*. New York: Oxford University Press, 1995.

——— . *On Becoming Cuban: Identity, Nationality, and Culture*. Chapel Hill: University of North Carolina Press, 1999.

Pérez Montfort, Ricardo. *Hispanismo y Falange: Los sueños imperiales de la derecha española y México*. Mexico City: Fondo de Obras de Historia, 1992.

Pérez Stable, Marifeli. *The Cuban Revolution: Origins, Course, and Legacy.* New York: Oxford University Press, 1993.

Perloff, Harvey. *Puerto Rico's Economic Future: A Study in Planned Development.* Chicago: University of Chicago Press, 1950.

Perz, John Raymond. "Secondary Education in Spain." PhD diss., Catholic University of America, 1934.

Pettavino, Paula J., and Geralyn Pye. *Sport in Cuba: The Diamond in the Rough.* Pittsburgh: University of Pittsburgh Press, 1994.

Picó, Fernando. *1898: La guerra después de la guerra.* 2nd ed. Río Piedras, Puerto Rico: Ediciones Huracán, 1998.

Picó, Rafael. *Puerto Rico: Planificación y acción.* San Juan: Banco Gubernamental de Fomento para Puerto Rico, 1962.

Pike, Fredrick B. *Hispanismo, 1898–1936: Spanish Conservatives and Liberals and Their Relations with Spanish America.* Notre Dame IN: University of Notre Dame Press, 1971.

Pope, Steven, W. "An Army of Athletes: Playing Fields, Battlefields, and the American Military Sporting Experience, 1898–1920." *Journal of Military History* 59 (July 1995): 435–56.

Power, Margaret. "Nationalism in a Colonized Nation: The Nationalist Party and Puerto Rico." *Memorias: Revista Digital de Historia y Arquieología desde el Caribe* 10, no. 20 (2013): 119–37.

———. "The Puerto Rican Nationalist Party, Transnational Latin American Solidarity, and the United States during the Cold War." In *Human Rights and Transnational Solidarity in Cold War Latin America*, edited by Jessica Stites Mor, 21–47. Madison: University of Wisconsin Press, 2013.

Prieto, Alberto. *Albizu Campos y el independentismo puertorriqueño.* Havana: Editora Política, 1986.

Puig Barata, Núria. "Emociones en el deporte y Sociología." *International Journal of Sport Science* 8, no. 28 (2012): 106–8.

Putney, Clifford. *Muscular Christianity: Manhood and Sports in Protestant America, 1880–1920.* Cambridge MA: Harvard University Press, 2001.

Quintero Rivera, Ángel G. "Clases sociales e identidad nacional: Notas sobre el desarrollo nacional puertorriqueño." In *Puerto Rico: Identidad nacional y clases sociales*, edited by Quintero Rivera et al., 13–44. Río Piedras, Puerto Rico: Ediciones Huracán, 1981.

———. *Patricios y plebeyos: Burgueses, hacendados, artesanos y obreros. Las relaciones de clase en el Puerto Rico de cambio de siglo.* Río Piedras, Puerto Rico: Ediciones Huracán, 1988.

Rama, Ángel. *Ciudad letrada*. Montevideo, Uruguay: Fundación Internacional Ángel Rama, 1984.

Ramírez, Rafael L. "National Culture in Puerto Rico: Class Struggle and National Liberation." *Latin American Perspectives* 3, no. 3 (1976): 109–16.

Ramos Méndez, Mario. *Posesión del ayer: La nacionalidad cultural en la estadidad*. San Juan, Puerto Rico: Editorial Isla Negra, 2007.

Ramsay, Jack. "The World Is in the Zone." ESPN.com, August 15, 2004. http://espn.go.com/espn/print?id=1860107&type=story (accessed May 15, 2015).

Regalado, Samuel O. "Roberto Clemente: Images, Identity and Legacy." *International Journal of the History of Sports* 25, no. 6 (2008): 678–91.

——. *Viva Baseball: Latin Major Leaguers and Their Special Hunger*. Urbana: University of Illinois Press, 2008.

Rein, Ranaan. "'El Primer Deportista': The Political Use and Abuse of Sport in Peronist Argentina." *International Journal of the History of Sport* 15, no. 2 (1998): 54–76.

——. *In the Shadow of Perón: Juan Atilio Bramuglia and the Second Line of Argentina's Populist Movements*. Stanford: Stanford University Press, 2008.

Renda, Mary A. *Taking Haiti: Military Occupation and the Culture of U.S. Imperialism, 1915–1940*. Chapel Hill: University of North Carolina Press, 2001.

Ribeiro, Luiz Carlos, ed. "Futebol, sentimento e política." Special issue, *História: Questões e Debates* 29, no. 57 (2012).

Richardson, Lewis. *Puerto Rico: Caribbean Crossroads*. Produced under the sponsorship of the Board of Publications, University of Puerto Rico. New York: U.S. Camera Publishing Corporation, 1947.

Rico Velasco, Jesús A. "Modernization and Fertility in Puerto Rico: An Ecological Analysis." PhD diss., Ohio State University, 1972.

Riordan, James. "The Impact of Communism on Sport." In *The International Politics of Sport in the 20th Century*, edited by Jim Riordan and Arnd Krüger, 48–66. London: E&FN Spon, 1999.

Riordan, Jim, and Arnd Krüger, eds. *The International Politics of Sport in the 20th Century*. London: E&FN Spon, 1999.

Rioux, Georges. "Pierre de Coubertin's Revelations." In *Olympism: Selected Writings*, edited by Norbert Müller, 23–31. Lausanne, Switzerland: International Olympic Committee, 2000.

Rivera Batiz, Francisco L., and Carlos E. Santiago. *Island Paradox: Puerto Rico in the 1990s*. New York: Russell Sage Foundation, 1998.

Rivera Medina, Eduardo, and Rafael Ramírez, eds. *Del cañaveral a la fábrica: Cambio social en Puerto Rico*. Río Piedras, Puerto Rico: Ediciones Huracán, 1985.

Rivera Ramos, Efrén. "Deconstructing Colonialism: The 'Unincorporated Territory' as a Category of Domination." In *Foreign in a Domestic Sense: Puerto Rico, American Expansion, and the Constitution*, edited by Christina Duffy Burnett and Burke Marshall, 104–19. Durham NC: Duke University Press, 2001.

———. *The Legal Construction of Identity: The Judicial and Social Legacy of American Colonialism in Puerto Rico*. Washington DC: American Psychological Association, 2001.

Rodríguez, Ilia. "Journalism, Development, and the Remaking of Modernity: News Reporting and Construction of Local Narratives of Modernization in Puerto Rico during Operation Bootstrap (1947–1963)." PhD diss., University of Minnesota, 1999.

Rodríguez Berríos, Luis Guillermo. "Nationalism, Socialism, and Modernization in Puerto Rico during the Muñoz Era 1898–1980." PhD diss., University of Minnesota, 1982.

Rodríguez Castro, María Elena. "La 'Escritura de lo Nacional' y 'Los Intelectuales Puertorriqueños.'" PhD diss., Princeton University, 1998.

Rodríguez Juliá, Edgardo. *Cortijo's wake = El entierro de Cortijo*. Translated and with an introduction by Juan Flores. Durham NC: Duke University Press, 2004.

———. *Las tribulaciones de Jonás*. Río Piedras, Puerto Rico: Ediciones Huracán, 1981.

———. *Peloteros*. Río Piedras: Editorial de la Universidad de Puerto Rico, 1996.

Rodríguez Tapia, Ismael. *Rafael Hernández Marín: Cantor de la afirmación nacional puertorriqueña*. San Juan, Puerto Rico: Publicaciones Yuquiyú, 2005.

Romany Siaca, Celina. *La verdadera historia de Roberto Sánchez Vilella*. San Juan, Puerto Rico: Ediciones Puerto, Inc., 2011.

Rowe, David, Jim McKay, and Toby Miller, "Come Together: Sport, Nationalism, and the Media Image." In *MediaSport*, edited by Lawrence A. Wenner, 119–33. London: Routledge, 1998.

Roy-Féquière, Magali. *Women, Creole Identity, and Intellectual Life in Early Twentieth-Century Puerto Rico*. Philadelphia: Temple University Press, 2004.

Ruck, Rob. *The Tropic of Baseball: Baseball in the Dominican Republic*. Westport CT: Meckler, 1991.

Ruiz Patiño, Jorge H. *La política del sport: Élites y deporte en la construcción de la nación colombiana, 1903–1925*. Bogotá: La Carreta Editores EU and Editorial Pontificia Universidad Javeriana, 2010.

Rush, Anne S. *Bonds of Empire: West India and Britishness from Victoria to Decolonization.* Oxford: Oxford University Press, 2011.

Russell, James W. "Operation Bootstrap and NAFTA: Comparing the Social Consequences." *Critical Sociology* 21, no. 2 (1995): 91–107.

Sánchez Agustí, María. *La educación española a finales del XIX: Una mirada a través del periódico republicano La Libertad.* Lleida, Spain: Editorial Milenio, 2002.

Sánchez Tarniella, Andrés. *Trayectoria de las actitudes políticas en Puerto Rico.* Río Piedras, Puerto Rico: Ediciones Bayoán, 1975.

Santiago-Valles, Kelvin. *Subject People and Colonial Discourses: Economic Transformation and Social Disorder in Puerto Rico, 1898–1947.* Albany: State University of New York Press, 1994.

———. "The Unruly City and the Mental Landscape of Colonized Identities: Internally Contested Nationality in Puerto Rico, 1945–1985." *Social Text* 38 (1994): 149–63.

Santori Coll, José. *Tiempo y Escoar.* Self-published, n.d.

Scarano, Francisco. "The *Jíbaro* Masquerade and the Subaltern Politics of Creole Identity Formation in Puerto Rico, 1745–1823." *American Historical Review* 101, no. 5 (1996): 1398–431.

———. *Puerto Rico: Cinco siglos de historia.* Mexico City: McGraw-Hill, 1993.

Schoenrich, Edwin. "An Interscholastic Basketball League for Porto Rico." *Porto Rico School Review* 4, no. 9 (1920): 38–40.

Seijo Bruno, Miñi. *La insurrección nacionalista en Puerto Rico, 1950.* San Juan, Puerto Rico: Editorial Edil, Inc., 1997.

Setran, David P. *The College "Y": Student Religion in the Era of Secularization.* New York: Palgrave Macmillan, 2007.

Sheinin, David. "The Caribbean and the Cold War: Between Reform and Revolution." In *The Caribbean: A History of the Region and Its People,* edited by Stephan Palmié and Francisco A. Scarano, 491–503. Chicago: University of Chicago Press, 2011.

Silén, Juan Angel. *Colonialismo, literatura, ideología y sociedad en Puerto Rico (Comentarios a la obra de José Luis González).* San Juan, Puerto Rico: Librería Norberto González, 1997.

———. *Pedro Albizu Campos.* Río Piedras, Puerto Rico: Editorial Antillana, 1976.

Silva Gotay, Samuel. *Catolicismo y política en Puerto Rico bajo España y Estados Unidos: Siglos XIX y XX.* Río Piedras: La Editorial Universidad de Puerto Rico, 2005.

———. *Protestantismo y política en Puerto Rico, 1898–1930: Hacia una historia del protestantismo evangélico en Puerto Rico*. 2nd ed. Río Piedras: La Editorial Universidad de Puerto Rico, 2005.

Smith, Anthony D. *The Antiquity of Nations*. Cambridge, England: Polity. 2004.

Sotomayor, Antonio. "Colonial Olympism: Puerto Rico and Jamaica's Olympic Movement in Pan-American Sport, 1930 to the 1950s." *International Journal of the History of Sport*, forthcoming.

———. "Operation Sport: Puerto Rico's Recreational and Political Consolidation in an Age of Progress." *Journal of Sport History* 42, no. 1 (2015): 59–86.

———. "Patron Saint Festivities, Politics, and Culture: Celebrating the Colonial Nation in San Germán, Puerto Rico, 1950s." centro *Journal* 20, no. 2 (2008): 100–125.

———. "Un parque para cada pueblo: Julio Enrique Monagas and the Politics of Sport and Recreation in Puerto Rico during the 1940s." *Caribbean Studies* 42, no. 2 (2014): 3–40.

Sotomayor, Orlando. "Development and Income Distribution: The Case of Puerto Rico." *World Development* 32, no. 8 (2004): 1395–406.

Stein, Steve. "The Case of Soccer in Early Twentieth-Century Lima." In *Sport and Society in Latin America: Diffusion, Dependency, and the Rise of Mass Culture*, edited by Joseph L. Arbena, 63–84. New York: Greenwood Press, 1988.

Steward, Julián H., et al. *The People of Puerto Rico*. Urbana: University of Illinois Press, 1956.

Stewart, Raymond. *El baloncesto en San Germán: Tomo II*. San Germán, Puerto Rico: First Book, 1998.

Suárez Findlay, Eileen J. *Imposing Decency: The Politics of Sexuality and Race in Puerto Rico, 1870–1920*. Durham nc: Duke University Press, 1999.

Symes, Carol. "When We Talk about Modernity." In "ahr Roundtable: Historians and the Question of 'Modernity.'" Special issue, *American Historical Review* 116, no. 3 (2011): 715–26.

Tenorio Trillo, Mauricio. *Mexico at the World's Fairs: Crafting a Modern Nation*. Berkeley: University of California Press, 1996.

Tesche, Leoman, and Artur Blasio Rambo. "Reconstructing the Fatherland: German Turnen in Southern Brazil." In *Europe, Sport, World: Shaping Global Societies*, edited by J. A. Mangan, 5–22. London: Frank Cass, 2001.

Thomas, Brooke. "A Constitution Led by the Flag." In *Foreign in a Domestic Sense: Puerto Rico, American Expansion, and the Constitution*, edited by Christina Duffy Burnett and Burke Marshall, 82–103. Durham nc: Duke University Press, 2001.

Thomas, Lynn M. "Modernity's Failings, Political Claims, and Intermediate Concepts." In "AHR Roundtable: Historians and the Question of 'Modernity.'" Special issue, *American Historical Review* 116, no. 3 (2011): 727–40.

Thompson, John W. *Puerto Rico: Where the Americas Meet.* New York: Hastings House, 1940.

Tomasini, Juan B. *Honor a los maestros de educación física y propulsores del deporte puertorriqueño.* N.p.: n.p., 1992.

Tomlinson, Alan, and Christopher Young, eds. *National Identity and Global Sports: Culture, Politics, and Spectacle in the Olympics and the Football World Cup Events.* Albany: State University of New York Press, 2006.

Toohey, Kristine, and A. J. Veal. *The Olympic Games: A Social Science Perspective.* Wallingford, England: CABI, 2007.

Torres, Arlene. "La gran familia puertorriqueña 'Ej prieta de beldá' (The Great Puerto Rican Family Is Really, Really Black)." In *Blackness in Latin America and the Caribbean: Social Dynamics and Cultural Transformations,* edited by Arlene Torres and Norman E. Whitten Jr., 2:285–306. Bloomington: Indiana University Press, 1998.

Torres, César R. "'Corrió por el prestigio de su país': El maratón Olímpico y el nacionalismo deportivo en Argentina y en Chile (1924–1936)." *Latin Americanist* 53, no. 3 (2013): 3–28.

———. "The Latin American 'Olympic Explosion' of the 1920s: Causes and Consequences." *International Journal of the History of Sport* 23, no. 7 (2006): 1088–111.

———. "The Limits of Pan-Americanism: The Case of the Failed 1942 Pan-American Games." *International Journal of the History of Sport* 28, no. 17 (2011): 2547–74.

———. "Peronism, International Sport, and Diplomacy." In *Diplomatic Games: Sport, Statecraft, and International Relations since 1945,* edited by Heather L. Dichter and Andrew L. Johns, 151–82. Lexington: University Press of Kentucky, 2014.

———. "'Spreading the Olympic Idea' to Latin America: The IOC-YMCA Partnership and the 1922 Latin American Games." *Journal of Olympic History* 16, no. 1 (2008): 16–24.

Torres, J. Benjamín. *Pedro Albizu Campos: Obras escogidas, 1923–1933.* Vol. 1. San Juan, Puerto Rico: Editorial Jelofe, 1975.

———. *Pedro Albizu Campos: Obras escogidas, 1934–1935.* Vol. 2. San Juan, Puerto Rico: Editorial Jelofe, 1981.

———. *Pedro Albizu Campos: Obras escogidas, 1936.* Vol. 3. San Juan, Puerto Rico: Editorial Jelofe, 1981.

Torres, Jose Arsenio. *Memoria pública, 1949–1999: Medio siglo de recuerdos y reflexiones.* San Juan: Editorial de la Universidad de Puerto Rico, 2000.

Torres, Wilfredo. *Historia de las Justas, 1929–1998.* San Germán, Puerto Rico: n.p., 1999.

Torres Saillant, Silvio. *An Intellectual History of the Caribbean.* New York: Palgrave Macmillan, 2006.

Torruella, Juan R. "One Hundred Years of Solitude: Puerto Rico's American Century." In *Foreign in a Domestic Sense: Puerto Rico, American Expansion, and the Constitution*, edited by Christina Duffy Burnett and Burke Marshall, 241–50. Durham NC: Duke University, 2001.

Trevor-Roper, Hugh. "The Invention of Tradition: The Highland Tradition of Scotland." In *The Invention of Tradition*, edited by Eric Hobsbawm and Terence Ranger, 15–42. Cambridge, England: Cambridge University Press, 1983.

Trías Monge, José. "Injustice According to Law: The Insular Cases and Other Oddities." In *Foreign in a Domestic Sense: Puerto Rico, American Expansion, and the Constitution*, edited by Christina Duffy Burnett and Burke Marshall, 226–40. Durham NC: Duke University, 2001.

———. *Puerto Rico: The Trials of the Oldest Colony in the World.* New Haven CT: Yale University Press, 1997.

Trouillot, Michel-Rolph. *Silencing the Past: Power and the Production of History.* Boston: Beacon Press, 1995.

Tugwell, Rex. *The Stricken Land: The Story of Puerto Rico.* Garden City NY: Doubleday, 1946.

Turits, Richard. *Foundations of Despotism: Peasants, the Trujillo Regime, and Modernity in Dominican History.* Stanford: Stanford University Press, 2003.

Ubarri, José L. *El deporte ayer y hoy.* Hato Rey, Puerto Rico: JLU, 1989.

Ulman, Amanda, and Ruth Machado. "Marchers in Puerto Rico Say: We are a Nation." *Militant* 60, no. 28 (1996), http://www.themilitant.com/1996/6028/6028_5.html (accessed May 18, 2015).

Unger, Corinna R. "Industrialization vs. Agrarian Reform: West German Modernization Policies in India in the 1950s and 1960s." *Journal of Modern European History* 8, no. 1 (2010): 47–65.

United Nations, Department of Public Information, News and Media Division. "Special Committee on Decolonization Approves Text Calling upon United States to Initiate Self-Determination Process for Puerto Rico." June 17, 2013. http://www.un.org/News/Press/docs/2013/gacol3255.doc.htm (accessed November 20, 2013).

Urbina Gaitán, Chéster. "Origen del deporte en El Salvador (1885–1943)." *Realidad y Reflexión* 6, no. 17 (2006): 13–106.

Uriarte González, Carlos. *De Londres a Londres*. San Juan, Puerto Rico: Editorial Deportiva CAIN, 2012.

———. *80 años de acción y pasión, Puerto Rico en los Juegos Centroamericanos y del Caribe, 1930 al 2010*. N.p.: Nomos Impresores, 2009.

———. *Puerto Rico en el Continente 1951–2011: 60 años de los Juegos Panamericanos*. N.p.: Nomos Impresores, 2011.

Van Dalen, D. B. "Physical Education and Sports in Latin America." *History of Physical Education and Sport* 1, no. 1 (1973): 65–89.

Van Hyning, Thomas E. *Puerto Rico's Winter League: A History of Major League Baseball's Launching Pad*. Jefferson NC: McFarland, 1995.

———. *The Santurce Crabbers: Sixty Seasons of Puerto Rican Winter League Baseball*. Jefferson NC: McFarland, 1999.

Van Hyning, Thomas E., and Franklin Otto. "Puerto Rico: A Major League Steppingstone." In *Baseball without Borders: The International Pastime*, edited by George Gmelch, 160–71. Lincoln: University of Nebraska, 2006.

Varas, Jaime. *La verdadera historia de los deportes puertorriqueños: De 1493 a 1904*. San Juan, Puerto Rico: n.p., 1984.

———. *La verdadera historia de los deportes puertorriqueños: De 1905 a 1919*. San Juan, Puerto Rico: n.p., 1985.

Villa-Flores, Javier. *Dangerous Speech: A Social History of Blasphemy in Colonial Mexico*. Tucson: University of Arizona Press, 2006.

Villahermosa, Gilberto. "Honor and Fidelity: The 65th Infantry Regiment in Korea 1950–1954. Official Army Report on the 65th Infantry Regiment in the Korean War." U.S. Army Center of Military History, September 2000. http://www.valerosos.com/HonorandFidelity3.html#The_Korean_War:_1950 (accessed May 18, 2015).

Villares, Ramón. *Historia de Galicia*. Vigo, Spain: Editorial Galaxia, 2004.

Villaronga, Gabriel. "Constructing Muñocismo: Colonial Politics and the Rise of the PPD, 1934–1940." *CENTRO Journal* 22, no. 2 (2010): 173–97.

Villena Fieno, Sergio. "Fútbol, *mass media* y nación en la era global." *Quórum: Revista de pensamiento iberoamericano* 14 (Spring 2006): 40–54.

———, ed. "fUtopías: Ensayos sobre fútbol y nación en América Latina." *Cuaderno de Ciencias Sociales* 160 (2012): 7–107.

Wagg, Steven, and David Andrews. *East Plays West: Sport and the Cold War*. London: Routledge, 2007.

Wangerin, David. *Distant Corners: American Soccer's History of Lost Opportunities and Lost Causes*. Philadelphia: Temple University Press, 2011.

Weber, Eugene. *Peasants into Frenchmen: The Modernization of Rural France, 1870–1914*. Stanford: Stanford University Press, 1976.

Wells, Henry. *The Modernization of Puerto Rico: A Political Study of Changing Values and Institutions*. Cambridge MA: Harvard University Press, 1969.

Wenner, Lawrence A., ed. *Mediasport*. London: Routledge, 1998.

Whitten, Norman E., Jr., and Arlene Torres, eds. *Blackness in Latin America and the Caribbean: Social Dynamics and Cultural Transformations*. Vol. 1. Bloomington: Indiana University Press, 1998.

Wilbur, Ray L., H. E. Barnard, Katherine Glover, and Winifred Moses, eds. *White House Conference on Child Health and Protection*. New York: Century, 1931.

Wilson, Tamar Diana. "Recent Works on Tourism in Latin America." *Latin America Research Review* 46, no. 2 (2011): 259–64.

Wimmer, Dick, ed. *The Schoolyard Game: An Anthology of Basketball Writings*. New York: Macmillan, 1993.

Winter, Thomas. *Making Men, Making Class: The YMCA and Workingmen, 1877–1920*. Chicago: University of Chicago Press, 2002.

Witherspoon, Kevin B. *Before the Eyes of the World: Mexico and the 1968 Olympic Games*. DeKalb: Northern Illinois University Press, 2008.

———. "'Fuzz Kinds' and 'Musclemen': The US-Soviet Basketball Rivalry, 1958–1975." In *Diplomatic Games: Sport, Statecraft, and International Relations since 1945*, edited by Heather L. Dichter and Andrew L. Johns, 297–326. Lexington: University Press of Kentucky, 2014.

Wojnarowski, Adrian. "No Longer America's Sport." ESPN.com, August 15, 2004. http://espn.go.com/espn/print?id=1860101&type=story (accessed May 18, 2015).

Wood, David. "Sport and Latin American Studies." *Bulletin of Spanish American Studies* 84, nos. 4–5 (2007): 629–43.

Wuest, Deborah A., and Charles A. Bucher. *Foundations of Physical Education, Exercise Science, and Sport*. Boston: McGraw Hill Higher Education, 2009.

Wulf, Steve. "The Great Escape: Fleeing Their Troubled Island, More than Three Dozen Cubans Defected During a Competition in Puerto Rico." *Sports Illustrated* 79, no. 23 (1993): 24.

YMCA. *Yearbook of the Young Men Christian Association*. New York: Association Press, 1898.

———. *Yearbook of the Young Men Christian Association*. New York: Association Press, 1899.

———. *Yearbook of the Young Men Christian Association*. New York: Association Press, 1900.

———. *Yearbook of the Young Men Christian Association*. New York: Association Press, 1901.

———. *Yearbook of the Young Men Christian Association*. New York: Association Press, 1902.

———. *Yearbook of the Young Men Christian Association*. New York: Association Press, 1903.

———. *Yearbook of the Young Men Christian Association*. New York: Association Press, 1904.

———. *Yearbook of the Young Men Christian Association*. New York: Association Press, 1905.

———. *Yearbook of the Young Men Christian Association*. New York: Association Press, 1906.

———. *Yearbook of the Young Men Christian Association*. New York: Association Press, 1907.

———. *Yearbook of the Young Men Christian Association*. New York: Association Press, 1908.

———. *Yearbook of the Young Men Christian Association*. New York: Association Press, 1909.

———. *Yearbook of the Young Men Christian Association*. New York: Association Press, 1910.

———. *Yearbook of the Young Men Christian Association*. New York: Association Press, 1911.

———. *Yearbook of the Young Men Christian Association*. New York: Association Press, 1912.

———. *Yearbook of the Young Men Christian Association*. New York: Association Press, 1913.

———. *Yearbook of the Young Men Christian Association*. New York: Association Press, 1914.

———. *Yearbook of the Young Men Christian Association*. New York: Association Press, 1915.

———. *Yearbook of the Young Men Christian Association*. New York: Association Press, 1916.

———. *Yearbook of the Young Men Christian Association*. New York: Association Press, 1917.

———. *Yearbook of the Young Men Christian Association*. New York: Association Press, 1918.

Zapata Oliveras, Carlos. *Nuevos caminos hacia viejos objetivos: Estados Unidos y el establecimiento del Estado Libre Asociado de Puerto Rico, 1945–1953.* Río Piedras: Comisión Puertorriqueña para la Celebración del Quinto Centenario del Descubrimiento de América y Puerto Rico, 1991.

Zauhar, John. "Historical Perspectives of Sports Tourism." *Journal of Sport Tourism* 9, no. 1 (2004): 5–101.

Zeigler, Earle F., ed. *A History of Physical Education and Sport in the United States and Canada (Selected Topics).* Champaign IL: Stipes, 1975.

Zolov, Eric. "Showcasing the 'Land of Tomorrow': Mexico and the 1968 Olympics." *Americas* 61, no. 2 (2004): 159–88.

Index

Page numbers in italics refer to illustrations.

National Basketball Association (NBA), 1
National Convention of the Communist Party of the USA, 163, 178
national identity: colonialism and, 7–9, 22–23, 206–7, 220n50; Cuba and, 28–29; formation of, 16–19, 205, 217n9; Generación del 30 and, 113; Martinique and Guadaloupe and, 103; of 1930s, 65, 100–101, 228n4; Olympism and, 6, 11, 14, 80, 132–33, 201, 214–16, 231n38; sport and, 7, 25, 26–27, 45, 65, 125; U.S. citizenship and, 14; without sovereignty, 127–28
nationalism: Blanton Winship and, 94–95, 96–97; CACG and, 91–94, 96–97, 101; Latin America and, 228n4; Olympism and, 4, 6–8, 16, 133; sport and, 25, 28, 29–30, 201
"Nationalism as a Practical System" (Lomnitz), 217n9
Nationalist Party. See Partido Nacionalista (PN)
National Olympic Committees (NOC), 10, 114–16, 141, 149–53, 210–11. See also COPR (Olympic Committee of Puerto Rico); OAPR (Olympic Association of Puerto Rico)
Nations and Nationalism (Hobsbawm), 7
Negotiating Empire (Moral), 15, 51
Negrón-Muntaner, Frances, 31
New Deal, 63, 77–78, 105
New Physical Education System, 59
New York Athletic Club, 60
New York Herald, 138
New York Times, 138

Nieto, José Luis, 166
NOC. See National Olympic Committees (NOC)

OAPR (Olympic Association of Puerto Rico), 153–54
"Of Greeks and Russians" (Cramer), 149
Olmo, Nicasio, 60
Olympic Association of Puerto Rico (OAPR), 153–54
Olympic Centenary awards, 202–3
Olympic Charter for Central American and Caribbean Games, 81, 99
Olympic Committee of Puerto Rico. See COPR (Olympic Committee of Puerto Rico)
Olympic Games: 1912, 59; 1936, 94, 97, 116; 1948, 103–4, 106, 109, 114–26, 118, 142, 145, 237n40; 1952, 141–44, 146, 149, 241n33; 1956, 144–45, 147, 150, 152; 1972, 3; 1980, 18, 211–12; 1988, 3; 1992, 1; 2004, 1–3, 210, 215–16; selection of athletes for, 71–72, 76
Olympic Games (Athens), 1–3, 2, 27, 210, 215–16
Olympic Games (Barcelona), 1
Olympic Games (Berlin), 94, 97, 116
Olympic Games (Helsinki), 141–44, 146, 149, 241n33
Olympic Games (London), 103–4, 106, 109, 114–25, 118, 142, 145, 237n40
Olympic Games (Melbourne), 144–45, 147, 150, 152
Olympic Games (Moscow), 18, 211–12
Olympic Games (Stockholm), 59

CPSIA information can be obtained at www.ICGtesting.com
Printed in the USA
LVOW08*2222130516

488206LV00004B/10/P